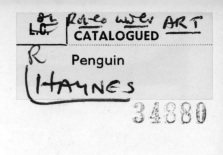

PELICAN BOOKS

A 166

GLASS THROUGH THE AGES

E. BARRINGTON HAYNES

GLASS

THROUGH THE AGES

*

E. Barrington Haynes

PENGUIN BOOKS

Penguin Books Ltd, Harmondsworth, Middlesex
U.S.A.: Penguin Books Inc., 3300 Clipper Mill Road, Baltimore 11, Md
AUSTRALIA: Penguin Books Pty Ltd, 762 Whitehorse Road,
Mitcham, Victoria

—

First published by Penguin Books 1948
Revised edition 1959

Made and printed in Great Britain
by Richard Clay & Company, Ltd, Bungay, Suffolk
Collogravure plates by Harrison and Sons

CONTENTS

PREFACE TO THE REVISED EDITION   7

LIST OF PLATES   9

PART ONE

The Glass of the Eastern World

INTRODUCTION   13

I BEGINNINGS   17

II THE FIRST FOUR CENTURIES

   1. The Glassmakers   24

   2. The Glass They Made   29

III THE SECOND FOUR CENTURIES

   1. The Western Empire   35

   2. The Later Roman Empire and Islam   40

IV THE EMPTY AGES

   1. Western Europe and Germany   47

   2. Eastern Glass   52

V THE RISE AND FALL OF VENICE

   1. Her Fortunes and Misfortunes   59

   2. Her Glass   65

VI THE REVIVAL IN WESTERN EUROPE

   1. The Turn of the Tide   74

   2. French and Spanish Glass   78

   3. Lotharingian and Netherlandish Glass   84

   4. Scandinavian and Russian Glass   91

VII GERMAN GLASS   102

VIII GILDING THE LILY

   1. Painting and Enamelling   110

   2. Engraving   117

CONTENTS

3. Gilding   125

4. Moulded Decoration   129

5. Cut Glass   131

6. Other Decorative Techniques   134

IX   GLASSMAKING IN ENGLAND

1. The Pioneers   142

2. Mansell   150

3. The Glass Sellers Company   154

X   JACOBITE GLASS   164

XI   COMMEMORATIVE GLASS   178

PART TWO

English Glasses of the Eighteenth Century

NOMENCLATURE AND CLASSIFICATION   193

Group I. Baluster Stems   209

II. Moulded Pedestal Stems   217

III. Balustroid Stems   222

IV. Light (Newcastle) Balusters   234

V. Composite Stems   240

VI. Plain Straight Stems   245

VII. Air Twist Stems   254

VIII. Hollow Stems   262

IX. Incised Twist Stems   264

X. Opaque Twist Stems   267

XI. Mixed and Colour Twist Stems   277

XII. Faceted Stems   284

XIII. Other Glasses with Short or Rudimentary Stems   290

POSTSCRIPT   300

INDEX   301

PREFACE TO THE REVISED EDITION

THE generous reception accorded to this volume on its appearance eight years ago and continuing inquiries for copies have demonstrated a wide demand for a simple and reasonably illustrated account of the history of glass and particularly of drinking-glasses.

That has indeed been gratifying to its author, and, more importantly, sufficiently encouraging for its publishers to project a re-issue.

The exigencies of a post-war existence have spelled delay and still more delay, but at length something has emerged more like a re-write than a reprint. Some at least of the original errors have been eliminated, and many dubieties and inconsequences smoothed out. In other places the sequence has, it is hoped and thought, been improved, and a certain amount of new matter inserted, as in Chapter VI. Advantage has been taken of new specialist publications to include a summary of Scandinavian and Russian glass, with due acknowledgements to the experts concerned, without whom the author would have had but little to say. Last but not least, the publishers are providing a further invaluable thirty-six plates whereon the competition for inclusion has entailed almost unbelievable deliberation.

In conclusion, I have to make my acknowledgements to those earlier writers whose works have been consulted or referred to in the text or in the bibliographical footnotes; among these Mr W. B. Honey's *Handbook* has been an ever-present help in difficulty.

On this occasion I also record grateful thanks for guidance to Mr A. J. Charleston, Dr D. B. Harden, Capt. W. Horridge, Dr Ada Buch Polak, and Mr A. Vecht of Amsterdam, and lastly to Mr Ray Winfield Smith who has most kindly advised on the chapters concerning ancient glass. To these, named and unnamed, any usefulness or reputation of this book will largely be due.

Part 2 has been entirely re-written. Originally it consisted of a skeleton classification of our English eighteenth-century glasses, based on stem formation. The skeleton having been largely clothed in its proper flesh, there was no point in repetition, though it can usefully be referred to.

Instead I have surveyed the various stem groups and outlined their size and scope, indicating unassuming rarities or undeserving favourites. The survey is based on the original classification which stands with but small amendment and will display itself as the reading progresses. New readers may be assured that the data given have been statistically and faithfully reached after years of systematic tabulation. I think it is fair to claim that a study and memorization of the classification will give a perspective view of our eighteenth century drinking-glasses unobtainable in any other way.

At the foot of each chapter a note is given of the standard works in English which treat of the subject in question. Our own literature on Continental glass is very inadequate. A full if necessarily incomplete bibliography will be found in Thorpe's *History of English and Irish Glass* and elsewhere.

LIST OF PLATES

1. Egyptian Glasses in *pâté de verre*, conventionally 500 B.C.
2 to 4. Roman Glass, 1st to 4th century
5. Gallic Glass, 1st to 4th century
6. Gallic Glass
7 and 8. Glass of the 5th to 8th century
9. Islamic and Early German Glass
10. Islamic Glass, 8th to 10th century
11. Islamic Glass, 10th to 13th century
12. Syrian and Islamic Glasses
13. Glass Made in Iran or for the Iranian Market
14. Scale-gilt and Jewelled Venetian Bowls
15 to 18. Venetian Glass
19 and 20. French Glass
21. Spanish Glass
22. Spanish and Lotharingian Glass
23. Rhineland and Antwerp Glass
24. Glass of the Low Countries, 16th to 17th Centuries
25 to 28. Glass of the Low Countries
29. Norwegian Glass
30. Swedish and Russian Glass
31. Glass of Indecisive Origin
32. German Enamelled Glass
33. German Engraved Glass
34. German Enamelled and Painted Glass
35. Enamelled and Painted Glass
36 and 37. Painted Glass
38 and 39. Diamond-engraved Glasses
40. Stippled Glasses (English, with Dutch engraving)
41. German Surface-engraved Glasses
42. Surface-engraved Glasses
43. Engraving in Low and High Relief
44. Decorated Overlaid and Flashed Glass
45. Gilded and Silvered Glasses
46. Moulded Glass, English Cut Glass
47. Irish Cut Glass
48. Hyalith Glass and Other Decorative Techniques
49. Other Decorative Techniques
50. Paperweights and Millefiori Glass, mid 19th century
51. Various

LIST OF PLATES

52. Modern Glass
53 to 56. English 17th-century Glass
57. Some Types of Decoration to English 18th-century wines
58. English 17th-century Glass
59. Glasses of the Later 17th Century
60. Further Types of Bowl, Rim, and Foot
61. Baluster Glasses (Group I)
62. Baluster and Moulded Pedestal Stems. (Groups I, II)
63 and 64. Moulded Pedestal Stems (Group II)
65. Moulded Pedestal Stems and Balustroid Glasses (Groups II, III)
66 to 68. Balustroid Stems (Group III)
69. Balustroid Glasses and Light (Newcastle) Balusters (Groups III, IV)
70 to 73. Light (Newcastle) Balusters (Group IV)
74. Light (Newcastle) Balusters and Composite Stems
75. Composite Stems (Group V)
76. Composite Stems
77. Plain Straight Stems (Group VI)
78. Plain Stems. Hollow Stems (Groups VI, VIII)
79 to 81. Air Twist Stems (Group VII)
82. Air Twists and Incised Twist Stems (Groups VII, IX)
83. Incised Twists and Opaque White Twist Glasses (Groups IX, X)
84. Hollow Stems. Incised Twist Stems
85. Opaque Twist Stems (Group X)
86 and 87. Stem Types
88. Opaque Twist Stems (Group X)
89. Mixed Twist Stems (Groups XI) 1760–70
90. Mixed Twist and Faceted Stem Glasses (Groups XI, XII)
91. Faceted Stems (Group XII)
92. Jacobite Glasses
93 to 96. Other Rudimentary Stems (Group XIII)

PART ONE

THE GLASS
OF THE EASTERN
WORLD

*

INTRODUCTION

THE chapters which follow are in no way intended to compete with the standard text-books on glass. Still less are they to be regarded as a comprehensive story of a product known to man for at least thirty-five centuries and one which (in some eyes at least) is as yet in its infancy.

It may be doubted whether any one author is qualified to write such an encyclopedic account, and in any case it would certainly neither appeal to the publishers of this series of booklets nor to the general public which reads them. What follows will indeed give nothing but a bird's-eye view of what may be called the table glassware of other lands, and a somewhat closer view of that of the British Isles, but it will serve to direct attention to more exhaustive works on particular phases of its history. It is designed to arouse interest rather than to give instruction; to show where knowledge can be found rather than to offer it; and to excite inquiry.

The phases of early glassmaking about which we know something have always seemed to me to stand in undue isolation in our popular text-books. In these chapters an effort has been made to link these phases, and it is hoped that some connected picture will disclose itself. It may prove to be distorted, since speculation has so often to replace knowledge, but with a glance at history and logical possibilities, even an imperfect picture will enable the less instructed reader to visualize the inception, the rise and decay, and the revival of a manufacture which has had as profound an influence on human convenience, happiness, and well-being as has any other discovery whatsoever, the printing press not excluded. What that thirty-five-century-old discovery may yet lead to can only be guessed at. Its conveniences in daily life and its services to scientific knowledge have stretched far indeed, yet its industrial application on a really large scale has perhaps hardly begun.

If, never having known such a thing, you were suddenly to

find yourself able to manufacture an infinitely tractable substance that could be either opaque or transparent at will, in a wide range of colours or without colour at all, and one that was impervious to moisture and unaffected by any ordinary chemical, and if, further, you could do all this at insignificant expense and by employing the commonest raw materials, you might justly anticipate public enthusiasm and applause. And that is precisely what did happen when glass-blowing was discovered, and it had precisely that result on the Roman world which saw it happen.

If, on the other hand, you endeavour to picture a world without glass, without any glass or equivalent substitute at all, you will quickly be reduced to speculation as to what our civilization would now be. Could the more northerly latitudes, for instance, ever have developed much more than an Eskimo standard of living without window glass? Indeed, it is hardly too much to assert that the major ancient civilizations and cultures existed in the Mediterranean and Near-Eastern areas simply because – lacking window glass – only in those warm climates was any noticeable civilization or culture possible.

And, further, consider where science would stand had there been no glass. Medicine, without the microscope and the test-tube, might still be fighting disease with herbal remedies, charms, and incantations, our years but two score and ten. Chemists would still be alchemists and astronomers remain astrologers.

Travel might still be limited to the pace of horse or sail. There would be no wireless and no electric light. Many of us would peer dimly through spectacles of horn and all of us grope forward in a permanent Dark Age. We would shave and our women would powder before a metal mirror. Diamonds would have to replace paste. There would be no cinemas, no cameras, and no illustrations to these essays. As it is, thanks to some unknown experimentalist and the glass he blew, progress seems illimitable.

Clearly enough, the place of drinking-vessels in this wonderful development is relatively unimportant, but it is not therefore a humble one. That is because the bowl and the beaker could also be a vehicle for art, and possess a human value as well as a mechanical or useful one. So drinking-glasses become collectable, are studied, valued, and preserved. In the same way, perhaps in lesser degree, the stained glass that has served to enrich so many ancient buildings possesses human value, whereas the oldest of plain window glass arouses little interest. I count that a pity, even though these pages will deal so exclusively with table glassware.

There are many other objects made of glass well worth study. We in England neglect them because they are seldom beautiful, because they lack the personal touch, or again because we do not know for what they were intended and are insufficiently interested to find out.

There are, for instance, certain jug-shaped objects with a long spout, an over-sized handle, and a wide top. They look like crude tea- or coffee-pots, adequately but not attentively made. These were designed to hold oil for filling the lamps so widely used in the days when, or places where, gas had not begun to creep smokily through a cobweb of iron pipes. Nowadays they are made of metal, presumably for reasons of safety rather than of cleanliness. Then there are numbers of lamps themselves, growing daily fewer through carelessness and neglect. There is a whole host of semi-scientific glass appliances, chemical apparatus, bottles and phials, and odd little things whose purpose is obscure or unknown – trivialities, some of them, but they had their place in bygone days.

Where you may pay pounds for a wine glass and find it matched in the next collection you chance to see, you will pay pence or shillings for these unpopular and unsought-for things, a good collection of which will tell posterity something fresh and not repeat the already known.

That is not to say that the study of drinking-vessels is completed. It has very far to go yet and finality will never be reached. Very much has been written and much more has been copied. It is the hardest thing not to be over-influenced by what authoritative writers have unanimously laid down, and once a theory receives general acceptance it is almost impossible to eradicate it even when it has been utterly discredited.

The classic instance in glass is of course the popular belief that Waterford glass has a distinct bluish tinge. Waterford is a euphonious name and for all I know a lovely and romantic spot. Its glass certainly is lovely and has many qualities, but a bluish colour is not among them. That is romance indeed.

It will be fair, then, to ask every student to read what others may have written, to hold their views in mind, but to accept nothing as completely true – not even what he is about to read here – if it should conflict with his own experience and deductions. But he will not fail to recall that experience comes only from the constant handling of specimens, and deductions only from the inquisitive mind and eye. Glass-knowledge can be acquired from books to a considerable extent, but connoisseurship cannot, and an opinion based on academic learning alone is obviously untrustworthy and in extreme cases but the reflection of tradition. And that is why actual possession and active collecting are so valuable.

CHAPTER I

BEGINNINGS

*

MOST books on glass refer quickly to the picturesque story told by Pliny, writing in the first century A.D., how certain merchants encamped on the sands of the River Belus placed their cooking-pots on some of the cakes of natron they were engaged in transporting. In the morning they found that the sand and the soda had fused together, forming glass.

This story, purporting to explain the origin of glass, is probably one of those myths which are born to account for a fact, the fact in this instance being simply that Syrian glass-makers did make use of the sand deposited by this particular river. A good judge, however, avows the possibility of some foundation for the tale, although nothing like the glass we know could have resulted. A lower temperature than that required for blowing glass would have sufficed. Even so, it may be guessed that the merchants would have found their dinner a trifle over-cooked.

Strictly speaking, the earliest glass we know of is a product of nature herself, who anticipated man by some thousands or millions of years by manufacturing obsidian, a natural glass of shiny blackish aspect where fractured, differing little in analysis from our own wine bottle glass. Some considerable use of it has been made by the Mexicans, and visitors to the Yellowstone National Park in the United States can hardly escape being shown the Glass Mountain, one of the many marvels there, but less impressive than some others for looking much like any other tree-and-herbage-clad mountain.

An axe, or knife, or arrow-head might logically be the starting point for any glass collection, but there will be a vast gap before any man-made specimen can be found. Still, we have since made amends, and when our first glass does come to light it is found, as might be expected, in that ancient and most favoured of civilizations, the Egyptian. Most favoured because so well-protected from outside interference, with deserts on east and west, with sea and desert on the north, and with a narrow defensible boundary (wherever it might chance to be) on the south. To such fortunate geographical circumstances the Egyptians owed their comparative immunity. It must be seldom that ribbon development has had so lucky a result. Elsewhere, and less favoured because oppressed by both man and nature, there was Mesopotamia, where there has been found glass ancient enough to suggest a manufacture as early as that of Egypt.

It must not be imagined that there have been no changes in conditions. It is believed that the Nile raises the level of the adjacent land by $4\frac{1}{2}$ inches in a century, that is (neglecting other factors) by some 13 feet during the period under review. It can therefore easily be understood that the Nile was formerly more widespread in its annual flood. The rainfall may have been heavier and Egypt's western boundaries more distant and more habitable. That would be in keeping with the encroaching tendency of the desert band which stretches from the Atlantic to the Persian Gulf and beyond. Elsewhere the Sahara and the Libyan deserts have encroached, slowly but remorselessly. Timbuktu, once Queen of the Sahara, is now Timbuktu the Mysterious. South-west of Cairo, Lake Moeris is gone and ancient water-courses are now always dry. Even the barriers of Niger and Nile may not always stand.

The important point to us is that Egypt was formerly much more wooded. The primary requisites for a glass-maker are silica, alkali, and fuel. There could be no shortage of silica, the natron lakes supplied soda with ample generosity, and acacia groves were there for fuel. So the people made glass.

At some date prior to 3000 B.C. they had learned how to make a vitreous glaze, opaque and highly coloured, and with it they covered the objects of stone they modelled or the sandy compositions they moulded. A few hundred years of practice endowed them with a high degree of skill, and in due course it was found that if the glass was made thick enough it needed no substance to support it, and it could be made into beads or cut into small pieces and used at discretion for inlay or surfacing work. Then someone discovered that it could be gathered on a suitable core of the requisite shape and the core removed, to leave a small vase or bottle which would not collapse in use and which could be made to stand up. All this may have taken time, for, as will be seen, Egyptian glass-makers (and perhaps other of her craftsmen) were of a conservative disposition.

Some of the books already referred to speak of certain wall-paintings of the twelfth Dynasty at Beni Hasan which are, or were, alleged to portray glass-blowers at work. The amended view is that they were iron-workers, and as no glass vessel, blown or otherwise, has been found of any earlier date than the eighteenth Dynasty, that is c. 1500 B.C., this view may easily be accepted. There can be no doubt as to these particular vessels because three of them carry the cartouche of Thothmes III. The names of his three immediate successors have also been found on one kind of glass or another, which brings us to, say, 1375 B.C.

But two things are worth noting. First, that no less than 1,700 years had elapsed since the first specimen of glazed ware had been manufactured, and second, that these vases suddenly appear, fully fledged so to speak, without the trace of an ancestor. It cannot be excluded that earlier and cruder specimens may have been made, but none has been recognized.

The natural location of Egyptian glass-makers was in the Delta and the Fayum, in proximity to the natron deposits and fuel. But Akhenaten, who abandoned the monumental city of Thebes, c. 1375 B.C. and founded El Amarna, 200 miles to the north, had the fancy to order that glass should be made near by, and the actual site has been discovered, a by-no-means-suitable spot for lack of – at least – fuel, but Egyptian monarchs had a way of disregarding the exigencies of time and place. Here, as elsewhere in ancient times, convenience may have been served by transportation of the metal in pigs. During the next 1000 years or so our Egyptian glass-makers demonstrated their lack of enterprise. There was a decline, and then an apparent cessation from c. 1100 to 600. Some likely Asiatic glasses have been dated to the eighth and seventh centuries. Then there was a long period of reproduction of the sand-core glass in the twenty-sixth and later Dynasties, but it is not therefore of proven Egyptian origin. Other sources in the Mediterranean were probably responsible, and the area of distribution barely included Egypt, whose glass-makers must surely have followed suit in some small degree, for all that the fashion was for them deplorably *vieux jeu*. It is from this later period that the specimens we possess are mostly derived, and production went on until about the birth of Christ. It would indeed have been strange if people had resumed an ancient manufacture after a gap of centuries, and equally surprising if the gap had not been filled by some alternative glass style, but of such there is no record.

One might have expected a so-long-fashionable style to have survived into the blown-glass era, but it vanishes almost as suddenly as it came. Some reminiscent surface-trailed blown forms are known from the Greek Islands, and some decadent hybrids from Syria, but the technique hitherto practised completely disappears.

It was simple enough, although with the available conveniences no small degree of skill must have been necessary to produce the really beautiful results which were so often obtained. On the end of a tapered metal rod a core of sand or clay was modelled to the desired shape. This was dipped into the crucible of molten metal (for specimens with surface bubbles or blow-holes may be found), or on occasion the metal may have been otherwise applied. Continued re-heating and 'marvering', i.e. rolling on a flat surface, made the vessel homogeneous and ironed out most irregularities.

When sufficiently coated, and whilst still hot and therefore soft, threads or trails of opaque colour might be superimposed, and these were not only rolled into the body of the vessel until flush, but the surface might also be dragged into a series of bands or zigzags to fulfil the fancy of or the orders to the workmen. A feathery 'palm-leaf' pattern (Pl. 1b) can be most effective, and obviously a discreet use of contrasting or graded colours could give a highly decorative result. A hand finish could be given and a final re-heat would produce what is now called a fire-polish. Some bottles have so smooth a surface that they look as if turned and polished. When cool the rod was withdrawn and the sand core extracted.

The possible variations of pattern were naturally many. In practice certain types were a good deal more common than others. While decoration might be confined to neck or shoulders or might cover the whole of the vessel, a dark opaque blue was most commonly chosen for the body, and yellow and pale blue predominate in the decoration. A delightful green is sometimes found, a jasper red, and white with or without black or deep violet decoration, evidently in imitation of the much-beloved native aragonite. Generally speaking, the colours have survived the years surprisingly well and the condition of specimens is often admirable. There are frequent fine hair-cracks due to pressure or inherent strains, and cunning repairs may be looked for both here and in all ancient glass.

Opaque colours were a matter of preference, not necessity, for during the early period both translucent and transparent colourless glass could be made. In the case of bottles, it was presumably the decoration which was of value and opacity was therefore a virtue, for the colours would not then have been marred by any tinted contents.

The forms found in most collections are of the later period and of three main types (Pl. 1). A cylindrical phial or *alabastron*, varying to fat cigar-like shape, is the simplest form. There is a pear-shaped amphorisk with a pointed base finishing sometimes with a little ball or button; a short-necked globular phial with rounded base may be called an *aryballos*. Most of the *alabastra* have a pair of applied rudimentary handles or diminutive loops, or tiny pegs, though some are entirely without. Amphorisks are more likely to be adequately supplied. Both these types are somewhat or entirely unstable. The third type is a small ewer or jug with a flat base on which it could rest, and this had a single handle one could safely use. So useful a shape naturally occurred again and again, and very noticeably in Ravencroft's English glass some 2,000 years or so later.

Specimens of the early period are rare. They include footed cups, goblets, and standing flasks or *unguentaria*, but their plurality is modest. In olden Egypt glass must have been a luxury article, and exclusive. Of the later period, stretching over some six centuries, our museums hold considerable numbers, and not a few are in private hands. Conventionally they get called *c.* 500 B.C., but many are much later. Dating presents difficulty and exactitude is a specialist's affair; it has been studied by Fossing. But even the late sand-core glass is now hardly a common commodity, and for every example we may well have fifty Roman pieces. It is true that we owe the latter to a widespread burial custom, yet they were made in a shorter time, in far greater variety, and in view of their fragility and often trivial nature even the protection of the tomb was limited. It would seem that the output of the earlier world never approached that of the Roman during the first four centuries after the discovery that glass could be blown. It cannot then be wondered at that on all the counts of antiquity, beauty, and rarity, the sand-core vases rank highly in a collector's estimation.

It is supposed that cosmetics were carried in all these things. Indeed, an illustration in Nesbitt's *Catalogue of the Slade Collection* shows an eighteenth-Dynasty lotus-headed *alabastron* with a spatula still inside it. Kohl, for darkening the eyelids and rendering the eye more lustrous, has been in immemorial use in the East, and no doubt then as now there was a wide choice of preparations an Egyptian beauty could command or have foisted upon her. Yet these vessels must have had their disadvantages. Their interior was far from smooth and the relics of the sand-core can often be seen, which suggests a gritty hazard to a smooth Egyptian skin.

Both preceding and post-dating these vases are beads of similar metal, occasionally reaching a considerable size. There are a few glass scarabs and there are little amulets of glass, both much commoner in other materials. There are mosaics, button-like objects, and, later, bracelets, for an account of which recourse must be had to archaeological literature. These are fascinating little fellows, and more indicative of a nation's customs and beliefs than all its priceless artistic treasures.

*

FOR FURTHER REFERENCE

EISEN, G. A. *Glass*, 2 vols, New York, 1927.

FOSSING, P. *Glass Vessels before Glass-blowing*, Copenhagen, 1940.

HONEY, W. B. *Glass*, Victoria and Albert Museum Handbook, 1946.

NEUBURG, F. *Glass in Antiquity*, 1949.

SMITH, RAY WINFIELD. *The Significance of Roman Glass*, Bulletin of the Metropolitan Museum of Art, New York, Oct. 1949.

CHAPTER II

THE FIRST FOUR CENTURIES

*

1. The Glassmakers

ALREADY it has been suggested that the exploitation of the blow-pipe to fashion what we call 'blown glass' was one of man's most far-reaching achievements. Like so many truly great innovations, it was one of the simplest character, and one of which there is no record whatever.

It is established without much doubt as having taken place about half a century before the birth of Christ – by whom now matters little. Possibly an unusually enterprising Egyptian, for there is reliable evidence that the sand-core process had already been supplemented by a press-moulding process (Pl. 2d). More probably the discovery was a Syrian triumph of ingenuity over tiresome monotony, the incentive a high commercial reward. The profit motive has contributed far too much to human progress always to be anathematized as selfish or vicious.

It was not a discovery to arouse surprise. The surprise is rather that it did not come earlier, for it only needed somebody to think of replacing the original iron rod by a hollow and longer one, to ease manipulation, and to render the use of hotter furnaces more bearable. Then sooner or later somebody's lips were bound to stray to the free end and puff – and the discovery was there.*

Once the blow-pipe was in common use the manufacture of glass developed with a rapidity altogether surprising, and more progress was made in fifty years than had been made in

---

* To avoid a break in the story it has been thought best to assume a knowledge on the reader's part of glass-blowing, the tools and technique of which have never changed in essentials. The processes are fully explained in several accessible text-books.

1,500. All this glass of the first four centuries is generally termed Roman, but that only means that it was made in the Roman world, not necessarily at Rome or by Romans. Two styles or trends in manufacture soon showed themselves.

There were the Syrian and the Egyptian sides of the industry, with Alexandria as the natural distributing centre for the latter. Both sides made utility glass for household and commercial purposes, the Syrians because they wanted to and had their eye on the popular and middle-class markets, the Egyptians because they could not ignore such competition and the quick profits the demand offered. The Syrian trend was towards simplicity and lightness. It did not concern itself unduly with the character of the metal, i.e. the substance of the glass, and perhaps at first had not the necessary knowledge and experience. So its products come in a wide range of green and yellowish tints which are difficult to gauge because the depth of every colour varied with the thickness of the glass. There was at times a naturalistic leaning in Syrian glass, bottles or vases being made to represent shells, bunches of grapes, dates, and pomegranates. Some of the latter (Pl.3b) complete with ribs or spines and rootlets look more like cacti which now grow in the Jerusalem area, an instance of unconscious foresight on the part of the makers, for it seems that cacti of this nature were not indigenous but a modern importation into Palestine. Others were moulded in the form of heads of various types, not always very decisive, and some (the Janus bottles) had two heads (Pl.3c). There are little bottles moulded to resemble basket-work, while a fortunate survival is a tiny basket with a thin loop handle, fashioned rather like a coal-hod (Pl.4b). Then there is an *unguentarium* shaped like a crocodile and a feeding vessel like a duck. In all, an immense variety, much easier to illustrate than to describe. As attractive as any are bottles with elaborately moulded classical designs, of the 'Temple' series (Pl.2c). Cups or beakers with moulded or painted gladiatorial designs are far rarer and found as widely apart as Britain and Afghanistan. Colour, especially blues and purples, was used, but at first there was no particular accent on it.

The Egyptians had always liked colour and their Alexandrian glassmakers, knowing the technique of old, were already using ambers, blues, and greens for self-colour drinking bowls, both press-moulded and blown. They quickly showed their pre-eminence by adding to their repertoire infinitely variegated mosaic and millefiori bowls (Pl.4a) and other colourful articles resembling marble or streaked stone. It does seem that the Alexandrian side of the industry turned as by instinct towards the elaborate and expensive glass in which ingenuities of technique and patient craftsmanship counted before all else.

But their people wanted household glass, bottles (flasks) and jugs for liquor, cups and beakers to drink it from, bowls for food, and oval plates off which to eat it. They used, too, stirrers and spoons as well as conical lamps. The Egyptian glass-masters had to supply the demand, and by reason of the excavations at Karanis we have a clearer knowledge of this everyday Egyptian glass than we have of the Syrian, but the one indicates the sort of articles the other employed. The 'murrines' of antiquity have been guardedly or perforce accepted as identical with the marbled and mosaic glass referred to. But very good authority has reinforced an opinion of earlier years and has identified *murrina* as objects made of fluorspar, not glass at all. The glass bowls were imitation murrines and were recognized as such by the ancients themselves. Pliny (A.D. 23–79) records the sale of two cups for 6,000 sesterces – something between £50 and £60 in our money. He also mentions a vase destroyed by Petronius to prevent its falling into Nero's hands; one modern writer values this vessel at £50,000 by adopting the earlier valuation and mistaking *sestertii* for *sestertia* and so magnifying the result a thousand times.

The Alexandrian shops also introduced the art of working upon glass with a wheel – lathe-cutting in fact – and developed their tools to produce grooved or faceted glass and linear cutting. They contrived further to carve glass in relief and so produce among other things cameo glass. A vessel was formed of glass of two colours, such as opaque white overlying blue; the outer white layer was then cut, carved, and ground away to leave a design in white and in relief on the basic blue glass. Intricacies of shadow were attainable by controlling the degree to which the white layer was removed. The best known example of this is the Portland Vase in the British Museum, and there are a few others and a considerable quantity of fragments. Wedgwood and Webb & Sons in England, and Gallé and others in France reintroduced the technique in the last quarter of the nineteenth century. Work of the Portland Vase quality has not been a commercial proposition despite time-saving tools and devices. Whether modern workmanship and artistry are the equal of the ancient each must decide for himself; given the halo and tone assured by the lapse of much less than nineteen centuries, I have come to think that the best of our work will be as warmly acclaimed.

The summit of technical achievement was surely reached by those *diatretarii* who combined carving and undercutting in such a way that a bold design – as of conjoined circles, for instance – would remain attached to and yet stand boldly out from the walls of a bowl or cup and appear as a network around it. Lettering could be incorporated in the design. Such objects are appropriately known as cage-cups, and there is a theory that one of the places at which they were made was Aquileia, at the head of the Adriatic.

In a different direction Egyptian artists learned to decorate glass in fired colours, a craft later to be elaborated, indeed one might say perfected, and doubtless there was a parallel development in Syria. Much of what we possess is fragmentary, and some not so unlike the vivid but crudely drawn figures on the lesser German enamelled glasses of the seventeenth century. But the early colours are not so opaque, and are more properly described as 'painting' than 'enamelling'.

Such is my interpretation of the individualities of the Syrian and Egyptian schools, open to much amendment in detail and to the presumption of a certain amount of duplication, for glassmaking has always been a competitive industry.

Other areas where glass has been found are Syria, Transjordan, and Palestine; Cyprus and Crete; eastwards, Mesopotamia and as far beyond as Afghanistan; westwards, Tripoli and Tunisia. We must infer from Strabo, writing early in the first century, that Rome had already established glasshouses of her own. So we can visualize an early penetration by glassmakers wherever Roman culture, which is to say Roman arms, ruled, from Syria to Rome, from Rome to the Rhône valley, thence west and south to the Spanish littoral and North Africa, and northwards to the Seine and Amiens, and to the Ardennes, the Rhine, and the Cologne area. And there is nothing to prevent our assuming that it reached Britain and such places as Colchester and Faversham.

A good many glassmakers are known to us by their names or trade-marks moulded on the vessels they blew. Of them all, Ennion and Artas, both of Sidon, and Frontinus in Picardy are perhaps the most famous. Their marks will appear on the body or handle, or, as in the case of Frontinus, on the base (Pl.5c). And that is virtually all we do know about them, but we can infer a considerable measure of competition from the very existence of their various names and marks, coupled with an occasional impressed slogan exhorting the user to remember the maker, a simple form of advertisement which glass collectors must regret was discontinued. We might also assume that such makers were the firmly established ones, but there is no real evidence.

Otherwise, the simplicities of glass manufacture were such that a small company of peripatetic craftsmen could travel from site to site, set up a simple furnace, supply a local market, and move on again when business or welcome languished. It was easier to take the furnace to the market than to face the risks and difficulties of dispatching the finished article. Equally it was easier to take the furnace to the fuel than *vice versa*. Such a restlessness has always been a feature of the trade, a tradition followed by the workers themselves as late as the nineteenth century, although the glasshouses had perforce stabilized themselves.

2. The Glass They Made

Something has already been said of this, but mention of rare artistic glass must not obscure the fact that the great majority of Roman glass is of the simplest kind. There were plates and dishes, bowls and beakers; there were bottles innumerable, square, squat, globular, tapered, and many-sided, all to be regarded as household goods. At first blown and flattened beneath so that they would stand up, a foot-ring either tooled or applied came to be added, in order to improve stability and line. A 'double-blown' foot was also used, that is to say, a secondary inflation was formed at the base and then flattened out and pushed upwards in the centre so that the vessel rested on a double rim. Stemmed vessels (Pl.2b) are relatively scarce, and as might be expected the simple inexpensive pieces are normally single-piece glasses blown and fashioned from one gathering only.

The minor variations of form are innumerable and impossible of survey here. The eye always looks for the specimen which is different, but I think it is the exception for a collector to find two identical pieces of Roman glass. The terms in use are confusing, for a drinking bowl is properly a cup, a vase may really be a bottle or alternatively an urn, which in turn can appear as a near-spherical bowl; and a lamp for oil looks like a beaker with a pointed base.

Besides this household ware there were very many *unguentaria* (Pl.3d, e), i.e. toilet and scent bottles, for oil and scent took precedence of soap in Mediterranean lands when a hardier North disdained both. The tradition is not yet extinct. All these vessels could be, and were, deposited in the graves of deceased persons without too great a strain upon the family exchequer. Even the deceased himself might be deposited in a glass urn (Pl.6a) after cremation. For those too poor to provide or spare such things there were tiny conventional alternatives of the cheapest sort, and in spite of their complete unimportance they are not without charm. Most of this glass was of the Syrian school. Needless to say, 'tear-bottles' did not contain tears, and one need not credit stories of lamps still burning when an ancient tomb has been opened.

While at least one authority thinks that little, if any, glass was especially made to serve as grave-goods, there are these tiny inconsiderables and also other vessels of greater consequence and size, but blown so thinly that it is difficult to believe they could have been intended for daily use. I have, for instance, a $9\frac{1}{2}$-in. carafe understood to have been found in a crypt in Jerusalem. This holds no less than three pints (60 liquid oz.), but it weighs only $4\frac{1}{2}$ oz., whereas the water-bottle in my bedroom holds 24 oz. and weighs a pound. When filled it seems eminently desirable to raise this Syrian carafe with care, and to support the base with one hand, lest either the neck come away from the body or the bottom fall out of the whole. Quite a number of beakers are equally fragile, some having a rough, unaccommodating rim never smoothed by fire or tool (Pl.2a). There is this mass of cheap glass, and, as stated, there was simple household glass of fair quality, already described. To illustrate the fine glasses available there is the small but illuminating collection excavated at Begram, in Afghanistan, once believed to have been founded by Alexander the Great (Alexandria ad Caucasiam) but most probably the ancient Nikaea, a bare fifteen kilometres therefrom. Begram appears to have enjoyed a reasonably placid existence until destroyed by the White Huns about the fifth century. Neither this deposit (of the first four centuries) nor the Karanis finds included grave-goods, and they therefore better represent what the passably rich and the relatively poor could possess and enjoy. The Begram find is divided between Kabul and Paris, where in the Musée Guimet something over a score of items is exhibited, with a surprising proportion in blue glass, and some in excellent condition.

Among the nearly two hundred specimens of this find there were both blue and uncoloured goblets caged somewhat in the manner of Pl.9b, some uncoloured with faceted hexagons for decoration, and others rather fragmentary painted in polychrome with gladiators or other figures. There were vases, blue and uncoloured, caged and plain, in line with the goblets aforesaid, as well as faceted jugs, and a longish series of fish-like flasks, again blue and uncoloured (which hardly means clear glass), termed ichthyomorphs, fragile and seemingly decorative rather than useful; the fish did become an important Christian symbol, but whether these fish at this early period and distant spot had such a significance is perhaps rather doubtful.

Coming back to what we now call the Near East, there were graceful *amphorae*, not all stable, and some tall ewers of delightful line, both plain and wrythen, and often furnished with handles or applied ornament in a different colour. Such pieces are scarce here; while the demand for them was smaller, their size and quality may have meant a reluctance to consign them to the grave, but Levant museums hold a number. They may be said to come between the utility glass and the luxury items already referred to. It would seem from the early classical writers that this luxury glass was far more plentiful than the few relics of it which we now possess would indicate. We may find it difficult to imagine anything finer than the first century A.D. Portland Vase, but it need not represent the uttermost of ancient achievement; nobody can say, but all must wish that the artist had signed his work and so ensured for himself a place in honour no less high than that of the Emperor (Alexander Severus) he is wrongly supposed to have served.

One other type of glass predominantly of the fourth century must be mentioned, although little enough of it, and that but fragmentary, will be seen outside a museum. It comes almost entirely from Roman catacombs and is peculiarly but not invariably associated with contemporary Jewish and Christian life. To the bases of the glasses a layer of gold leaf was applied, and this was etched with a needle to show conventional Christian scenes. Occasionally colour was employed in addition, and when the work was complete a further disc of glass was laid over the gold and fused to the plate or vessel used. It is chiefly to these bases, found cemented into the tombs, that we owe acquaintance with this special technique, one which many centuries later came into great popularity in Bohemia.

By the third century A.D. the picture is one of a Roman

world everywhere producing or using glass in a profusion not to be equalled until another fifteen centuries had passed. This glass ranges from real crudity through all grades of service-ability and beauty to artistic heights at which we still reasonably wonder. And it was not confined to table-ware and magnificent ornaments.

There was the slit-window glass, designed rather to keep out the weather than to let in light, as is evident from excavations at Pompeii. The use of glass mosaics over the walls of Roman rooms, and especially Roman bathrooms, became most fashionable, and it was occasionally used for mosaic floors in place of the usual stone or pottery *tesserae*. There its disadvantages will quickly have been realized by careless bathers or carefree diners. In this as in many other respects Rome had a modern trend all her own.

In the year A.D. 200 Rome may well have seemed stable and strong enough, and withal rich and amusing enough. In the year A.D. 300 it may not have appeared very different, but a century of struggle to maintain an unknit Empire had sown the seeds of disaster. To glass students the great events of this fourth century are, first, the recognition of Christians in 313 and of Christianity as the religion of the Empire in 324, and second, the building of Byzantium (Constantinople) and the transfer to that city of the seat of government in the year 330, together with a presumptive migration of glassmakers but is there certain evidence of a single glass made there?

In the year A.D. 400 there can have been little complacence. Alaric was invading Lombardy and in 410 was to sack Rome herself. It happened again in 455, and twenty years later the break-up of the Western Empire was complete.

But for the time being it was business as usual. If they thought at all of the future, the glass-masters may have reflected how invulnerable were their works and how mobile their workers. The industry was by now widely spread and securely rooted, and particularly so in the assumedly prosperous and populated Seine–Rhine area. There, some notable styles had quite early been developed, for instance the attractive chain-handled jugs and, from the aforesaid firm of Frontinus, mould-blown bottles of barrel form (Pl.5c) on which latter it had the forethought to impress its mark in a considerable number of letterings, not invariably however. Now still more desirable are the Western snake-thread drinking and other glasses, trailed in the same fashion as Pl.12a but in colour; they belong to the third century. In England evidence of the technique exists but is limited to very small fragments. Blown glass at the Amiens end may have a peculiar bright greenish tint and a surface texture or sheen of its own. The tint of specimens from the Rhine end, Cologne and Andernach, for instance, can be a duller green, relatively lifeless, but no generalization is warranted. It would be surprising if there had not been a deterioration in the output of provincial furnaces when the Roman world began to crack, yet in the disruption to come the distant provinces and cities of Gaul may have preserved the arts they owed to Rome more successfully than did their Italian counterparts.

And Constantine had not migrated to his new capital without good reason. It was from the East that the wealth and resources of the Empire had been derived, and the Rome on the Tiber could not control them as could the New Rome on the Bosphorus. There was nothing to prevent the Syrian and Alexandrian glasshouses from switching any required part of their exports to Constantinople so that for the remaining seventy years of the period under review (A.D. 330–400) there need have been no more alteration in the kind of glass they made than that due to natural development and elaboration. But the change must have put Egyptian competitors at a disadvantage, if only for reasons of propinquity. Besides, any glassmakers who moved with Constantine or joined him may have settled down and worked with a gradual orientalization of style until what had been Roman glass developed into Byzantine, whereof we know just nothing. They may indeed have been but merchants on the trade routes, forwarding the glass of Mesopotamian and Sassanian houses westwards and northwards to the Baltic coasts, at least until the irruption of Attila across the routes. Equally they may have traded eastwards from Syria into the Crimea.

By the end of the fourth century the Eastern Capital was well and truly established. The enduring magic of the very word Rome must not be allowed to obscure the reputation and vigour of the Empire centred on Constantinople, which, for all its chequered history-to-be, was yet able to stand a bulwark between Europe and the Asiatic hordes, and to remain the centre of the world's culture for 1,000 years. Unhappily, it is at this point that the hitherto plentiful supply of Roman glass begins to fail.

FOR FURTHER REFERENCE

Works as listed for Chapter 1.

HARDEN, D. B. *Roman Glass from Karanis*, Michigan, 1936.

THORPE, W. A. *English Glass*, 1935 (2nd edition 1949).

And for glassmaking technique.

McKEARIN, G. S. and H. *American Glass*, New York, 1941.

PELLATT, ASPLEY. *Curiosities of Glassmaking*, 1849.

POWELL, H. J. *Glassmaking in England*, 1923.

THORPE, W. A. *History of English and Irish Glass*, 2 vols, 1929.

CHAPTER III

THE SECOND FOUR CENTURIES

*

1. The Western Empire

WHEN history itself becomes confused it is not surprising that the story of a minor art should be obscured. A study of the times is needful to realize how anarchical conditions became in the fifth century and how chaotic daily life must have been; it is essential if even the vaguest comprehension of contemporary arts and crafts is to be obtained. The impact of history upon civilized progress is all-important, for civilization cannot yet dictate events.

The fourth century had been one of depression and depopulation, of tyranny and taxation – evils accentuated no doubt by luxury and waste in high places, but of which the root cause was the increasing strain of maintaining the Empire's boundaries. The pressure upon them had been slowly increasing since the beginning of the first century, and the more or less controlled admission of very many barbarians, and their enlistment in camp and at court, had become a dangerous if inescapable palliative. Its source was the northern Teutonic lands in the basins of the Oder, of the Spree, and of the Vistula, where the tribes were wholly pagan. This would have mattered less had they not also been predatory by instinct and destructive by nature – characteristics which twenty centuries have not sufficed to eradicate from our world.

As long as Rome could firmly hold the barriers of the Rhine and the Danube, the expansionist fervour of these barbarians could only be directed eastwards, and some at least of the Goths did move to what is now South Russia: the Dniester–Dnieper area. It seems probable that others, as well as tribes disturbed by that early drive to the east, sought or gained admittance to the Empire, and to this result both the spread of Christianity and a real appreciation of Roman civilization may have contributed.

When, however, Roman power no longer sufficed to maintain the barriers, a westward and southward surge of the northern barbarians inevitably followed. And when Attila and his all-devouring trans-Caspian Huns decided to press westwards, they added to the confusion by driving both the West Goths and the East Goths within the Empire's gates, where they (the Goths) seem to have behaved with relative propriety and even friendliness. Indeed, since many of their blood had preceded them and had been assimilated, a stable Romano-Gothic State would doubtless have emerged eventually, in spite of an Italian abhorrence for the unorthodox (Arian) Christianity now professed by the Goths.

It is also to the credit of all concerned, and the Visigoths in particular, that they turned with one accord upon the Hun and eliminated that danger in the Châlons area (A.D. 451). He at any rate was an inexcusable interloper to no man's fancy, and Western Europe had good reason to be thankful for his disappearance.

One gets the impression that the main migrations, being genuine migrations, were carried out with some measure of order. A certain amount of lip service at any rate was at first paid to the nominal supremacy of the Emperor, and no doubt a certain amount of real deference was felt for the traditional reputation of Rome and the value of her civilization. It is even possible that the migrants may themselves have desired something better, something more progressive, than their age-old savagery.

For it need not be supposed that any of the immigrant processions was either very numerous or, in the fifth century, totally pagan. The hazards of their journeying and their contacts with Christianity would in any case soon have abated their numbers and modified their paganism.

All these incursions of Franks, Burgundians, Vandals, Sueves, and Goths took place within the first fifty years or so of the fifth century. Their peregrinations are a matter of history, as those of lesser tribes and even more predatory bands are not. And so, collisions of these moving bodies were bound to occur, not only with the relics of Roman power but also with each other and with their forerunners, with unhappy results for those already settled in the vicinity.

Hence any fusion in Italy was delayed, and at just the wrong moment the Eastern Empire, Justinian ruling, found enough means and strength to destroy the kingdom of the Vandals in Africa (533) and, much less easily, the kingdom of the East Goths in Italy (533–55), but it had not the strength to hold either of them. Justinian had ample excuse, because the African Vandals had not only turned pirate but had sacked Rome in 455 with every sort of persecution of its religion. Still, it was unfortunate for Italy, because the northern vacuum was quickly filled by Lombards from the Brandenburg country, still plundering pagans, and at their hands much of Italy was subjected to massacre, destruction, and pillage.

Rome, Ravenna, and certain maritime cities – Venice and Pisa among them – found a measure of independence in self-reliance, and remained under the ineffective jurisdiction of the Empire. It is said that Venice was founded by refugees fleeing from the barbarian invaders. It is quite possible that its lagoon and island population was reinforced, and certain that Venice eventually replaced Aquileia, destroyed by Attila in 452, as the first strategic and commercial centre in the northern Adriatic. And if it is true that Aquileia was a glassmaking or glass-carving centre – as is also possible – Venice may well have acquired a tradition that was to stand her in good stead in the future.

The Lombards did gradually adopt orthodox Christianity and assimilate something of the Italian civilization, but their modes and their manners had evoked such detestation that when, by invitation, Charlemagne overthrew the Longobard kingdom (773) the world was the gainer and there was no Italian discontent.

In all this long-continued strife learning almost perished in the Western Empire, and when learning dies the other arts will already have gone, and not last the art of fine glassmaking, while pillage, plunder, and the mere lapse of time must have wrought havoc with the glass already in existence. It was the monasteries which performed a real service by maintaining the continuity of learning and of the arts and crafts, and somehow trade continued to flow from the Mediterranean and penetrated into parts as distant as Britain.

Whether, and to what extent, common glass continued to be made in Italy is a matter of opinion rather than of evidence. For only now, three quarters of a century after the all-important official adoption of Christianity in 324, does the significance of that event become clear to the student of glass. Hitherto the tombs have furnished material in plenty from which the evolution of glassmaking can be deduced, while leisure and learning have bequeathed at least some contemporary comments on and references to it. The burial of glass was, however, a pagan practice which ceased as Christianity spread. By the year 400 the tombs largely fail us for specimens, and by 450 even the Christian gilt glass is no longer found.

I am going to assume that despite all commotions, the relics of the Western Empire and the old provincial centres such as the Rhône valley and Catalonia still made common glass as and where possible. It is a reasonable assumption, remembering the simplicities of its manufacture and the conveniences of its use, and the lack of evidence is no argument against such an assumption. The record is imperfect, and some of the traditional forms are likely to have been adhered to, and if any such were deposited in late pagan tombs they might not be recognizable as post-fourth-century glasses.

So far as Italy is concerned there is no evidence of any continuance of fine glassmaking. Yet the successful self-reliance of the maritime cities may be remembered and the courage and tenacity of the Church in adversity had been notable. Throughout the seventh and eighth centuries the influence of the Papacy in world affairs had been increasing. Surely a certain state must have been maintained by the Popes, sufficient to attract a nucleus of craftsmen. If so, it is impossible that there should not have been glassmakers among them; actual remains of glass mosaics found in Rome, Ravenna, and elsewhere, confirm Nesbitt's belief that such mosaics continued to be made until the ninth century.

The case is rather different in northern Gaul. Of all the immigrant Germans, only the Franks from the Rhineland contrived to combine wisdom with force and thereby succeed in establishing a permanent state. By the middle of the sixth century their boundaries stretched from the Atlantic to Thuringia and from the Mediterranean to the North Sea. It is from the Seine–Namur–Rhine area of this relatively stabilized kingdom that clear evidence of continued glass manufacture is found. It was obviously in the northern regions far distant from Rome that paganism was likely to linger and ancient burial customs to persist. And so from Frankish tombs in Gaul and across the Rhine, and from Saxon graves in England and southern Scandinavia, we get a series of Merovingian (c.400–c.750) glasses (Pl.6d), among them some of distinguished and distinctive appearance, possessing what has been called a 'northern appeal'. They include ribbed drinking bowls (Pl.8c), and particularly the cone-beakers and their companions the claw-beakers (Pl.6e). Especially 'northern' are drinking-horns, though very few examples have been found in England. Such glasses were for the rich, and the finest of them will stand comparison with any hand-made glass since blown. They date up to the seventh and eighth centuries, when their story also closes. Specimens will be found in the British Museum, and also scattered in small local museums where their presence is little known and their importance likely to be overlooked by visitors. Few examples are in private hands.

For the poorer there were palm-cups (Pl.5d) – little beakers such as might cap a modern thermos flask. Much more may have been made. Utility glass will not be expected to have survived unless deposited in tombs, and although the Seine–Rhine populace can hardly have been universally Christian, it may have become indifferent, or universally too poor to provide grave-goods, or possibly the old custom died out irrespective of religious considerations.

As to glass, fine or common, being made in England from the fifth to the eighth century, it is generally believed that the fine pieces referred to above were brought over from the Continent. Even if that be so, it does not follow that common glass was not made in this country. The same must be held to apply to Spain.

2. The Later Roman Empire and Islam

The term Eastern Empire, so often and conveniently used, is really a misnomer until A.D. 800, when Charlemagne's Empire in the West could legitimately claim the title of 'Roman'. The Later Roman Empire is the best title for the eastern portion of the old empire. Its history begins with the establishment of Constantine's new capital (indifferently New Rome, Byzantium, or Constantinople) in A.D. 350. Its traditions and population were predominately Greek. Its official language from the middle of the sixth century was Greek. Its civilization and culture were inevitably Graeco-Roman. But its peoples were still Roman in the old political sense of the word, and until A.D. 800 there was only one Roman Empire, varying indeed in extent and in power with circumstances, but still a single entity even if (as at first) there were two capitals and generally two emperors.

For this civilization now centred on the ancient city of Byzantium the term Byzantine is preferable. Its importance as a world influence ought not to be overlooked. For as heir to the past, and as the greatest city of the world and the only one which had always been Christian, Byzantium naturally stood supreme in civilization. From its situation it linked East with West, and so was of immense importance commercially. As a state, the Later Roman Empire was always what we now call a world power, and almost always the first world power. The services it rendered for a thousand years as a bulwark to a somewhat undeserving West were inestimable.

For there was always an actual or potential menace from the east and the north. We have seen how the western provinces of the Empire were lost in the fifth century and partially and temporarily regained in the sixth. It was unfortunate on all counts that after a truce lasting some two and a half centuries, and despite a very recent promise (how history repeats itself) of eternal peace, hostilities with that rival empire of Persia – the Parthia of earlier times – should almost immediately have broken out (A.D. 540). It took nearly a century of consistently unfavourable war before the Persian power dissolved at the hands of Heraclius (A.D. 628). With a loss of the greater part of Italy, of all Syria and Egypt, and much of Illyria, and with herself dangerously threatened (A.D. 626), it was by little that New Rome had escaped extinction. But the disappearance of the Persian power was an event of such magnitude that all and more than all might have been recovered. Time and the unexpected denied such rewards.

The surprise was the sudden rise of Mohammed, which must have seemed inexplicable to the Romans, so long and so often dominant in the East and now apparently without a rival. Christianity had permeated Syria and Egypt and had spread to Abyssinia; it was converting the Teutonic barbarians; it had its centres and an increasing influence in Arabia. And Persia had, if not a religion, at least a beneficent philosophy.

To a thoughtful mind these facts must have demonstrated that paganism could never stand before the new faith. If, then, a non-Christian mind rebelled at the thought of Christianity, it might easily conclude that some alternative belief was imperative. Mohammed's was such a mind, and his teachings were in fact, if not in design, a competitive religion. Though they seem to have been tolerant enough on their inception, they were received as coldly as all new teachings are. But once established, not so tolerantly, their spread was as rapid as anyone could have wished. First haltingly preached in 610, the new religion so quickly became a political force that in twenty years Mohammed felt strong enough to demand the conversion of both Heraclius and Chosroes II of Persia. As conversion implied submission, it is not surprising to find no record of the replies of those rulers. In 634 Damascus was selected as capital of the new Power, and by the middle of the seventh century Islam controlled not only Syria but also Arabia and Egypt;

she quickly added Persia and Armenia, and by the end of it dominated Africa, had besieged Byzantium (A.D. 673–7), and was shortly to do so again. Of all this territory only portions of Syria were recovered by the Empire, and these but inter-mittently.

A religion no more difficult to understand than Christianity, one which was satisfied with an affirmation of faith rather than a demonstration of it, and one which, moreover, encouraged conversion by the sword and rewarded the converter with the spoils – such a religion could hardly fail for lack of enthusiastic adherents. But as a world power Islam could and did fail just because of them and their mutual rivalries and jealousies.

With the defeat of the second attempt on Byzantium (A.D. 717–18), egress from the drier and desert lands was checked, and the constant indeterminate warfare which followed for the next two centuries did nothing to promote progress on either side and much to retard it in areas in which these mutual hostilities took place.

Generally speaking, the eighth century was for the Eastern Empire one of prudence and reform. Stepping ahead, we find that the ninth saw a resurgence of its power and a period of re-conquests. The eleventh saw the beginning of a final de-cline, when the familiar and hereditary dangers on the north and east were accentuated by political aggression on the part of the Normans and commercial aggression on the part of Venice. And at last the Franks and Venetians exploited the situation created by the Turks and captured Byzantium in 1204. It was not the end, but it was the beginning of the end, and the world cannot thank them.

What, then, of the glass of the Later Empire during these second four centuries? That Byzantium itself made glass, and glass of quality, can hardly be questioned. Could it have been otherwise in a capital but recently established, with the skill at hand and at call, and a hereditary delight, and indeed a neces-sary delight, in pomp and circumstance? Since the elaborate embellishment of St Sophia with coloured mosaic and window glass was possible, there ought to have been the artistry need-ful for the fashioning of fine vessels. Yet nothing corroborates the theory and such fragments as have been found have been Syrian types. Of suggestive pieces there are some in the Treasury of St Mark at Venice, brought from Constantinople in 1204, mainly of the fifth and sixth centuries, inaccessible in the ordinary way of things and outside the scope of this book.

Of its day-to-day glass we seem to know nothing, but should not therefore assume that Byzantine styles or techniques are lost to us. It seems very likely that the styles then popular in the East, in Syria, Palestine, and Egypt, were equally popular in the Roman capital.

Glass of considerable merit was, naturally enough, being made in Syria in the fifth and first half of the sixth centuries, that is, until the Persian war, perhaps without much development of style, colour, or decoration. Such glasses included *unguentaria* and vases with zigzag stringing or distorted loops stretching from the shoulder or neck to the rim of the mouth. Horizontal stringing in a colour different from that of the body was also a feature of this period, as was a similar type of zigzag trailing to the body (Pls 2f, 3e, and 8b). This use of contrasting colours is still more definite in two-colour *amphorae* (Pl.7a), in amber with green or blue (Pl.7d) and ewers in amber and blue or green and blue. Plate 8a illustrates a sixth-century water pitcher of a form which Ruth might have carried centuries before.

As stated, the Christian gold-glass persisted until the middle of the fifth century, and, even later, Syria was making rather crude mould-blown bottles with Christian emblems, such as the Cross or the Jewish seven-branched candlestick, on the sides.

Another form of trailing in self-colour belongs more firmly to the fifth or even sixth century, namely a circuit of large irregular oval loops linked together and sometimes extended above and below to form subsidiary loopings, as in Pl.4f, but more emphatically rendered; there were comparable patterns (Pl.7c).

There were still made for a while cups, vases, and conical oil containers commonly called lamps, decorated with irregular blobs of colour, dark green or blue. These lamps, which are not so unlike cone-beakers, were dropped into holes in a suspended circular metal frame, the counterpart of our modern electrolier or gasolier.

But when all is said and done, the uncertainties of nearly every ancient glass are such that precision of dating is impossible, and that of provenance usually unknown. Style may betray, but still remains the safest feature whereby to assess any specimen, and we need not be too exigent.

From now on one may or may not observe a certain decadence in these many glasses of traditional type; in every century there had been careless, cheaply executed work, just as there has been in every country since. What had been Syro-Roman had devolved into Syro-Byzantine, and a fairer judgement would be possible if the quantity of fifth- to eighth-century glass at our disposal was anything like so great as that of the first four centuries. Unhappily it is infinitely less, chance rather than formal burial having been the cause of its preservation.

But there was a parallel orientalization which provides a group-type of oddly trailed or patched globular and cylindrical bottles (Pl.9a) and similar incurved hemispherical bowls, generally looking as though made of glass of mud. They have a hard incrustation which does not flake away at all easily, and beneath it the metal is good, and pale amber or honey-coloured. The glasses are liberally trailed, sometimes with a sort of starfish pattern; flat circular prunts are also applied, and both the trailing and prunting may be in purple, blue, or pale green, perhaps a development of the blob or blotch decoration of the fourth to fifth centuries. They will have looked very well when new. More fanciful are some *unguentaria* enclosed within a grille or lattice and mounted on the back of an even more fanciful horse (Pl.9b). Lamm dates this group-type to the fifth and sixth centuries, and the grille around the horse-mounted *unguentaria* is certainly reminiscent of the caged Begram beakers of Chapter II. In such glasses a coarser Arab influence may fairly be inferred, and the term 'Arab' is a good title for orientalized yet pre-Islamic glass, which betrays little of the Semitic craftsmanship of the first four or five centuries, but which may evidence the versatility of the craftsmen.

During the Persian war from the mid sixth century to well

into the seventh, the power and prestige of the Empire were sorely strained. It is not likely that these unhappy circumstances had any effect on the glass of Byzantium, but if so there was no time for any revival before the Empire had Mohammed as a foe in place of Chosroes, and it took exactly the same time to neutralize the danger – that is to say, another eighty-eight years (630–718).

War was more desultory then than it has since become, and Persia or no Persia, Islam or no Islam, I do not think that enterprising glass-makers would easily have relinquished the market which the capital of the Later Empire offered, and there is nothing to show that the domination of Mohammed and his successors implied direct interference with trade relationships. But it is a question whether Syrian glass-makers were as enterprising as before, after two centuries of trouble. It may be that the initiative had passed to Mesopotamia or Persia rather than to Egypt, happily situated outside the disturbed area. It may not be at all related to the Mohammedan overlordship just established in Damascus (634) that from the middle of the seventh century further and eventually far-reaching changes in style, and particularly decoration, began to show themselves.

Blown, mould-blown, and cut styles such as those shown in Pl. 10 appear in the eighth century and carry on into our next period. The moulding tended to be emphatic, deeply impressed if not always sharply, and covering the body of the vessel; the sharpness seems relative to the thickness of the metal, the lighter glasses giving the best definition, as in Pl. 7e, a fragile vessel indeed. Simple forms of cutting naturally preceded elaboration, and here a substantial wall of metal was, for a long time, essential.

With the accession of the Abbasid Dynasty the Mohammedan capital was removed to Baghdad in 749. This was a different thing, and from now on Mohammedan art came more and more under Persian influence. It is one reason for postulating that Persia was already at least abreast of any other country in the art of glass. We can this time picture a Mohammedan world, from Egypt to Iraq and Syria to Persia, making glass in considerable profusion, yet of it we still possess comparatively little which is not fragmentary. As anticipated, more material is coming to light, preserved on abandoned city sites or in rubbish-dumps. Yet we still know much less about it, though it is some six to eight centuries younger than our first blown glass. The full blooming of Islamic into Saracenic glass was still distant, but the promising buds were appearing, to open in our next period.

FOR FURTHER REFERENCE

DILLON, E. *Glass*, 1907.

EISEN, G. A. *Glass*, 2 vols, New York, 1927.

HONEY, W. B. *Glass*, Victoria and Albert Museum Handbook, 1946.

LAMM, C. J. *Glass from Iran*, Stockholm, 1935.

THORPE, W. A. *English Glass*, 1935 (2nd edition 1949).

CHAPTER IV

THE EMPTY AGES
(A.D. 800–1400)

*

1. Western Europe and Germany

THE period now to be dealt with may be regarded by collectors as one which cannot be adequately represented in the cabinet except by the grace of fortune and a purse long enough to command a Saracenic mosque lamp. It remains true that in so far as European glass is concerned no age is so empty and the cabinet is likely to remain in a similar state despite the most accommodating of purses. That this should be so after some thousand years of civilization is an uncomfortable reflection.

The East, however, now offers an increasing range of interesting glass of good quality, quite apart from its expensive enamelled glass; as time goes on this Islamic glass will become better known, and if provenances and dates can only be estimated within a century or so and a few hundred miles, nobody is very much the worse, and in due course fuller knowledge will become available.

There may be hardly anything to find of European make, but there is still evidence that glass continued to be made. There are treatises on its manufacture, not very comprehensible, not always original, and never free from a certain alchemistic leaning. Fact and fancy are mingled in a truly medieval manner, but were there no other evidence, the mere existence of such treatises would be enough to prove that glass was needed and was made.

In A.D. 800, in what is now France, the practice of burying glass in pagan tombs was finally dying out. Glassmaking continued, though the Franks, with a law and a church and an empire to sustain, may have envied the profitable Semitic glass trade and have implemented their covetousness. In any case it seems that there were reasons strong enough to persuade these glassmakers to migrate in the ninth century, this time to l'Altare in Montferrat, not far from Genoa, a movement which had both an immediate and a delayed effect. The disorders consequent on the break-up of Charlemagne's empire doubtless contributed. Populations were rural, not urban; the local market was small, and the lack of law and order deterred movement, even a peaceful penetration by itinerant glassblowers. On the other hand, the Roman road system was disintegrating and the transport of goods was becoming more hazardous.

And so far as the Normandy–Picardy glassmakers were concerned, it seems reasonable to suppose that their migration was powerfully influenced by the depredations of the pagan Northmen. It is at least significant that their exile corresponds so closely with the official existence of the Duchy of Normandy (911–1204), carved out by Rollo after a century of incursions and rapine. Rouen, Paris, and Picardy especially suffered, though the raiding went far wider than that, inland as far as Bourges, and coastwise to Bordeaux, and to Nîmes and Arles near the mouth of the Rhône.

It would seem that those who remained in the old glassmaking centres, and any of the Franks who may have been tempted to exploit the trade, found fine glassmaking beyond their powers. Deprived of technical skill and commercial enterprise, one would expect markets to have fallen away irrespective of hostile incursions, and the craft to have degenerated into the making of utility vessels presumably in the simplest of the ancient forms, but of which we possess some fragments only. Much of the glassmaking effort was insistently devoted to window glass.

Towards the end of the period, that is to say in the fourteenth century, there is evidence of a very considerable output of serviceable glass, and of some elaborate glass, all still seemingly *verre de fougère*, but again few recognized specimens exist. Latterly also inventories demonstrate that royal and other owners possessed and prized a certain amount of fine glass.

This too is mostly lost, and descriptions which have come down leave us little wiser than before. The conventional view is that such pieces came directly from the East as gifts, or as souvenirs of a crusade. Doubtless some did, but there is no means of gauging the true quality of this inventoried glass. Some may have been made locally by straggling oriental craftsmen.

There is also that delayed effect of the Semitic expulsion to consider. When conditions permitted, those Altarist descendants began to migrate once again, and their dispersion is generally dated to the sixteenth century. But that gives them an Italian home for some seven centuries, and of their handiwork during that extended period there is no trace. I would prefer to think that it was the thirteenth century at latest which saw this dispersion begin. It would account very easily for that large *verre de fougère* output in the Dauphiné in south-eastern France during the fourteenth century and also for at least a part of the inventoried glass. If that Laurence Vitrearius who, as we shall see, settled near Chiddingfold in 1226, could be shown to be an Altarist, the case would be proved. He is known to have come from Normandy, which had fallen to Philip Augustus of France in 1204, and it does not follow that he was a native of that Duchy, an early and likely goal for any Altarist whose forefathers had migrated thence.

In the Rhineland, and elsewhere in the eastern areas owing allegiance to Frankish dominion, a *waldglas* tradition reigned, comparable to the *verre de fougère* further west and south. The one was based on the use of beech or other wood-ash for the necessary alkali, the other on the use of 'fern' or bracken, but no doubt local conditions determined the choice; there did not have to be exactitude, and in any case the resultant glass was much the same. Again, the simplest vessels were to be expected, such as palm-cups, jugs, and bottles, but nothing is recognizable until we come to a very few examples, little sealed pots of heavy glass enclosing relics, found embedded in altars. One at least belongs to this period, being dated 1252. Others are dated to the end of the fourteenth century and to 1519. There are pictorial records of comparable and concurrent little prunted cups and an actual example of the mid fifteenth century. Later these developed into the prunted roemers and beakers of the Rhineland.

In the northern parts of Germany paganism lingered on, and more glass might be expected from graves in parts of Poland and along the Baltic shores. Indeed, eastern Prussia and Lithuania were not converted until the thirteenth and fourteenth centuries, and then by the knightly Teutonic Order which had founded itself during the Crusades. Conversion in this case meant coercion, and in due course a cohesion which turned the tables and wrecked the Order. Its practice of, and services to, real Christianity are not impressive. There are grave-glasses from Scandinavia, and Kisa mentions a few as late as the tenth century, but the records suggest a dwindling either of the ancient burial customs or a lack of contacts with glassmaking areas, which latter would not be surprising in view of the state of Europe at that time.

In England no grave-glass is known later than the seventh to eighth centuries, and as we find requests from English churchmen for French workers to make window glass, it can be inferred not only that any such home industry had disappeared but that the Frankish workers could supply the need. It was not until the second quarter of the thirteenth century that Laurence Vitrearius, hailing from Normandy, established himself in the Surrey–Sussex Weald, and glass was again certainly made in England. Primarily it was window glass which was made, but there was naturally a certain output of vessel-glass. It was doubtless a profitable business, as Laurence was followed in due course notably by the Schurterre family in 1343, again specializing in stained glass, and they by others. It is not possible to identify the window glass they made, even though it is known to what churches it went. Of the vessel glass there remain only indecisive fragments discovered on glasshouse sites and stray finds on various excavated sites.

Both in England and on the Continent the importance of the demand for window glass, and especially church window glass, must be given full weight. It went a very long way towards restricting the manufacture of vessel glass; indeed, consciously or unconsciously, the Church checked this latter by prohibiting the making of chalices in glass. This would be understandable even without having to remember the un-exampled influence and power of the Church. Both rich and poor could do without beakers, jugs, and bowls, or get them in alternative materials, but there was no substitute for win-dow glass. Comfort had to come before convenience, and that fact goes far to explain the paucity of even fragments of medieval utility glass.

Some few glasses found in Spain may have been made there during this period, for if glassmaking did not entirely cease elsewhere, there was no special reason why it should have died out in Spain. Some *lipsanotecas* – flasks for salves or unguents – are recorded of the eleventh and twelfth centuries, but they remain Arab or Islamic in style, even though some were found in Catalonia, liberated from the Moors centuries before by Charlemagne. Fine glasses will have been imported from the East.

Italy contributes no recognizable glass of the period under review, that famous specimen in the British Museum known as the Aldrevandini beaker being now regarded as of Eastern manufacture, *c.* 1300. Its inscription, *Magister Aldrevandini Me Feci(t)*, suggests that the glass is as good as could then be made, or at least that its maker – presumably a European – took great pride in it. It is, however, rather poor work, surprisingly so in view of Venetian connexion with Syria, cognizance of the graces of Constantinople, the existence of a guild of glass-blowers in 1224, and records of an export trade in 1279. There was acquaintance, too, with the glassmakers of l'Altare in the (Genoese) Marquisate of Montferrat, competitors and rivals of Venice with similar interests in the eastern Mediterranean and (*c.* 1200) with far more territory.

Glass furnaces also existed in other places in Italy, such as Padua and Bologna. It is rather surprising, too, to read that Murano craftsmen reinforced the Altarist workers in the four-teenth century. Perhaps this happened earlier, because there was always the keenest rivalry between the Venetians and the Genoese, and from 1253 to 1380 often actual war. Possibly it was simply that individuals crossed to l'Altare not so much with the idea of cooperating, as with a desire to escape the trammels at home and then to carry their art into new and more profitable fields abroad.

No example of Altarist work has come down to us. But if Italy is devoid of any indigenous glass of the period, it still contains the largest collection of medieval glass in existence. Elsewhere there are preserved in churches a few specimens to which tradition assigns romantic histories which we may credit or not, according to taste, and at St Mark's in Venice there are some thirty examples with a claim to be regarded as a Byzantine group of glasses brought from Constantinople on its fall in 1204. They include cups, and shallow bowls cut and mounted as hanging lamps or patens (Honey, p. 43), and there are two differently coloured bowls cut in relief with hare-like animals. The collection is of course not necessarily all of the same date.

It seems beyond the bounds of probability that nothing whatever remains of thirteenth- and fourteenth-century Venetian and Altarist glass, and one easy explanation offers. From the eleventh century both Venetian and Altarists had been particularly in touch with the age-old glass industry of Syria, and must have been acquainted with Egyptian glass also. It would be surprising if they had not adopted selected Eastern styles and had not reproduced them at home faithfully enough to prevent our distinguishing a quite variable Asiatic product from an as yet unknown European manufacture.

2. Eastern Glass

In the East, Egypt continued to make glass, to export it, and probably to export its glassmakers as well. Colour, inherent and applied, cutting, and relief carving were its specialities, but the production appears to have included all the recognized techniques. Yet the question remains, whether leadership in the art had not passed to Mesopotamia and Persia. Certainly some of the styles attributed to Egypt were made elsewhere, some indeed anywhere in glassmaking centres in the East.

There seems no reason to attribute a somewhat unanimous choice of forms and techniques to any common religious concept. But a somewhat unanimous acceptance of a religion may have formed a cultural tie between peoples formerly aloof or even distant in both senses of the word, and so the glass of Syria, Iraq, and Persia, as well as that of Egypt, can now be termed Islamic, and further differentiation left to specialists.

Just such a glass was the bicoloured striped and threaded ring-beaker (Pl.10b), so narrow in diameter that nobody but a child could comfortably have used it; or could it have been a dice-beaker? Gaming is not a modern obsession and it knows no frontiers.

Small palm cups in colour, with moulded rosettes in raised dots, were again on the simple side, though more imaginative, accompanied by a more important range of bicoloured bottles showing also a well-favoured decorative device of concentric circles (Pl.11a). In this case, as with the ewers of similar style, the upper part was in blue glass and the lower in what may have been intended for clear metal, but which in fact was pale green or pale amber. Alternative colours were used. Their manufacture must have offered considerable technical difficulty. So, too, must have the decoration on the flask at Pl. 7b. It commences beneath the base as a continuous white trail rising in close horizontal spirals, but quickly being interrupted, to appear first as dashes growing shorter and shorter, and ultimately as small dots: this was no mean feat.

Patterned and deeply impressed mould-blown glasses of the eighth century were carried over into this period, perhaps gaining in weight and strength as time went on. There were many more bottles, commonly given a little bulb or bulbs in the cylindrical neck (Pl.10a). Bag-shaped ewers with a thumb-piece to the handle were rather crudely moulded with an indefinite design, occasionally with an apparent inscription (Pl. 11b). Common and rather remarkable characteristics were the inadequacy of the handle and the narrowness of the mouth of the vessel. Indeed, to a modern eye not many of the ancient glasses illustrated here would be regarded as of utility value. Sprinkler bottles in heavy green glass emerged in the twelfth

century, the bodies moulded as before, the necks with a vermi-
cular collar at the base (see Pl.11d). A later and related form of
this bottle is the Damascus sprinkler of Pl.12c. From further
east – that is to say the present Persia – the twelfth and thirteenth centuries give us some opaque white bottles and vases
(Pl.13a) smoothly finished and delicately fashioned.

Utilitarian and too ephemeral were small light perfume-
flasks in blue or green glass; more substantial ones were
stronger and cylindrical, as in quite early centuries. Very substantial, indeed something like unbreakable ones, were circular, or with four or more sides (Pl.10c), of thick crystalline or
even granular glass, cut in greater or less degree, some provided with molar-like feet, almost legs. These must have been
made in great profusion in the ninth and tenth centuries.

Less mechanical and geometrical than the foregoing was
faceting such as appears on the bottle at Pl.10d, and a further
step forward was the vivid intaglio representation of animals
and birds (ninth to eleventh century). Much of this work is
fragmentary, but it evokes great praise from those who have
studied it closely. Relief carving is exemplified in a small group
well known as the Hedwig glasses, something over a dozen in
all, mainly preserved in mid-Europe. They are short, thick
beakers with stylized eagles, and other animal forms, bold and
possibly attractive work which can hardly be termed beautiful.
They can now be reasonably and confidently attributed to
Persia, eleventh to twelfth century. No specimen has yet been
found in Egypt, but it remains a possibility that an emigrant
Egyptian may have been responsible. Somehow these glasses
have found their way into cathedral treasures as reliquaries,
though they carry no outward indication of holiness, and from
a Mohammedan source none was to be expected.

The ultimate achievement was the cutting of vessels in high
relief with elaborate designs in imitation of rock-crystal carving, and somewhat in the style of the earlier trailed work on
the bottles of Pl. 12a, b. Such work as this is now greatly prized,
and it came not only from Egypt but from further east, and
indeed may have been a Persian innovation. If so it strengthens
a growing belief that the glass of Persia was for long as im-

portant and artistic as any other. Here, as in a good many other respects, it seems that the story of ancient glass requires and will doubtless receive recasting.

Mention should be made of the varieties of pigmental decoration, some of very ancient origin. Painting was recorded in Chapter II, and to this can be added decoration in lustre colours and a staining process now apparently lost. A few glasses were gilt and not coloured, although touches of gilding were to become common. Examples of any of these processes are of very great rarity, but they were perhaps not very satisfactory, and were superseded in the end by an enamelling which gave a thickness and a depth of colour as well as relative permanency. This, the most important work of the period, and as important perhaps as that of any later period, will be mentioned immediately.

The end of the eleventh century saw the beginning of the Crusades, which led to the establishment of a long coastal belt of European kingships and countships, incorporating the ancient centres of glassmaking – Sidon, Tyre, Hebron, and Tiberias. What effect this occupation had on the industry is problematical. There was booty and no doubt a certain demand by the more important expeditionaries for the curious luxuries they had never before seen. But the self-seeking proclivities of the Crusaders in general and the debased standards of the rank and file seem more likely to have checked the industry than to have promoted it. However, it is certain that glassmakers were working at Damascus, whence they could exploit the appetites of the invaders without residing within reach of their jaws. A very important result was the practical knowledge of the craft the Venetians could have acquired in their capacity as shipping agents and purveyors in general to the crusading forces, and they were not the men to let any opportunity slip.

Beakers of every conceivable variety had been made since glass-blowing began. Now they became rather more substantial, with an everted mouth, and gradually taller and more flared. Forms which were somewhat waisted were also made (Pl.12d), again a shape quite suitable for a dice-beaker. The decoration included blobs or bands of colour and also circuits or zones in red colour, as if drawn with a pen; this is now usually obscured by flaking or incrustation, but originally it was merely decorative, or on occasion inscriptional or pseudo-inscriptional, in character. Gilding might accompany colour-work.

These beakers will serve to introduce the so famous enamelled glass of Syria and, it is suspected, minor sources further east. Honey gives an account of it from which it appears that the earliest types of glass were of clear metal with heavy enamel work, inscriptions, and the free use of bead-like drops. This class is attributed to Rakka, dating from the late twelfth to the middle of the thirteenth century. Before and after the virtual ending of the Crusades, which can be put at 1292, after the unrewarding capture of Acre, a certain number of vessels were brought away, and have been preserved in France, Germany, and in England, whereof we know best two flared beakers: the 'Aldrevandini' glass assumedly by an Italian in a controlled Syrian shop, and the more striking *Hope* glass in the British Museum.

As the thirteenth century wore on the enamelling developed and the metal was allowed to be tinted. Specimens heavily and boldly enamelled are assigned to Aleppo, even though some of them may have been made in Iraq, but perhaps not after 1258, when the country was overrun by the Mongols. The 'Luck of Edenhall', another flared beaker, is of this class, as is the bowl in Pl. 13c, decorated on the inside only, in part with superimposed enamel colours which exhibit a different design when viewed from the outside. There is a use of gilt tracery and an 'inscription' in pseudo-Kufic characters. Lamm (*Mittelalterliche Gläser*) gives it a date of *c.*1260, and records its reputed discovery between Baghdad and the Persian border; there is no question but that the decoration is Persian in feeling, wherever the bowl was made.

Specimens delicately and sometimes sparsely enamelled are assigned to Damascus; the work varies from relatively insignificant pieces to specimens of the highest quality and artistry. Of the former, there were such things as sprinkler bottles of flat, oval-bodied form with a tall, slender neck (Pl. 12c), which reproduced a much earlier style, but with a device in true enamel colour on the shoulders, encircling the base of the neck. Again, the beaker at Pl. 12d has banded red and gold decoration at top and bottom, and is a substantial glass. Of the latter, and especially after the disaster at Baghdad in 1258 which caused glassmakers to concentrate within Syria, fine vases and lamps were made whereon the decoration is often centred in some portrayal of horsemen, animals, birds, or figures delicately and meticulously executed, in contrast to the colourful and arresting design-decoration of Aleppo. Towards the end of the thirteenth century there appeared decorative styles derived from Chinese influences, maybe a result of the incursion of the Mongols.

Thus in the late thirteenth and the fourteenth centuries we have the peak of Saracenic glass, in a remarkable range of themes wherein colour, design, and figuring all play a sometimes competing part. It is chiefly the mosque lamps (they are really lamp shades or lanterns) which have survived, but there are also bowls and vases. They are the outstanding glasses of the Empty Ages and would be outstanding glasses in any Age. They are numerous, as rare glasses go, but museums prize them – Cairo alone has some seventy lamps; the Metropolitan Museum of New York boasts as many as thirteen examples; English museums too are not without a quota. So there are not enough to go round and prices have reached towards a four-figure mark; what they will reach remains to be seen.

So it went until history intervened, this time in the shape of Tamerlane. His shadow had appeared a century before over Damascus, and such were the intricacies of Eastern power-politics that then there was welcome for a potential ally, for Damascus had had experience of Christian allies as well as Christian customers. But the substance, in 1402, had become wholly predatory, and Tamerlane's ubiquitous incursions culminated in the capture of Damascus and the enforced transfer of its craftsmen to embellish his capital of Samarkand. Yet somebody made a few lamps believed to be of fifteenth-century date, whether evasive Damascenes or men of Aleppo is not known. Of the fortunes of the transferees at Samarkand we are equally ignorant.

To us now, a more important result was the opportunity it gave Venice to usurp the ancient Syrian industry, and to develop without competition the glass techniques it had not omitted to acquire. One era had passed away. Another, that of modern glass, was in sight.

*

In three short chapters some slight account has been given of the blown glass of the first fourteen centuries. When it is considered how little we know of the earliest single century of English blown glass proper – that is to say the period 1550–1650, a mere three hundred years distant, when men could read and write and print what they had written – one may fairly postulate vast gaps in our knowledge of, and important errors in our reconstruction of, ancient glass history. How great are our misconceptions we may never know, but I suspect that those who best understand the subject are most conscious of the incertitudes.

Slowly, by study, interpretation, and assessment of fresh material, specialist archaeologists have added much to the knowledge which we who have never seen an ancient glass *in situ* must gratefully accept, at least as a working hypothesis susceptible of variation as research progresses. It is with that reservation in mind that the preceding chapters have been written.

FOR FURTHER REFERENCE

DILLON, E. *Glass*, 1907.

HARTSHORNE, A. *Old English Glasses*, 1897.*

HONEY, W. B. *Glass*, Victoria and Albert Museum Handbook, 1946.

LAMM, C. J. *Glass from Iran*, Stockholm, 1935, and *Oriental Glass*, Stockholm, 1941.

THORPE, W. A. *History of English and Irish Glass*, 1929, and *English Glass*, 1935 (2nd edition 1949).

WINBOLT, S. E. *Wealden Glass*, 1935.

* Within whose pages something will be found on all phases of old glass.

CHAPTER V

THE RISE AND FALL OF VENICE

*

1. Her Fortunes and Misfortunes

IT may be observed how strangely the fortunes of Venice were determined by events never to have been foreseen. Mention has been made that refugees from Aquileia may have reinforced the original fisher-folk when Attila destroyed their city in 452, and it is unlikely that they were the first refugees, for Goths and other barbarians had passed through the land with customary thoroughness. Still, they had passed. The destruction of Aquileia marked a change, in that it coincided with the fall of the Western Empire. If many of those unhappy refugees now gave up hope of rehabilitation and sought security through their own unaided efforts, they were wise in their generation. The domination of the Lombards was still to come.

Hardly any more unsuitable site could have been found for a great city than those watery islands and unstable lagoons of the north Adriatic. Yet it was a case of safety first, and those overgrown islets of the lagoons formed an almost unassailable refuge from the land-bound barbarians. And with Aquileia gone, Venice, as she may now be called, found herself the port of entry nearest to central Europe. Her citizens could and did control the traffic routes from Egypt, Syria, and the East to mid-Europe and the Baltic. The amber of the North and the manufactures of Alexandria alike paid their dues in passing.

Whether the refugees brought from Aquileia their reputed knowledge of glassmaking cannot be said. It seems possible, even if opportunities for practical use of it were limited. For it must have been a matter of immense labour and no common ingenuity to build such a city as Venice on such a site. It was indeed the last and greatest example of European lake dwellings, and seemingly its mere construction was the main preoccupation of its citizens, because history has little to say about Venice until the ninth century.

The Venetians could not be content with a static role. They naturally and quickly became carriers as well as merchants, and developed first into a maritime power, landless and invulnerable, and later into a world power by conquest, negotiation, and an indifferently peaceful penetration, but were then more open to challenge. It was the lying athwart the north-to-south trade route which brought Venice her earliest opportunity.

The reasons for and the vicissitudes of the Crusades make strange reading, but little else was to be expected when the interests involved were so diverse and so conflicting. Not the least of these was the ambition of traders to found a controllable route to the East, and as Venetians were among the most ambitious of traders, their cooperation, upon terms, was whole-hearted. Had the primary effort been directed towards Egypt the course of history might have been a very different one.

So from the year 1096 the Crusades went forward, and Venice was there to provide shipping, services, and supplies to those who needed and could pay for them. It was a profitable business, though the terms of the bargains struck included some curiously indefinite provisions that Venice should receive a given proportion of the conquests made, provisions the self-seeking Crusaders could hardly be relied upon to implement or the Venetians be in a position to enforce. Yet they sufficed to secure special privileges, such as exemption from tolls, and in some cities special quarters were allotted to the Venetians, with churches and even a justice of their own. They could then carry on trade with both friend and enemy with true commercial dispassion, and in something like complete independence. By 1124, and at the height of crusading successes, they were firmly established in Jerusalem, Acre, Sidon, and especially Tyre. It is not necessary to suppose that all these establishments were abandoned when Saladin retook Jerusalem in 1187. There was no particular enmity between Christian and Moslem; even the respective leaders seem to have been on quite as good terms with their enemies as with their allies.

The only fly in this so satisfactory Venetian ointment was the competitive activities of the Genoese, and for the next two hundred years the history of Venice was largely one of struggle with her rival for trade supremacy in the eastern Mediterranean. It was one reason for the attack on Constantinople, with its resultant capture in 1204. The Emperor Manuel had been persuaded by the Genoese and others to dispossess the Venetians trading in Constantinople, and an indignant declaration of war by Venice had been disastrous (1171). Putting business first, she had not been ashamed to treat successfully with the Ottoman Turks on their occupation of Syria (1189–91) for the retention of her trading rights. And, exploiting the fact that Byzantine pickings were not only much easier to obtain than Saracenic but also much more valuable, Venice, jealous and revengeful, succeeded in diverting the Fourth Crusade to Constantinople. The Wheel of Fortune turned once more. The city, so long the guardian of Europe, was captured and, characteristically, viciously sacked, Venice emerging from the invidious adventure with great possessions stretching from the Adriatic to and into the Black Sea. Crete was bought from Boniface of Montferrat, and Venice had suddenly become a world power.

Much knowledge must have been acquired by the enterprising and competitive traders of the day, including some acquaintanceship with the techniques of Syrian glass-blowers. Glass must have inevitably formed a part of the goods of trade, and it could not but have occurred to both Venetians and Genoese what advantages and what profits there lay in making such fragile wares at home. Each had at least a traditional knowledge of the art and probably an actual experience of blowing simple glass forms. Whether either could justly claim higher skill or could approach the finer styles of Eastern glass cannot now be known. In any case, it would have been a natural commercial move for Venice to have included competent Byzantine glass-blowers among her loot from

Constantinople in 1204, thereby assuring herself of practical tuition, if not also theoretical knowledge.

For certain it is that as early as 1224 there was a glass-blowers' guild at Venice, that in 1268 they could make 'graceful objects' in glass, and that in 1279 they were sufficiently well known to attract German pedlar-purchasers, while other Venetians were working glass furnaces elsewhere in northern Italy.

The thirteenth and fourteenth centuries were busy ones for the Venetians. They were occupied with carrying other people's goods and with territorial expansion, with many weighty matters to preoccupy them in a not too friendly world. None the less, these centuries quite certainly saw the establishment rather than the foundation of their glassmaking industry. Its production may have been imitative and also simple, and yet in advance of any other in Europe. Its future could not have been visualized even at the end of the fourteenth century. Chance had already played an unusually large part in the fortunes of Venice; one merit of its citizens was their power to exploit the unforeseen, and an opportunity for demonstrating that power was at hand.

Between any presumptive establishment of the Venetian industry about 1200 and its first recognized series of fine glass around 1450, at least two and a half centuries had to elapse, unmarked by any known home-made specimen. Two centuries had to elapse before there is any record of exportation to the Low Countries or to England (1394-9), and even then such exports were insignificant glasses (see Pl.15d). It would appear, then, that over this long period fine Venetian glass was not made, and that Venice could not rival the wares of Syria. It may be that any Byzantine workers brought away from Constantinople were less skilful, less willing, or less long-lived than was expected. Moreover, European notables as a whole condemned the attack on the Eastern Empire, and were probably disinclined to put profits into renegade Venetian pockets as long as they could buy the glass of the East; as for European populations, they had still some way to go before becoming buyers of any good glass at all.

But in 1402 unforeseen opportunity arrived. Tamerlane descended upon and captured Damascus, and virtually extinguished the Syrian glass industry by deporting its craftsmen. Venice was then able to make the most of this further stroke of fate and in no long time to replace the East as the world's centre of fine glassmaking. Tamerlane was not a man to do things by halves, and one may guess that his deportation of the Damascus craftsmen was thorough. Yet human beings can be strangely elusive if put to it, and a certain number escaped the net, some to keep alive the Syrian industry for a while, judging by a few fifteenth-century lamps in Egypt, others perhaps to serve the occidental traders rather than the oriental tyrant. Certainly such men would have been invaluable to Venice, as yet, so far as the evidence goes, by no means mistress of the art of glass. Perhaps twenty or thirty years, certainly fifty years later, she undoubtedly was, and with no sort of competition but that of the Altarists. How much such a favourable position came to be valued may be judged by the extreme measures the authorities took to promote a monopoly of the art. Substantial European competition, outside Italy, was appreciably postponed by these measures which authorized severe reprisals on workers who escaped to practise and pass on the sacrosanctified mystery of glassmaking. Nevertheless, it was often not possible or politic to enforce the drastic edicts.

It is possible, then, that some unknown Syrian had a considerable part in the ascendancy of Venice glass. Indeed, there exists a lamp presumed to be Venetian work of the third quarter of the fifteenth century, but there is little Saracenic influence remaining in the first fine series known to us, the magnificent Gothic standing cups or goblets of the second half of that century. Colour there is – an abundance of it – but no more. On the other hand, much may have been done in the half century 1402–50, and it is highly unlikely that we possess the earliest of Venice's *chef d'œuvres* or her only style of vessel. How many English-made glasses of the much later but rather comparable period 1549–1600 can be pointed out? The answer is, eight acceptable specimens, the earliest dated 1577 and the latest 1590. Furthermore, we know nothing about Altarist production of the same fifteenth-century period – it must surely be presumed – could we possibly have attributed to Venice any glass of her competitor?

The two centuries of rivalry between Venetians and Genoese had ended with the supremacy of the former, but the prize – control of the precious trade routes to the East – would not long have benefited either. In the naval war the honours were not uneven, but Venice secured the last battle by counter-blockading the apparently victorious Genoese fleet in her very own lagoons. This action in 1380 settled the matter, though perhaps a Pyrrhic victory. The threat had been one of starvation, and it was doubtless with regret that Venice was driven into a not unsuccessful attempt to become a land power, her peak being reached at the end of the fifteenth century. But the effort required had been great, and it coincided with less fortunate contests with the Ottoman Turks, from 1453 supreme in Constantinople. Europe had no sympathy for monopolist Venice, and demonstrated its feelings by forming the League of Cambrai against her. Venice could justly claim a great position and a world reputation, but she could not include extra-national goodwill among her acquisitions. It does not appear that this was a common commodity anywhere during the later Middle Ages, and Venice had done little to merit even a small share of the world's sympathy and respect. Her rulers, then, had to congratulate themselves on a lucky escape when the League which had pressed them almost to extinction fell to pieces on account of internal jealousies.

These reverses might have been foreseen. What could not have been foreseen was Diaz's discovery of the Cape route to the Indies (1488). Fate had struck again, and this time directly at the foundation of Venetian prosperity, for the overseas route was not only quicker but also safer and cheaper, and in-valuable trade passed into the hands of the ocean-going nations – the Portuguese, the Dutch, and the English. Venice had been effectually by-passed and ceased forthwith to be a world power. The gradual loss to the Turks of her remaining possessions was then a foregone conclusion, despite her best and bravest efforts. The process was complete in 1716.

It is difficult to regret this sixteenth- and seventeenth-century decline because it coincided so exactly with the ascendant period of Venetian art, not only in glass but in painting and in other fields. It is as if Venice, recognizing her failure to dominate in commerce, had resolved in consolation to dominate in art. It will be conceded that her second thoughts brought her the greater glory.

2. *Her Glass*

The early and entirely documentary history of the glass of Venice has been referred to, the evidence being suggestive of a considerable output of simple serviceable glass which was nevertheless in advance of anything made elsewhere in western Europe, other than, possibly, the products of l'Altare, as to which our knowledge is not even documentary, and of Catalonia, first notable in the fifteenth century but then well advanced. The Catalans themselves had not been uninterested in the Eastern trade.

As, then, this documentary history begins about 1200, manufacture on a considerable if possibly unambitious scale must have been proceeding at the same time. One likely reason why we know nothing more of Venice glass prior to 1450 is that we have been looking for something distinctive, whereas the ordinary Italian production was quite likely a *façon de Syrie*, and if and when found, specimens have been confused with Mohammedan glass. Plate 15d shows the sort of glass I have in mind: a simple little phial, excavated in Finsbury, London, according to the label on it, and it may even be one of the 'little bottles' recorded as reaching London from Venice at the end of the fourteenth century.

So far as we today are concerned, Venetian glass begins after rather than before 1450, two and a half centuries after the latest possible establishment of the industry. It begins with those richly coloured pedestal-footed goblets in Gothic style which will always stand in the forefront of the world's glass. Their makers relied on metal colour, heightening it with gilding

and 'gemming', i.e. with little pearl-like spots of coloure
enamel. Some few specimens such as the famous marriage cu
by Berovieri in the Civico Correr at Venice, were also pictor
ally enamelled, and are therefore known as procession glasse
and to that extent are commemorative. Plate15c shows an ex
cavated wine glass which may easily be allocated to the six
teenth century, though its simplicity denies exact dating.

Interesting and instructive as these goblets are, it seems a
most a pity to have thus overwhelmed the beauty of the met
itself. This particular type of richly coloured glass passed a
too quickly, but it had its descendants in certain colourful im
tations of ancient techniques. It is as though the tradition:
styles of Alexandria and Syria had arisen again, colour an
glassmanship waging a losing battle against crystal an
dexterity.

From the Berovieri side came vessels built up of millefio.
canes, but not, as anciently, finished on the wheel. They wer
not particularly successful, and indeed it remained for th
nineteenth century to show what could be done with mille
fiori glass. Another derivative which has been given a date a
early as the late fifteenth century, but which corresponds we
enough with forms being made a century later, was *calcedon*
or *schmelzglas*, imitating streaky stone, agate, or onyx, for ir
stance (Pl.18b). Our Greene who appears in Chapter ix, calle
it *calsedonia*; the colour was not a surface effect, but a throug
colour. Splashes of avanturine looking like gold or gold
spangling came to be added.

The milk-coloured glass, technically *lattimo*, may fairly b
correlated with the foregoing; this might be anything from
dull opaque white to a more or less transparent and shade
opalescent glass, and it took gilding, painting (rather tha
enamelling), and splash decoration very well. Early Venetia
examples of millefiori, chalcedony, and milk-glass are rare.

Crackle-glass or, more properly, ice-glass (Pl.15b) was als
a decorative process, the hot half-blown vessel being suddenl
cooled and then reheated, expanded, and finished, when notice
able fissures were left all over it. Or the hot paraison – th
incipient vessel – could have fragmentary glass particles rolle

ito the surface and then be fully blown and finished in the
rdinary way. Glasses of this kind probably looked better
hen new than they do now, with the dust of ages inextricably
ttled within the cracks and fissures.

These styles were re-introduced in the nineteenth century, the
hmelzglas in smoky purplish-greenish colours; the others
ay be misleading, but generally betray themselves. The
olour cult did not of course cease with the introduction of the
ear alternatives, but it cannot be said that it was very popular.
he sixteenth century saw the other school arise and attempt
ie production of crystal-clear metal. Enamelling and gilding
rocesses were still commonly used, and so we find the scale-
ilt and gemmed bowls (Pl.14). These and comparable circu-
r dishes can have armorial coats enamelled in medallion-like
yle and set in the centre; not every such coat is genuine. The
owls in particular had a lengthy vogue, and they seem to me
o represent a compromise between the colour and the *cristallo*
chools. Some of a heavier greenish-grey metal rather crudely
iade, without gemming or scale-patterning, indifferently or
arely gilded at all, and with a heavy blue band laid on and
round the margin of the foot, seem very non-Venetian to me,
ut seventeenth-century *façon de Venise*, and my present view is
ill that they may well be of English origin.

Gilding alone would appear to belong to the school of clear
lass, and it is uncommon. Plate 17a shows a circular dish of
robable early seventeenth-century date whose gilding, laid on
ie underside, demonstrates unusual stability. Similarly, gem-
iing might occur without any gilding; a lazy man's job.

Not only armorial bowls but armorial drinking-vessels were
Venetian product. It will be seen later how fond were the
erman nobility of their coats of arms, and even after the art
f enamelling was competently practised in Germany – that is
o say, in the last quarter of the sixteenth century – orders still
em to have been placed in Venice. Honey records several
lasses of the sort covering the whole of the sixteenth century.
Iere, Pl.18a shows an outstanding glass fitted with an ancient
opper foot. Other glasses which it resembles in form have
oot-mountings, for reasons of stability. There is the *Hope*

beaker and the *Palmer-Morewood* glass (Hartshorne, Pl.22) both thirteenth to fourteenth century, and the covered Lehmann beaker (Muhsam Cat. II, 115), of about 1592, though the latter is less flared. The glass now mentioned is undamaged and is dated 1584, despite the earlier style of the glass. It is enamelled most skilfully with the Fugger arms, a family whose exploits as the super-Rothschilds of the sixteenth century in commerce, finance, statesmanship, and the arts deserve the much that has been written of them. The colours are distinct and are laid on smoothly and in part on a background of gold leaf, in these respects contrasting with the heavy, vigorous enamel-work of contemporary German artists.

Despite the assumed attempts of the *cristallo* school to provide a crystal-clear metal, it is well to remark that the early Venetian *cristallo* is of a peculiar greyish tone and not so free from minute bubbles. It improved as time went on, in both respects, but it never approached the clarity of English lead crystal or German soda-lime glass of the eighteenth century. It may not have surpassed the best of Roman clear glass and the encomiums lavished upon it are justified only when comparison is being made with the sort of metal previously current. In some eyes, at least modern ones, this greyish tone is a merit, not a demerit; but it seems that it had the result of compelling the glassmakers to blow their glasses extremely thinly, for the thicker the vessel the more distinct did any colour tint become; it probably suited all concerned well enough.

Quite early in the sixteenth century stem formations under went a radical change, the simple classic pedestal being supplanted, or at least supplemented, by a hollow urn-stem displaying a pair of lion masks (Pl.15e). This stem was blown into a two-piece mould exactly as the ancient Roman 'Janus' bottles had been; it was often *semé d'or*, dusted with gold, and was a delicate and not too practicable stem, but it achieved an extremely wide popularity, and there is no reason to suppose that its makers were concerned about fragility. The same two piece mould was also used for bowl forms, though examples are hard to come by. Plate16a shows such a bowl, reminiscent of earlier Florentine decoration. It has been firmly wedded to an important English stem and foot (Pl.58b) of the late seventeenth century, a quite reprehensible union which, however, has so far defied dissolution.

Much more often the bowls were free-blown, and ranged from the perfectly straightforward forms to wavy-edged, widely flared styles which make such inconvenient drinking-vessels that they are often termed *bouquetières* (Pl.15e). Decorative devices were used much less on such bowls than they were on ewers, bottles, vases, and the like. But there was moulded fluting, and applied work such as ribbing, stringing, and masking, gilding, and a little gemming also. Masking meant the attachment of separate medallion-like facial representations to the glass. The Romans had used the head of Medusa (Pl.5b). Venetians preferred a lion's head (Pl.15a), doubtless in compliment to the Lion of St Mark.

Techniques based on *lattimo* glass followed. For other articles besides drinking-glasses, bands of opaque white were applied to the gathering before manufacture was far advanced and then dragged into a series of festoons. Types of this work can be seen on very many of our English Nailsea flasks. From festooning and its obvious alternatives, such as banding, we come to the true Venetian lace-glass or *vitro di trina*, notable because so striking and so often seen. In some of its many variations it was being made from the latter part of the sixteenth century and far on into the seventeenth. In its simplest form it was merely a spiral threading or narrow banding of opaque white enamel (Pl.17c), a form of decoration early enough to occur on glasses with the lion-mask stem. The threads were then multiplied and worked into true lacy bands in considerable variety and used to decorate the bowl or even to compose it entirely (Pls16b, 15a); the foot could be similarly made. The ultimate development was the intricate *netz glas* where two layers of lace-glass were fused together in such a way as to leave the threads forming a net pattern (*a reticelli*), each tiny square of which contained a minute air bubble (Pl. 17b). This was reproduced in the nineteenth century, as were other of the earlier techniques, and such reproductions should be guarded against, but not necessarily despised, for the work is good.

It was so easy a step to replace some of these white threads by coloured ones that an almost infinitely variable series of coloured lace-glass might have been expected. Examples do occur, usually with a ruby threading, but they are not common. There are, however, plenty of such beakers, ice-plates, cups, and saucers to be found of modern manufacture, those of this present century often displaying avanturine. Pl.17d shows a modest glass with an owner's label beneath, *Bought at Paris on his wedding tour by John Evans in 1850*. The coloured threading was in the main originally reserved for decoration of the stem, and was less in favour at Murano than at Amsterdam, though the difficulty of differentiation must be noted. The Venetian trend (Pl. 16c, d, e) about the end of the sixteenth century and into the seventeenth was rather towards a much-convoluted stem in colourless glass, the 'wings' or 'ears' often having a marginal pinched trail in a lovely translucent blue colour. Later on, maybe about the middle of the seventeenth century, there came simple knop and pillar stems, hollow and with wrythen ribbing. They were much liked by the Antwerp and Liège glasshouses, and in a plainer and stronger form may also be one of the productions of our own Mansell.

No undue elaboration of bowl form could easily be made in the intricate forms of lace-glass; the patterns were too likely to become distorted. I do not think that the glass-blowers were really happy until they hit upon the idea of *cristallo* bowls and convoluted stems. Then they could blow all the fantasies their imaginative minds desired, and support them on equally fantastic and fragile stems. There was still a home market rich enough to buy them or powerful enough to order them, and ready enough, it seems, to destroy them all in a single night of carousal. Were the glass-blowers not there to make more?

Not many of these whimsical drinking-vessels have come down to us, as can be understood, but there were glasses in the form of animals, monsters, ships, windmills, birds, and human figures, in sufficient variety to permit of a belief that still odder things were made. They were essentially ephemeral, fashioned for the hour, and not for posterity. They were blown so extremely thinly partly because they could not otherwise have been fashioned so well and partly because, as already stated, the *cristallo* was not particularly clear, and the thicker it was the less clear it became.

The convoluted stem may display something of the 'beast' motif. A serpent with a coiled tail may support a simple bowl, or the wings of a figure-of-eight stem may be topped by a pair of grotesque 'heads' which fancy may resolve into spitting monsters. Naturalistic floral devices were applied, and here coloured glass was introduced to simulate flower-heads, perhaps not too happily.

The moulded decoration of ordinary wine glass bowls is confined to simple dip-mould patterns, an over-all diamond design (Pl.16e) being as attractive as any. There were unobtrusive forms of applied work, milled cordons, vertical trails, fine horizontal stringing in clear or in blue, gadrooning, and occasionally small loops to the sides of a vessel suspending loose rings. These styles also appear on *façon de Venise* glasses from other countries. A certain number of bowls are found with delicate diamond-point or graver etching, generally with a repeat floral pattern incorporating birds and maybe the vine. But even these simplicities are relatively scarce, for the wheel could not favourably be used for engraving a very thin bowl, and even diamond or graver had to be used with extreme care. Beyond this, the casualties attendant on even normal daily usage would have inhibited engraving.

That so much remains to us is sufficient evidence of the quantity of glasses made. That hardly any specimen is of a commemorative character is equally good evidence that they were not expected to last. It will be seen how different in this respect were the glasses of England, Holland, and Germany.

Something of a decline is observable during the latter part of the seventeenth century. Not only were the territorial and trading losses disheartening and impoverishing the home market, but other nations had contrived to lure away Italian glass-blowers and had learned how to make their own glass.

The sequence is observable in the Greene–Morelli transactions mentioned in Chapter IX, and in fact Murano's export trade fell gravely away, and by the year 1700 was confined, so far as blown glass was concerned, to a relatively small trickle to such Eastern markets as were left to the former universal providers of fine glass. There remained the still important mirror-plate business, itself not untouched by competition, and the age-old manufacture of beads, in which Venice excelled. But one does not live on beads alone; the profits were inadequate and the glasshouses of Murano otherwise so stricken that glass collectors today hardly recognize an eighteenth-century Venetian glass at all. No doubt some were still made in the best-selling lines; to distinguish them from true seventeenth-century specimens seems not to be attempted.

There is one exception. Whereas Venice had formerly taught the world, there came a day when one Briati determined to investigate the secrets of the all-too-successful Bohemian competition. He worked disguised for three years in a Bohemian glasshouse, and on his return to Venice in the 1730s, not impossibly with certain Bohemian workers, he achieved a good deal of success for himself without noticeably advancing the welfare of Venetian glass in general. He gained especial note in making *vitro di trina* and *netz glas* at least equal in quality to the earlier glass of the same kind. But Briati's money was probably made out of his lustres or what we now call chandeliers.

However, all came to naught with the fall of the Republic in 1797, and not until 1838 was there any attempt to revive the industry. Then a large measure of success was achieved and is still being achieved. This modern glass with which the name of Salviati is so popularly linked receives little contemporary recognition, but some of it has much artistic merit, and the time to collect it is, after all, while it is still to be had, and particularly while it can be properly identified and labelled for the benefit of those to come. The volume, the diversities, and the similarities of modern glass will sorely puzzle future students unless some such record is made.

To close this summary, it ought not to be assumed that the glass Venice exported so widely was identical with that used at home. No doubt odd specimens of the latter sort reached foreign countries by one means or another, but much of it was inherently unsuitable for export, irrespective of considerations of the foreign taste. The Venetians were business men, and business men try to make what their customers want. That would be a fair assumption even if we had not the correspondence between Greene of England and Morelli of Murano, *. 1670, dealt with in Chapter IX, wherein the one sends specific designs with his orders and the other more or less fulfils the instructions given. These glasses were, in a sense, English glasses made in Venice. There is also evidence that the requirements of the German market were studied, and it is easy to appreciate the difficulties in discrimination between Venetian glass for export and *façon de Venise*.

Much thought and study has been given to this question and to the separation of corresponding *façons de Venise*. Yet except where some particular idiosyncrasy appears, it seems that the results have been inconclusive. Each and every country certainly desires to know what it made, exactly and precisely, but it is a good deal less interested in the manufactures of other countries. Accordingly it may be less important to know where a popular type of glass was made than when it was made. We seem to have permitted ourselves considerable latitude in dating Venetian and *façon de Venise* glass, using for instance the indefinite term sixteenth to seventeenth century which can indicate uncertainty or that the type in question was used in both centuries or part thereof. There is some reason to think that a common tendency to pre-date glasses applies as forcibly to Venetian glass as to any other.

FOR FURTHER REFERENCE

BUCKLEY, W. *European Glass*, 1926.
BUCKLEY, W. *The Art of Glass*, 1929.
DILLON, E. *Glass*, 1907.
HONEY, W. B. *Glass*, Victoria and Albert Museum Handbook, 1946.

CHAPTER VI

THE REVIVAL IN WESTERN EUROPE

*

1. The Turn of the Tide

WE have followed a tide of glassmaking, rising in the East about the time of Christ, flowing through Italy to Spain, Gaul, and perhaps Britain in the first and second centuries, and reluctantly receding, leaving at best a few stagnant pools here and there as a relic of what had been.

With its going went very much of the by no means negligible civilization installed by Roman power. For its going, and for the thousand-year hiatus in our glass history and all that that implies, we have primarily to blame the men of the Oder, the Spree, and the Vistula. Time has cast a cloak of romance over the barbaric invasions, but history has left an evaluation of their real meaning in its negative record.

Then we have seen the tide rise a second time in the East and flow quickly to Italy, and we have measured its subsequent strength and depth there. The further spread of that tide has now to be followed.

It will be remembered that the Semitic glassmakers of Gaul gave up the unequal struggle and retired, some of them, to l'Altare. It is not so apparent that the glassmakers from the Rhine end, Liège, Aix, and Cologne, followed suit, and if there was one pool left behind by the first wave which was wider and deeper than another, I suggest that it was the Rhenish pool. There the density of population was surely as great, and the Church as firmly and ambitiously established as anywhere north of Italy, and the vast influence which the Church had on glassmaking can hardly be over-stressed, even if it did not encourage vessel glass. When the tide began to flow again, it was not the Venetians who set the isolated pools rippling.

74

It was the Altarists, especially, and the Lorrainers. The story makes very confused reading, and if we had not had a portion of the Altarist archives we should know very little indeed. The records were extracted by Schourman, and they may innocently mislead us into thinking that there was at first no other influence at work. They suggest, for instance, that the Lorrainers, who will soon feature in glass history, were among Altarist pupils. That need not presuppose that the Lorrainers were altogether ignorant of the art of glassmaking, but it does infer a liberality of action entirely foreign not only to Altarists but to all others of the glassmaking craft. Above all, such men desired to keep their secrets to themselves. Some were prepared to make glass, on terms, for anyone who wanted it, but it is clear that they all endeavoured to avoid teaching the craft to others, and to this natural reluctance one may trace some of their troubles with imperious customers who expected a good deal more than they actually received.

Count Raymond of Toulouse with his Provençals, and Godfrey of Bouillon and Baldwin his brother with their Lorrainers, had together forwarded the First Crusade and had ruled in Tripoli, Jerusalem, and Edessa. Richard of England, Philip Augustus of France, and Frederick Barbarossa of Germany had been concerned in the Third Crusade. Baldwin, Count of Flanders, had had his own adventures and associations with Dandolo, Doge of Venice, in the Fourth. No important part of Western Europe was, then, ignorant of the arts of the East, and nearly every western potentate was ambitious; their cities were growing, their trade progressing, and their manufactures being established. That they were eminently desirous of adding glassmaking to the list goes without saying, and if ambition had not so dictated, comfort assuredly would have done so.

One may guess that the new tide began to flow into Western Europe somewhere between the establishment of French power over the Normans in 1204 and the middle of the century, and that is borne out by the recorded arrival from Normandy of our Laurence Vitrearius about 1226. It is not difficult to believe that some of the earliest Altarists would have immediately directed themselves towards their ancestral home in

Normandy. The first phase, however, must be attributed to individuals without much knowledge, and its first effects were probably insignificant.

Subsequently, and perhaps considerably before 1400, accredited Altarist craftsmen began to permeate France, and, in somewhat lesser degree, the Low Countries. Whether, and if so how soon, Lorrainers followed this example, we are unable to say, but from the fact that John le Alemayne, presumably a Lorrainer, was at Chiddingfold in 1350, it seems that they may not have been less enterprising. Their natural field lay northwards, where the peoples were at least as anxious as the French to learn the art of glass, and at least as ready to pay for the knowledge. They may also have moved eastwards into Bohemia, even though the reverse process has been suggested to account for their origin.

It is largely an academic question, for in spite of all this far-flung activity even less is known of thirteenth- to fifteenth-century glass in Western Europe than of the glass concurrently produced at Venice. It is therefore quite impossible to guess whether it differed. If it did – and that is the natural conclusion – it is much more likely to have been a difference in quality of metal than any striking difference in style. The important point is that it cannot have been better than the not so very good glass which Venice was then making, and it may have been notably worse, but, for all that, better than the hereditary *verre de fougère* and *waldglas*.

For these early Altarists and Lorrainers window glass was the primary and most profitable business. The world could not have too much of it, and utility vessels were a side-line. Among the latter, it may be conjectured that lamps – that is to say oil-containers – phials, and bottles took precedence over drinking-vessels. They come into view during the fourteenth century, and there may be more specimens than is realized. The difficulty is one of recognition, for unless the circumstances of the find are incontrovertible, the simplicities of form and similarities of metal buried over three centuries may easily confuse.

And so, for the first phase of the new tide of glassmaking, the term late medieval is appropriate. There could be no *façon de*

Venise until after 1450 because until then Venice had established no recognizable fashion of her own, and it was another half-century or so before it was approved and acceptable elsewhere.

A very different and much more important phase set in with the sixteenth century, by which time Murano glass was deservedly famous, and western potentates more anxious than ever not only to possess it but also to see it made within their own boundaries. Equally, the authorities at Venice were most anxious to retain a monopoly of their superior knowledge and skill. But money talks, and the discovery of the Cape route in 1486 had entirely changed the commercial situation. Portugal, the Low Countries, and Britain were well on the way to becoming the world's carriers and overseas traders. Their merchants were rapidly ousting the landlocked Venetians and Genoese from their earlier predominant position, with Antwerp, Amsterdam, and London clearly marked out as world ports of the future, to serve influential towns which had grown up inland.

And so, enough persuasion was forthcoming to induce ambitious Murano men to circumvent the prohibitions laid down by their masters and to travel north to work in more powerful States and to compete with Altarists already established there. What these men did not know of the possibilities of profit they could easily guess, and if their guesses were sometimes over-optimistic and too little regardful of local difficulties, that would only be in accord with human nature and normal commercial experience.

For competitive Altarists and Lorrainers, also advanced in the lore of glassmaking and now *gentilshommes verriers* who might work and trade without prejudice to their acquired or assumed nobility, there were other inducements. Britain was fast becoming a Protestant country and moreover a comparatively tolerant one. That suited those Huguenots and others whose religious tenets carried an inherent risk. Britain, too, was not unused to war, but her soil had remained inviolate for half a thousand years. Artisans as well as gentlemen glassmakers may easily have thought that as considerable an advantage as did those others who streamed to America in the eighteenth and nineteenth centuries, there to make American glass in all the pure European styles and in many more of hybrid origin. Britain in the sixteenth century bade fair to provide not only security but also an ever-expanding market. British ships were annoyingly ubiquitous wherever profitable trade was to be found, and distressingly indifferent as to how they found it. Britons held the obnoxious theory that the seas were free, particularly to those who had the better ships and the tougher sailors. They were making settlements and founding colonies in places so remote and so little known that popular belief turned their rivers into silver and their sands into gold. The prospects were eminently favourable.

In general, the development of glassmaking in all western countries was much the same. There were the sought-for beginnings, the trials, failures, and in due course the establishment of a *façon*, and then eventually some native style which might be truly individual, as in Germany, Spain, and England. This was not quite the case in the northern States of Europe, whose glass history is included in this chapter, as will be seen, but none the less derivatives of established styles might arise, as in Scandinavia, and hybrid growths as in America, all destined to continue the evolution until perchance the one-time tutor becomes a pupil.

The second phase, from 1500 to 1700, is important, not only because it brought with it *façon de Venise* but also because specimens of the glass exist and can be studied. Many Altarists and some Lorrainers felt, or were compelled to feel, its influence, so perhaps the term *façon d'Italie* would be a better one, for the flights of fancy of Murano were modified to suit a more stolid and practical North, and it was not only Murano men who were the exponents. This second phase can be followed in some detail.

2. French and Spanish Glass

France, for all her early traditions and despite a widespread Altarist penetration, failed to make good. Some sort of *verre de fougère* had probably been produced in wooded areas continuously from the Roman era, and window glass was very early a product of Normandy and was exported in medieval times.

But the industries of France were agriculture and war, ill-matched steeds for the chariot of any State. Whatever was won on the field of battle was more than offset by loss on ten thousand fields of peace. The people suffered on both counts, and it is the people who buy glass and the burghers who buy fine glass.

There are a few enamelled glasses of the fifteenth to sixteenth century. Plate 19a shows a specimen which especially appeals because of its simple sincerity; it is a marriage-glass with portraits of the contracting parties, and within the gilt band around the rim is the pious invocation DOMINE · LABIA · MEA · APERIES · ET · OS · MEVM · ANNVNCIBIT. It is probably no more than of average quality; others are in our two principal museums, and one with very finely executed enamelling is in the Wallace Collection, so London is fortunate.

In the sixteenth century also glassmakers from l'Altare settled at Nevers; there seems to be no certain example of their work, which soon concentrated on the making of little statuettes and models in coloured and varicoloured opaque glass (Pl.49a). Of devotional tenor were shrines, now generally termed 'grottoes', arrangements of caves, pools, and perhaps galleries set in a dust-proof box with a glazed front; they were lavishly embellished with shells and greenery, and there were affixed tiny birds and animals with larger figures in a central position, portraying for instance the birth of Our Lord or with His grown figure or that of Mary or those of Apostles and perhaps Saints. They were homely productions with a simple-minded sincerity of much charm. The little mirror pools, a disregard of the demands of scale, gravity, and balance, suggest composition by a child-like mind. It is to be feared that stability was not their strong point; most of the groups have undergone rehabilitation in some degree or other. Rather more sophistication attended later work of the kind, which Honey records as being carried out at Paris also, and at other places in the eighteenth century; fashioning continued well into that century.

The foregoing manufactures were distinctive rather than distinguished. More or less contemporary but hardly before 1600 were barrel flasks (Pl.20b) and other decorative glasses in bluish glass spotted all over in colours, particularly red, white, and blue. The style may have been made elsewhere – in the Low Countries, for instance – for a time it may have been a ready seller.

Glass from Normandy is better known; rather graceless ewers of the late seventeenth century (Pl.19b) and candlesticks of silver form matched or were matched by English examples in early lead glass (Pl.59f). Numerous very light, small wine glasses are still to be found in France, where they are regarded as of the early eighteenth century (Pl.20a). They vary considerably in merit. Comparable glasses (Pl.59a) with a reassuring provenance have been found in England, as well as a number of poorer quality there and elsewhere without any. It is known that France was a greater importer of glass in the eighteenth century (Honey, p. 140) from England and Germany, and probably also from Liège, to which town moulding of the type shown on Pl.20a is particularly attributed. Beyond suggesting that the style of these little glasses was international and not produced in England or Liège other than in the later seventeenth century, the problem, as yet unsolved, cannot be dealt with here.

There followed, rather later, Burgundian glass with a reddish tinge and, often enough, a considerable degree of crizzling. An example is shown on Pl.20d, and a Poitevin production is also recorded. About the middle of the eighteenth century a curious little cordial glass came into use in Normandy; who copied whom is obscure, but Pl.20c shows a definite example in lead metal, and there have been others. One is told that they played a customary part in weddings in north-western France, wherein bride, bridegroom, and a couple of cherries were mutually involved. Be that as it may, Normandy achieved a modest distinction in exporting rather a pleasant type of ewer to England (Pl.19c). Examples come, very naturally, from Hampshire, and sufficiently so to have given rise to a belief that they were English work made at a presumed glasshouse at Buckler's Hard, on the river Beaulieu, actually a shipbuilding site. They are of good quality soda metal. From a less competent source there were little crizzled tumblers, crudely engraved with a name and date, in one case *M. de La Fontaine 1774*. That such things can be remembered emphasizes the paucity of good French glass of the eighteenth century, a time of wars and exhaustion.

Of nineteenth-century date, and probably from Normandy, were simple milk-glass vases painted in soft colours with landscapes or beauty spots; one such pair was marked on the base with the name of a Christchurch vendor, a practice paralleled in Dublin and Belfast, where makers impressed a factor's name on such things as decanters and finger-bowls.

The fact is that France never became glass-minded until the rise of the Baccarat factory in the first quarter of the nineteenth century. This house revolutionized French glass by adopting a lead metal of superb quality. It produced what are now termed *sulphides*, silvery-looking incrustations enclosed in clear glass (Pl.49b). Crests in coloured enamels (Pl.30e) extended the range and secured a good market, leading up to the paper-weight age; something of both these processes may be read in Chapter VIII. Baccarat aimed high but did not therefore neglect a poorer public. It made a lot of moulded glass, strong and by no means devoid of design; a four-piece mould was often used, as was an impressed mark BACCARAT inside, not beneath, the recipient, and that after all is where it can most easily be seen (Pl.20e).

The second quarter of the century also brought *verre opaline*, a semi-translucent metal in milk-glass or pastel colours. It was decorative glass beautifully shaped and often in classical form; important pieces such as *garnitures de cheminée* were commonly given ormolu mounts. After 1850 the styles thereof deteriorated, though many of the numerous specimens made retain a strong appeal. Sharply-pressed glass of good design (as Pl.20f) in a good clear metal gave to the less wealthy something which had been initiated, or at least most highly developed, in America, where it became immensely popular; it is widely collected today.

A final chapter of French art has yet to reach conclusion. It began in the third quarter of the nineteenth century, when glass designers arose to construct decorative articles, and particularly vases and bowls in clear or coloured glass, overlaid, carved, scraped, and otherwise maltreated by mechanical and chemical processes to produce a wide range of naturalistic and impressionist and wholly unconventional and even inconvenient articles. Tall vases (Pl.44c) were probably more numerous than anything else, to judge by survivals, or perhaps they were merely less used. Many artists signed their work or used their signature as a factory mark. Of them all, Gallé of the older school and Lalique (Pl.52a) of the newer are the best known. Not long ago, work by most of these artists cost a matter of shillings; things are different now and really fine pairs of Gallé vases have realized high prices.

*

As in France so also in Spain it seems that some sort of glass is likely to have been made continuously from the Roman period onwards, though how many specimens still extant are indigenous is a question nobody can answer. However that may be, one may fairly suppose that after the fall of Rome, and indeed perhaps even before it, any fine glass had to come from Syria or Egypt.

On the whole, Spain seems to have been unimpressed by any need for glass, and showed little anxiety and less haste to develop it. The Catalans had had a share of the Eastern trade and may be presumed to have acquired a sufficient knowledge of glassmaking, and must have been making good glass in the fifteenth to sixteenth century. In proof we have the rare and attractive enamelled glass of Barcelona, something of a parallel with the Gothic glass of Venice, with a green colour predominating. Barcelona, indeed, might have supplied the western maritime cities of Italy and all those of Sicily and Sardinia more easily than could Murano. It seems that she would not, for her glass history becomes undistinguished, and one may conjecture two reasons. First, the transatlantic obsession, and second, Castilian scorn for meticulous trade, an apathetic refusal to contemplate progress, and perhaps a certain prideful disdain for competition. The void was naturally filled by others.

Hence there is nothing further to note until in the seventeenth to eighteenth century the Moorish styles of Andalusia and Granada appeared, in surprisingly original and indeed rather fantastic forms. They come in deep green tones and in olive-amber and sometimes ugly smoky yellows. There was a varied range of objects notable for the pinched trails to the handles, copious stringing, and novel prunting, in all a superabundance of applied decoration, and it is thought that the fashion spread elsewhere. There is an indescribable sprinkler termed an *almorrata* which is attributed to Catalonia. A kettle-like *cantaro* or water vessel was in wide use and exhibited the same peculiarities. Plate 21 shows some examples of these things, seemingly deliberately designed with an eye to impracticability and unregardedful of cleanliness. But at least there was ingenuity in the shell prunting (Pl.22g) and in the plume-like decoration of Pl.21b. Few glasses exhibit more individuality. Perhaps from the more northern Catalonia came rather unstable fragile vases (Pl.21c) less exuberantly decorated; the metal is of a dirty-water colour and distinctly bubbly, and in any other country it would be allocated to the sixteenth century, but not necessarily so in Spain.

In the late seventeenth century the originality was played out. *Latticinio* glass comes into view with a *porron*, something like a handleless watering-pot wherefrom wine was poured into the mouth (Pl.21d). No doubt imports from Bohemia, the Netherlands, and to some extent England in the eighteenth century, filled the possibly rather small demand for drinking glasses.

The royal glasshouse of La Granja de San Ildefonsa was opened in 1728, and after trials and failures turned out a quantity of clear glass of fair quality. Something of Spanish taste can be seen, but so overborne at the hands of the foreign craftsmen who made and decorated the glass that at best it seems but half Spanish, and in cases where shape did not enter into it the production was so like the foreign article that differentiation can be uncertain. The decoration was inclined to be crude; colourful conventional floral patterns were popular; coarse and even more conventional engraving was heightened by gilding. Still, they remain cheerful and in their way rather picturesque pieces. A certain amount of milk-glass was added to the repertoire; tumblers were made of this as well as of clear metal, both with enamelling in colours, as for instance Pl.37d, which is inscribed *Viva Carlos III Rey de Espana*, and case-bottles such as were made and painted in central Europe. These date from the middle of the eighteenth century onwards, a time when England was exporting cheap glasses of soda or near-soda metal (Pl.65f) and in such quantity, it would appear, that Ricart and de Artinano, in their *Vidrio* of 1935, attribute hardly anything else to us, which is understandable but unkind, particularly as collectors here would describe them as Dutch, with equal unkindness. We did in fact also send good soda glasses in appealing tints, though still simple glasses. Indeed, were it possible for a scrutinizing committee of all western European nations to sit in judgement on the cheap glassware of the eighteenth century, I believe a surprising proportion would have to be declared stateless for want of an acceptor.

3. *Lotharingian and Netherlandish Glass*

To this day there are glasses in production which are direct, if distant, descendants of the crude heavy *Igels* of the fifteenth century and before, and it is to the inhabitants of Lower Lorraine that we are indebted for the inception of the series and its development in the Aix–Cologne area, that is to say, the ancient Rhenish pool. These hereditary glassmakers no doubt spread over a wider space, and it will accord with the probabilities if we assume that Upper Lorraine – the wooded country south of the Ardennes and west of the Vosges – was no less able to make this Rhineland glass. Hence the better term Lotharingian which is sometimes applied to it, neither German nor as yet Dutch.

We have met with beakers from the very beginnings of blown glass, differing in no essential from our modern tumblers. In the Rhenish forms they were of green metal, and by the middle of the fifteenth century flat circular blobs of glass were being applied in rows around the lower portion of the cylinder; there was not much trace of the up-pointed thorn left when the tool depositing the pad of glass was drawn away. By the beginning of the sixteenth century the thorn was being accentuated of set purpose and was occasionally looped, while the base might be provided with an indented or even a clawed band. In the seventeenth century the familiar raspberry prunt (Pl.23b) became common as well as a form of blunt triangular hobnail or 'beechnut' (as in Pl.24c).

The *roemers* were most distinctive vessels, derived directly from the beaker, the top being first widened into saucer shape (Pl.22a) and later into a cone (Pl.23a). In the seventeenth century the cone became a more or less spherical cup (Pl.39b), the cylinder was narrowed to form a wide hollow stem which carried the prunts, and a 'coil' foot added beneath. Here again was originality, the basal rim of the parent beaker being developed on the roemers into a low 'spun' foot, formed by winding a trail of glass around a wooden cone. At first only a matter of two or three circular turns, the foot became gradually taller with the coils finer but more numerous – perhaps a score of turns in all, though the narrowness of the resultant foot left a good deal to be desired in the way of stability. In the modern art glass product – and it has its attraction – the foot has become a hollow, spreading pedestal moulded with horizontal rings, with the gain of, at least, stability.

Throughout the beaker-roemer series, metal improvement kept pace with design, the green glass in particular giving a strong impression of control, as opposed to the inherent green tints of the old *waldglas*. Its finish and texture were good, and it contained no more of the tiny air bubbles than was inevitable with the firing methods of the times. The pleasantly jocular 'unbreakable' beaker of Pl.23b exemplifies the excellence of the metal.

More or less allied to the foregoing were green glasses in the form of animals whose identity might give rise to conjecture, jest glasses as much as anything else. Little green barrel-flasks could be set longitudinally on four splayed peg-feet and given a hole on the upper side, neither ornamental or very useful; elsewhere and later they appeared in variegated colours. A few other glasses (Pl.22f), beakers, ewers, and conical wines in deep brownish-amber metal, the latter with little rings hanging from loops on the bowl (Pl.22e), would be of the early seventeenth century and may be related to the foregoing and accorded a Lotharingian origin, whereafter the term is better abandoned.

The term Netherlandish is a convenient one for glasses one knows were made in the Low Countries, particularly if a more precise origin cannot be given. The two terms are synonymous and also geographical, but the peoples who live there were already divided by sharp racial and cultural differences. It will then be more accurate to separate them, as far as one can, as they are separated today, into Belgians and Dutch, and to deal with the glass they made accordingly. Political boundaries change; racial characteristics endure.

The southern (Belgian) centres of population and influence in the early sixteenth century were the Flemish towns of Ghent, Bruges, and Ypres, then surpassing an Antwerp, Louvain, and Brussels group as well as another centred on Liège. Away in the north were the Dutch towns Dordrecht, Leyden, Delft, and Rotterdam in the province of Holland, and Middelburg in Zeeland.

The Flemish towns were too fully occupied – in the woollen industry, for instance – to be interested when Venetian glass was first made at Antwerp about the middle of the sixteenth century, an example soon followed by Liège, and also by Middelburg and particularly Amsterdam. There could hardly have been any more unfavourable period than the second half of the sixteenth century for the peoples of the Netherlands, oppressed as they were by the Spanish occupation and religious persecution. Intermittent revolt by the obstinate Flamands preceded and stimulated organized rebellion under William of Orange with its successes and disasters, but ended with expulsion of the Spaniard. The cost in wealth, lives, and suffering had been tremendous, and it is against such a background that we have to envisage Belgians and Dutchmen learning to make fine glass, persevering, and in no long time succeeding.

It seems that each nation made quite a lot of glass in competition with the other, such were trade conditions of the day, and any exports from Murano to the Netherlandish ports of Antwerp and Amsterdam added to competition then and to a correct attribution of origin now. It sounds like free trade all round; in fact, glassmaking was carried on much as in England, under a licence which policy might recommend or interest obtain. Such licences often carried material benefits, such as subsidies or freedom from tolls, and they might be supported by interdicts on competitive foreign glass. But it does not follow that they were always granted without some sort of consideration, or that the attached benefits were invariably implemented. Among other vicissitudes of glassmaking in the sixteenth and seventeenth centuries, internal competition greatly affected profits, but that these were potentially important can be inferred from the recurring attempts to realize them.

In Belgium the chief centres were Antwerp and Liège, the former very well suited geographically to obtain *barilla*, the soda derived from a Spanish coastal plant, an ingredient widely regarded as an essential if clear glass was wanted. The glassmasters of Antwerp, among whom Pasquetti, Mongarda, and Gridolphi, were prominent, preferred an imitative *façon de Venise* of more sober and economic design than the traditionally fanciful Murano styles, and not without idioms of their own, such as the Neptune masks and the little turquoise eyes in their raspberry prunts (Pl.23b). They made *latticinio* glasses, but also plainer ones in greater variety and quantity. There were many wines with plain or wrythen knops or knop and pillar stems which might or might not have simple winging; others were given multi-knopped and collared stem forms, a striking example (Pl.26d) being a parallel edition of the tall Nuremberg goblets of Chapter VII. All this and more was well within the power of the Antwerp glass industry; Pl.26

gives three illustrations of what could be done and Pl. 28d shows a more ambitious class of goblet no less favoured in Liège, Holland, and England.

That ancient town of Liège had traditions of glassmaking going back to the early centuries, and at the period under review had obtained a special position of its own. By the local wealth of timber, and subsequently of coal, it was well provided, and also well suited geographically to supply the Dutch market, with the river Meuse at hand for transport. Liège was still, in the seventeenth century, under the Bonhommes, working in what Baar called an Altarist style, or could it be a lingering Lotharingian one? It was a *façon de Venise* with more applied work than Antwerp liked, trailed work, gadrooning to the bowl, and finials with pinched wings to matching covers. Plate 25a shows a cup and cover of this description, made of thick clear dull green metal; in like specimens the finial may represent a bird, a fancy to be found in much later American glass. The style may have been made as early as the sixteenth century. A trick vessel, hardly a jug, requiring the drinker to suck from the bottom of the handle (Pl.25c), displays the same technique but is made in near-clear metal.

Antwerp had a century and a half in which to exploit the glass industry, during which time the growth of her trade and shipping interests greatly increased, and may have lessened application to a minor activity. However that may be, the rise of English crystal and Bohemian *cristallo* coincided with the cessation of serious glassmaking at Antwerp at the end of the seventeenth century.

Liège continued for another hundred years making undistinguished glass, only occasionally imaginative, as in the case of those always unfortunate bowls and baskets in trailed lattice-work which are so frequently attributed to Bristol. In the second quarter of the eighteenth century it was making simple wines with rib-twisted stems and mould-blown bowls of bucket or round funnel form with various types of decoration, particularly close spiral ribbing, beech-nut moulding, and short vertical flutes rising into honeycombing. This last pattern appears on English air twist glasses, though not commonly; it is also referred to in Section 2 of this chapter and will be mentioned again in Chapter IX, 3. The series consisted of strong light glasses, eminently wine-worthy, with well-proportioned high conical feet. Many have an English air about them and also show distinct traces of lead in their composition. Such specimens can either be regarded as a continental compliment to our English makers, and one which happened to use a certain amount of lead cullet in the making, or they can be called English glasses made for export with less than the usual amount of lead in the batch for economy or lightness, or again just with lead cullet. It does also appear that those glasses without any lead generally have a continental look about them.

In the third quarter, Liège was making, it is said, interior twist glasses, more white twists than air twists or colour twists. The Baar collection contained some of the former, indistinguishable from English glasses, and there were others of poor or very poor quality, mainly in soda metal, to which it is surprising any country should lay claim. Air twists seem to be relatively scarce in Belgium, and mostly of a soda metal form commonly found in England. As a whole the Liège output in this century was indeed an indifferent one, unreflective of the still redoubtable capacity of its glassmakers.

Amsterdam, with Middelburg, was not behind Liège and Maastricht in the making of Venice style glasses; the Hague and Rotterdam followed suit. The ascription too often remains uncertain. Bowls and beakers were more or less an international form; if decorated, there might or might not be a clue to origin. Both were made in the sixteenth century, as were urn-stemmed goblets (Pl.23c). The beginnings of *latticinio* glass appear in beakers and, about 1600, in a series of little biberons (Pl.28a).

By this time it seems that competition was developing and attacks – or reprisals – being made on the glassmakers of Belgium. Drinking-glasses with a flattened convoluted interior twist stem structure – *flugelgläser* to the Germans – outdid in elaboration anything Venice fashioned of this kind, so massive could the 'stem' be. The convolution was provided with a striking pinched and dentate outer trail in blue glass. Something of the sort might be used as a finial to a cover, but these are not now common, whatever was the fashion at the time, and covers were probably not made for short and later glasses of the same class with a cup or a trumpet bowl or over the knop and pillar stem with substantial wings (Pl.39c).

Holland made the popular and convenient goblets of Pl.24a in *latticinio* or with applied *latticinio* ribbing (Pl.27e); the bowl can have our own nipt diamond waies worked into the base, or it can be made of ice-glass. Certainly not less than half a dozen varieties of intrinsic or extrinsic decoration are known, the glass itself remaining exceedingly stable in form, so that one may easily suppose that various glasshouses in various parts of the Low Countries, and perhaps Normandy also, each had its own particularity.

Concurrently with the foregoing the green roemers continued and remained popular into the third quarter of the seventeenth century; towards its end, Holland was making glasses with quatrefoil knop formations, and many small conical bowl wines were fashioned with a single such knop (as Pl.56c) or a pear-shaped knop, just the sort of thing England was making and importing. Tall flutes and sizeable goblets appeared in this latter style also.

Dutch glass-blowers were as competent as any others to make fine things and spent a hundred and fifty years proving it, yet in all this period there was nothing inherently Dutch or of artistic novelty to compare with the green roemers, and by the end of the seventeenth century Dutch glass, like that of Antwerp, declined. Nature had not been kind in her provision of fuel; long before, England had found it politic to forbid the use of wood as fuel, and although there is some doubt as to the pertinence of the reason given, viz. a possible shortage of oak for shipbuilding, the same circumstances would have applied in still greater force to Holland without there being the same resources of coal as an alternative. Whether for that or any other reason, Dutch glass of the eighteenth century is undistinguished. But the Dutch were glass-lovers, and no people n the world could surpass them in the arts of living. They had, from the last quarter of the sixteenth century, applied themselves to engraving, first with the diamond-point or steel graver (Pl.38c,e), and latterly with the wheel (Pl.70d), and by so doing they conferred distinction and subsequent historical value upon many glasses not in themselves of great account.

If glassmaking could not become a profitable national industry in the face of German and, later, English competition, the Dutch had other lucrative resources overseas – a valuable carrying trade, and not least an industrious and intelligent population which saw no reason and had no necessity for reduction in their standard of living. If they could not compete in actual glassmaking they could still enjoy decorating other folks' glassware for their own delight and individual profit. Throughout the eighteenth century their craftsmen seem to have worked indefatigably on these lines, both at home and abroad, where their example was welcome enough. They chose our own lead glasses of Newcastle, to the extent that it is harder to find one of these without engraving than with it. Indeed, until fairly recently the glasses themselves were regarded as Dutch by more than one writer.

This engraved work will be referred to later. The best of it lives unexcelled, and some of it seems inimitable until it is remembered that what man has done once he can accomplish again. It has been suggested that some of the diamond-point work was the feat of gifted amateurs; even so, the varied and personal nature of the designs is almost proof of a commissioned order of a commercial character. In this latter field the Dutch had no competitors, and in surface wheel engraving none other than the late seventeenth- and early eighteenth-century artists of Nuremberg, and, for rather longer, those of Bohemia.

4. Scandinavian and Russian Glass

In Scandinavia and Russia it was not a revival which took place but a commencement, a natural spread of the art of glassmaking. Here in England one sees little of the glass of these countries and recognizes little of what one sees, other than the obvious armorial goblets of the two eighteenth-century Russian Tsarinas, Elizabeth I and Catherine the Great. The accounts which follow are largely drawn from the works cited, Norwegian glass having at last been comprehensively dealt with.

Ancient glass has been found in Norway attributable to the first seven centuries, and not all of it came from the northern provinces of the Empire. The trade routes from Italy at first and then from Byzantium provided a modest quota. The same applies to Sweden, but over a longer period stretching into Saracenic times. Needless to say, most of this glass is fragmentary. In view of their proximity to the sources of supply, South Russia and the Crimea in particular have naturally provided a quantity of ancient glass.

It may be that the Dark Ages were darker in those hardy northern lands than elsewhere, or let us say that the dawn came later and more slowly. In all three countries the accent is at first on engraved glass, fair evidence that the respective Courts, nobility, and gentry, in descending order, were to consume the output of the modest factories set up.

In Denmark and Norway, then united under one Crown, what glass was used in the sixteenth and seventeenth centuries was imported, from Venice in the first instance, but otherwise mainly from Germany. At the end of the seventeenth century, one George Kreybich of Bohemia was travelling personally with glass to sell (so it is alleged), taking with him his engraving tools; he visited London and noted that there were six glasshouses there producing fine glassware. On a subsequent trip, and possibly the very next one, he visited Denmark and Sweden. Denmark also must have noted the fine English glassware and appreciated its characteristics, for from the beginning of the eighteenth century English glass was well favoured and consistently imported, even though the popular market was supplied by Germany.

It seems that glass was first made in Norway in 1741. Progressive ideas were abroad, and in Denmark they took shape in a projected exploitation of Norway's resources, notably the timber trade, with glassmaking as an adjunct; in 1749 the 'Norwegian Company' was formed to actuate the plans, backed by the Court and the nobility.

A glasshouse was already in operation at Nøstetangen on the river Drammen with water communications to the sea. Germans were called in to run the glasshouse and the usual utility glass was at first produced. Soon, however, finer wares were being made, good enough for the Court, as was no doubt the intention, shapely covered goblets whereof one had the monogram of Christian VI, the cover with a Cross and crown finial; the stem was of baluster type, and the engraving done in Copenhagen. By 1748 it may be said that the glass-making project had been successfully launched – more success-fully, it seems, than the other plans, because in 1753, when the Norwegian Company was reorganized, glassmaking became its primary objective, to supply the markets of both Norway and Denmark. Further glasshouses were set up, notably Hur-dals Verk for crown glass. An enlarged Nøstetangen was to deal with crystal glasswares, and the organization became the Royal Norwegian Glass Works.

Hitherto it had been German skill which was employed, but in 1755 a young Englishman named James Keith was induced to leave South Shields.

He proved a most valuable man, with capacities beyond the mere blowing of glass, and he served the Glass Works faithfully until 1787, introducing lead crystal and bringing the spirit of Newcastle design into somewhat Germanic forms, and producing an air-twist *cum* baluster stem never made in England, on a domed foot which also was not ours, though the resultant glass could easily be taken for English. It was an important move.

So also was the issue in 1763 of an illustrated price-list, liberally used in Dr Ada Polak's book, from which it can be seen just what was made. One could wish that other nations had been as thoughtful. Roughly speaking, one might call it a series of German–English hybrids, with German influence dominant in the cheaper glasses and utility glassware, and English in the finer sorts of drinking-glass, with one feature never marred, the English multiple spiral air twist. Some things can be done only one way.

Of more important glasses made for the Crown and nobility, much must have been engraved, and finely engraved. Two names stand out in this respect: that of H. G. Kohler, whose period of activity ran from 1756 to 1770, when the Nøstetangen house was contracted; both he and his successor made a feature of sets of glasses with a series of linked scenes. Kohler was already a cutter and engraver when he joined the factory from Copenhagen; towards the end of his life he returned there, but his work deteriorated. The other engraver was Villas Vinter, first a glass-blower, but during the 1760s a pupil of Kohler's, and no mean artist, as the glass at Pl.29d demonstrates. He also left Nøstetangen, in 1773 – it shut down entirely in 1777 – and worked in conjunction with one Becker until at least 1797. Hurdals Verk took over the crystal work of Nøstetangen and made more types of glass, though generally of a simpler kind, such as air twist three-piece wines with gilded engraving (Pl.29a), colour twists with an English ogee bowl (Pl.29c), and cheaper German-type wines such as the loyally engraved wine (Pl.29b) in favour of Christian VII. Hurdals Verk survived until 1808, when in turn it handed over to Gjøvik.

The Becker referred to above worked as an engraver at Nøstetangen for six years, leaving in 1773, presumably with Vinter, for they set up in business together. He seems to have been a prolific and competent engraver, no more, and is not known to have signed any of his work; he died about 1807. There is a colloquialism – I respectfully borrow the term – running through the designs of these engravers; it can be seen in the mantle around the ciphers and monograms so often used and it is called 'the Norwegian cartouche', appearing in one of many variations around the inscription on Pl.29c, and, somewhat masked, on Pl.29a. Plate 61b shows an undoubted English baluster with the cipher of Frederick V (reigned 1746–66), quite possibly engraved by Kohler.

A little painting on glass was done, but only rather crude work on simple vessels either side of 1800 survives.

Collectable Norwegian glass is regarded as ending in 1843, when the crystal glasshouse at Gjøvik was closed. This house was started privately after 1803, when the State monopoly had expired; it had been able to absorb the traditions of the earlier houses, and during its time had all the chances there were. But the expiry of the monopoly opened the door to foreign imports, and political situations were adverse. Norway was separated from Denmark in 1814 and had then to stand on her own feet, an exacting financial posture. Gjøvik did what others did in a difficult period: experimented with coloured glass, cheap glass, and, it may be, copies of other people's glass. One particular pattern, sometimes seen without the handle in England, is shown at Pl.29e, an onion-shaped carafe, or *zirat flaske*, prunted and trailed and variously gadrooned. One has been recorded as made of lead metal (which is possible – no more) and as English of much too early a date; all those noted by myself have been of non-lead glass, the surprise being the number found over here.

The account of Swedish glass given by Heribert Seitz lays quite as much emphasis on its decoration, by wheel engraving, as on the glass itself, and in this respect it lines up with the glass of Norway and of Russia, and for very much the same reason.

As in Norway, so also ancient glass has been found in Sweden, and it has been recorded by Lamm. Of home-produced glass there is a record of two Venetians reaching Stockholm and making it there in 1556, a further instance of the mid sixteenth-century irruption of Italian glassmakers into other European States. There followed a series of glasshouses, the last-established of which was Melchior Jung's in Stockholm (1641–78). It is, however, doubtful whether any relic of these houses exists.

It is therefore from the Kungsholm glasshouse, Stockholm (1676–1815), that the first authenticated Swedish glasses emerged, and under successive managers quite a series of known engravers decorated the glasses produced. The first of these men, Kristoffer Elstermann (*fl.* 1691–1721), was a German, and he may be regarded as the most notable, partly because of his long reign, and partly because of the inauguration by him of particular colloquialisms such as the crossed palm and laurel branches which seem to out-Nuremberg the engravers of that famous centre; fields of small scattered flowers and sprigs, a pale reflection of which appears on English wines of the later eighteenth century in oil gilding; and particularly the radiant Sun and the radiant North Star. Both these last were multi-rayed, the former with numerous not very definite points, the latter with five pronounced points radiating from a near-solid nucleus. The Sun remained a favourite throughout the eighteenth century, the North Star keeping pace with it only until the 1750s, but not entirely disappearing even then. The scattered flowers make a recognizable feature, but vanish about 1725.

The names of the engravers are known only because they appear in Swedish documents and archives, not because they signed the glasses they decorated; it appears, indeed, that no single signature exists. For this reason the name of Kristoffer Fransysk (*d.* 1720) may be mentioned because the beaker illustrated on Pl.30a is initialled *C F fait A° 1706*, the use of the French justifying the *C*. Its story may be read in brief in Chapter XI.

No clear distinction existed between engravers and cutters, and latterly, at any rate, it appears that the glass artist could turn his hand to both techniques.

As to the glass forms made at Kungsholm, it is clear that they were designed under strong foreign influences, to say the least of it. An early series belonging to the first quarter of the eighteenth century had a stem partaking of both a Nuremberg and a Bohemian style, a multi-collared one with triple hollow knops; it settled down into a central large flattened and ribbed knop with smaller plain ones above and below, all hollow and separated by more or less exuberant collaring. Most of the feet were folded and a good many engraved with the crossed palms, laurel wreaths, or scattered floral field. Cylindrical beakers on triple bun feet are more definitely derived from Nuremberg, and solid, slightly waisted beakers from Potsdam.

At the same time Dutch influence is apparent in roemers with almost spherical bowls, beneath which there is a vermiform collar; the usual wide stem is generously provided with rather small raspberry prunts, and the pedestal foot is a low one, not coiled, but plain and also folded. Later on, cylindrical tankards with hollow handles, and low circular bowls with covers, a pair of handles again hollow, or possibly a gadrooned base in low relief, also recall Dutch taste.

Moulded pedestal stems carrying pointed round funnel bowls and set on folded feet bring to mind English styles, especially a four-sided stem with the words *Kung Hols Glas Bruk* moulded thereon in likeness to our own *God Save King George* specimens.

Parallel for a time with Kungsholm was the Skånska glass-house in North Scania; it worked from 1691 to 1762, when it fell victim to arson. On the whole its output was Germanic in style. Little squat tumblers with gadrooned bases seem to have been a speciality of its own. Conical carafes with a collar near the top and an everted mouth fulfilling the curves of the body were perhaps derived unknowingly from a Greene form. Further circular bowls on a low pedestal or ring foot were also made.

There were ten further glasshouses, of which Limmared and Kosta are still in operation, and a few glasses of no particular importance are known to have come from them. The production was utility glass, the best of Germanic in style and comparable to the Norwegian potash–lime glass; specimens such as Pl.29b were turned out in some quantity and engraved in much the same fashion. The engravers are known by name, but were as modest as their predecessors in omitting any signature on their work. Such of these houses as produced any glass at all in the nineteenth century will presumably have continued making various current styles; a covered cut rummer, for instance, must have had a French ancestor somewhere with its ovoid bowl, octagonally cut spreading stem, and solid square foot; it came from the Strömbäcks house and is dated 1809.

No inkling was there then, or could have been, of the renown the following century was to bring.

Until comparatively recent times the story of glassmaking in Russia is no more than one of glassmaking for the Court, for successive rulers from Michael (Tsar, 1645–76) to Catherine the Great deemed it inconsistent with their dignity not to be able to furnish the imperial tables with good Russian-made glassware.

That they largely failed despite all attempts to obtain foreign tutors is not surprising in view of the social state of the country, its people, and, as Peter the Great was later to demonstrate during his visit to England, its rulers. Yet one must not be too scornful, for few of our own peasantry in Mansell times but used vessels of leather, wood, or pottery; in Russia at the same period oiled paper or parchment served as window glass for the poor, the gentry and nobility being perforce content with mica; not until Peter set himself to build St Petersburg did glass begin to replace the mica. Naturally, imports of foreign glass made to order were necessary, and though little of it is known until the eighteenth century, it may be attributed to Saxony, Bohemia, and after 1672 to England, which country supplied medicine phials, possibly as much a necessity as window glass. The story of the Russian endeavour is, then, a chequered one, punctuated by inconsequences and queries of all kinds, but much of it has been extracted from Russian archives by Marianne Pelliot, whose *Verres anciens* deals primarily with glass of Russian interest and without which the present author would have had little to say.

It begins with an authorization of 1634, reasonably conceived and supported, but the undertaking produced no known result. Tsar Alexis tried in his turn, and one Manio, working from 1668 onward, must have had some success, for a palace inventory of 1687 records some 2,400 pieces of Manio-made table-ware and articles of more personal use. The ultimate fate of this venture is not disclosed, and of a certain Sveden, who set out in 1684 to make *façon de Venise* glass, we know nothing at all.

Peter the Great might have achieved greater success with less despotism. He decreed the erection of a factory at Kiev in 1720 and manned it with workers from other houses which had somehow sprung up. The reason reads strangely, but seemingly arose out of Peter's predilection for ships and forests, so important in his mind that he made it a capital offence to fell a tree, fit for a mast, within a given area, and underlined his point by erecting a gibbet every five miles along the Neva. As all the furnaces were wood-fired, glass-workers may have felt that the inconvenience of being whisked off to Kiev had its compensations. It is not revealed whether they made any glass there.

In 1730 the Empress Anna allotted a glasshouse at Yabino to an Englishman, William Elmzel, and also another in the same Yambourg district belonging to a disgraced Prince Menchikoff. The latter house was making a variety of objects in crystal, but Elmzel died in 1738 with nothing to show but failure.

Peter's policy of forest preservation was followed by his successors. In 1747 it was forbidden to erect any glasshouse or distillery within 200 versts of Moscow unless water communication permitted the bringing in of wood from afar. Six houses were accordingly 'displaced'. In 1754 all glasshouses within the said area were banned and two were completely destroyed, one of these having been founded in 1723 by the brothers Maltzoff. In the following year the houses in St Petersburg were transferred to Yambourg, and finally in 1759 it was forbidden to erect factories in the governments of both Moscow and St Petersburg.

In 1743 Elizabeth Petrovna took steps to improve her table by ordering the still existent glasshouses of St Petersburg to make wine glasses and carafes, both in crystal, each piece to be inscribed as the property of the imperial Court, and none to be sold elsewhere. She also wanted a colourful *façon de Venise*, and in 1752 set a Professor Lomonosoff of the Academy of Sciences to work, but evidently academic knowledge was not enough, for his failure was complete.

Thus far it seems that the encouragement given by one

imperial hand was all too quickly neutralized by the other. I
1760, however, the name of Thomas Maltzoff turns up, a Mos
cow merchant and presumably some connexion of the un
lucky man whose glasshouse was destroyed. Thomas suc
ceeded so well that in 1775 his successor Jacob was ennoble
by Catherine the Great. Two years later the *Manufacture Im
périale de Cristal* was founded, the property for a long time o
Prince Gregoire Potemkine; besides great quantities of fin
glass for the Court, it also made common glass.

But of all the Russian-made glass over a period of more tha
a century, very little seems recognizable. Pelliot figures fou
specimens, each fortunately inscribed, and dated respectivel
1722, 1730, 1758, and 1767. All four are enamelled. The earlies
and most desirable is a globular jug, perhaps for holy water
with trailing round the cylindrical neck; the enamelling show
Adam and Eve and the serpent in one view, and in another th
archangel Michael is driving them out of paradise. A barre
shaped flask is dated 1730, a goblet with the imperial arms
1758, and the final piece is a dark green bottle with scenes fron
the history of Joseph, arranged on the lines of the Germai
'Ten Ages of Man' *Humpen*. The four must be Russian-made
and there are a few other items; the total is indeed paltry fo
the effort expended, unaccountably so.

Catherine bought the Potemkine business for the State, an
its output of ordinary glass at once ceased; like other Stat
enterprises in other lands, it deteriorated rapidly. Alexander
revived it in 1804, and it continued to turn out fine glass ex
clusively for the Court until the end of the nineteenth century

Almost at the same time as the last-named house was that c
Bakhmeteff, which worked at least until the revolution of 191
(Pl.30d). It had had its vicissitudes, sabotage in 1773, and de
struction by fire when Moscow burned in 1812; after resusc:
tation it made what a more polite Europe thought fitting
under marked German and English influence. In view of thi
Paul I banned foreign imports, though making an exceptio
in his own favour. Alexander concurred, for he spent som
£1,900 on English glass in 1802 and the odd sum of 10,46
roubles and 23 kopeks in 1803, not one of our most-thought-c

eriods. Baccarat also made glass, if not for the Court itself,
t least for its entourage, and it is not to be supposed that
ohemian and Viennese glass could find no entry.

For most of us it is the Elizabeth Petrovna (Pl.30b) and
katerina II monogrammed and sometimes portraited goblets
hich grace our collections. It would be hazardous to say that
ey were made in Russia, but if so then only by German
orkers; Bohemia and Saxony are more probable birthplaces.
he goblets were engraved in similar style and the engraving
ilded, on a black background; some of their pristine appeal
as necessarily been lost, but at their best they were unques-
onably imperial glasses.

FOR FURTHER REFERENCE

uckley, W. *European Glass*, 1926.
uckley, W. *Art of Glass*, 1929.
illon, E. *Glass*, 1907.
oney, W. B. *Glass*, Victoria and Albert Museum Handbook,
    1946.
elliot, Marianne. *Verres anciens*, Paris, 1929.
olak, Ada Buch. *Gammelt Norsk Glas*, Oslo, 1953.*
eitz, Heribert. *Aldre Svenska Glas Med Graverad Decor*,
    Stockholm, 1936.*

* With summary in English

CHAPTER VII

GERMAN GLASS

*

SOMETHING has already been said of Lotharingian glass, which may lay claim to the title of German, in so far as it may have been made east of the Rhine at the same time as it flourished west thereof, and in fact the earlier Rhineland roemer are as often called German as Dutch. Further, the account in the following chapter dealing with the decorative processes applied to glass will say so much of German work that it may almost serve as a description of German glasses.

However, to call a glass German is so imprecise as to have little meaning, and here the term is applied to the people, lands, and glasses of mid-Europe lying north of Italy and east of the Rhineland. The term will then cover what was until 1918 known as the Austrian Empire, including Bohemia, or Czechoslovakia.

Originally these interior Germanic countries drew their supplies of (luxury) glass by barter from Rome-controlled sources by way of Aquileia; with the barbarian irruptions and the fall of the Western Empire that route was broken, but trade in glass was still possible with the Seine–Rhine area, so far as Western Germany was concerned. Bohemia, Poland, and the Baltic were better served by the Eastern capital of Constantinople, by the Danube route, but this also was cut in the fifth century by Attila and his Huns.

Except, then, for any knowledge and practice of glass-making derived from the Rhineland, Germany proper owed her knowledge of it to Italy, and we know that their pedlar purchasers were fetching glass from Venice in the thirteenth century. Buckley, in his *Art of Glass*, gives data concerning certain glasshouses and some dates at which they were at work. Not all these places are easy to identify, and the dates

iven are not necessarily those of their establishment, but
though remains to suggest that glassmaking may have pene-
ated by two routes. One of these ran more or less north-
ards from Venice to Trent (1468), then over the Brenner to
Hall in the Tyrol (near Innsbruck – 1534), onwards to Munich
Upper Bavaria – 1584) and Nuremberg (Middle Franconia –
542), further to Lauscha (Thuringerwald – 1597), and thence,
a north-west direction, to Cassel (Hesse – 1584).

The other route from Venice ran north-east, to Villach
Carinthia – 1468), and Vienna (1486), though some sort of
lass was being made there in 1428. The intermediate town of
raz is heard of in 1650. From Vienna, the penetration would
ave been to Prague, and thence fan-wise to the wooded
oundary ranges of the Erzgebirge and Riesengebirge, and
to Silesia. The northern glasshouses of Hanover, Bruns-
ick, and Brandenburg were later; Potsdam's requisitioning
and was not stretched out until 1674.

It has to be admitted that this theory of the spread of glass-
aking is no more than a reasonable speculation, and doubt-
ss as incomplete as are the records themselves. Bohemia, for
stance, has put in a claim to have been making glass as early
the second century B.C. For all that, glassmaking did reach
ermany from Italy, and the earlier the glass and the nearer to
aly, the more Italian in character it was likely to be. This
ould follow, seeing how often it was actually made by
alians or Italian-trained workmen.

Just as they adventured into other countries, so also Vene-
an craftsmen found their way to Germany, and there made
asses for new masters, notably at Hall in the Tyrol. During
e sixteenth century *latticinio* beakers are thought to have
en made, and perhaps wines in addition, but Germany
ems to have been less tolerant of foreign work than other
uropean countries. Germany wanted something more robust
d she certainly achieved that aim. Also, she wanted to be in-
vidual, indeed had to be, for everywhere different national
aits lead to different styles in art and crafts; here again she
as successful, to the extent that very many German glasses
ve a common characteristic – that of trying to impress. They

were meant to be original, but succeeded only in being diffe:
ent, though sometimes very different. It is doubtful wheth∈
any drinking-glass made east of the Rhineland could claiɪ
originality of form, even whether that was any longer possibl∈
Originality in form and convenience in use were not con
patible objectives, and in some cases, such as the greate
Humpen and *Passgläser*, neither was achieved. In others th
classic lines of forms adopted were marred by superfluities. I
particular, the bowl too often overshadowed the foot. A ta
stem, or a bowl necessarily rather heavy in order to accept th
decoration imposed upon it, was often given too light a foo
In such cases the result was a glass unbalanced in both sens∈
of the word, and if too high a centre of gravity was countere
by extra width to the foot, as in some Nuremberg goblets, i∎
beauty was still further impaired. The determination to b
different recurs continually throughout the whole of Germa
glass, as well in decoration as in form, and in the face of th
zweischengoldgläser goblets, and Kothgasser's painted beakers
century later, who will condemn it? From the collector's poiɪ
of view one recognizable *façon* is much more satisfactory tha∎
a series of similar *façons*.

Other than the palm cup and *maigelein* (Pl.9d), which d∈
rived from the Rhineland if not in fact made there, we do nc
now possess any German drinking-glass made before the si≭
teenth century. Then the Tyrolean glasshouse of Hall cam∈
into being. The glasses most safely attributed to Hall cam∈
from the royal Austrian collection, and are, we hope, pr∈
served among the treasures of the Kunsthistorisches Museuɪ
of Vienna. In the likely absence of corroborative data, a sim
lar attribution for comparable specimens must be speculativ∈
The *tazza* on Pl. 38 would certainly belong to Hall, judged b
the patterning of the engraving, yet the stem is extremely clos
to that of the Barbara Potter glass of 1602, accepted as Englisł
and Honey (p. 66) suggests the possibility of a Hall engrav∈
having come to England.

Dating from the mid sixteenth century the tinted fore∈
glass used for the nearly cylindrical *Humpen* (Pl.32) of Bavari∎
Franconia, and Bohemia, was perfectly in keeping with th

hearty enamelling so often applied to them; indeed, when this metal died out the enamelling did not long survive; it had had a run of a century and a half at least. *Stangengläser*, narrow cylindrical glasses on a pedestal foot, offered a smaller area whereon to enamel; they were decorated with armorials, family occasions, and rustic joys. They could come from Saxony when of nearly colourless metal. *Passgläser* were like the last but banded horizontally into zones (Pl.34c).

Nuremberg made towering goblets of character in an adequate *cristallo* from the middle of the seventeenth century until about 1730; the bowls were small, of U shape or nearly bucket form and a cover was possibly nearly universal, but that is by no means the case today. The stem was built up of hollow bulbs and multiple collars over a foot which was necessarily wide. No difficulty appears to have been presented by the metal, possibly because, for their size, the glasses remained light in weight. Colour was used, or used in part, for the stem might be parti-coloured; glasses in green (Pl.33a), amethyst, and blue are known, all of particular rarity and decided charm. There were also made smaller beakers of thickish metal such as would conveniently accept carving in low relief.

Bohemia followed suit with tall but heavier goblets, more workmanlike glasses with sturdier stems and often heavy knops with swirled lobing. Here moreover appeared ruby and gold spirals within the stem, on glasses early enough to be affected by 'glass disease', our crizzling (Pl.33e). As at Nuremberg, small heavy beakers were also made (Pl.43a).

At Potsdam, Kunckel had already made in the 1670s a fine ruby glass, a good green, and apparently blue, and opaque white also. The ruby was a cold colour, like red ink, and very different from the later warm tints of even raspberry red, from various quarters. A fair amount of the latter has been set in gilt metal mounts at one time or another, in emulation of late seventeenth-century fashions. The clear glass of Potsdam was also heavy; it included substantial goblets and heavy beakers, all thick enough to take deep intaglio engraving. Rather strangely, it suffered badly from glass disease, to the extent that beakers of about 1690 may be so decomposed as seriously to obscure the carving, and as late as 1714 the affliction had not been suppressed. The chief artists concerned are mentioned in Chapter VIII.

Somewhere about 1720–30, it may have been, when a change came about. The simple but inconveniently large *Humpen* faded out with the stately Nuremberg and Bohemian goblets. It may have been felt that honour was satisfied and that something more polite was called for, so glasshouses adopted the classical wine and goblet with conical or pointed round funnel bowl and inverted baluster stem (Pl.41b), with free local differences in proportion and treatment. The bowls remained on the large side, and what would be goblets in English eyes considerably exceeded wines in point of numbers. The bowl chiefly preferred was a rather deep pointed round funnel, as graceful as anyone could wish, so long as its size was not exaggerated. Of drinking-glasses with small bowls, like our mid eighteenth-century twist glasses, few indeed were made. It was perhaps considered that a glass of small capacity was a reflection upon both host and guest.

Thus, Bohemia, Silesia, Saxony, Thuringia, Hesse, Brandenburg, and many less important places made much the same kinds of glass in their different styles which are confusing to English collectors and not always clear to German ones. They might or might not be easier to identify if the cutting did not so often disguise them. Some baluster (Pl.41d) and plain-stemmed English designs were copied, with characteristic amendments. The frequent provision of a cover may be symptomatic of this, or it may reflect a convention that an uncovered vessel silently invited a refill, a covered one satiety. It may be added that in the course of two centuries the covers for German glasses have all too often been misplaced; they should not only fit but suit, showing some definite decorative affinity with the business end of the glass.

Metal underwent a considerable improvement in which it seems that the use of chalk played a decided part. Bohemia and Silesia in particular employed a soda–lime metal which had a clarity and hardness nowhere bettered (Pl.42b) and which was especially suitable for the delicate and intricate engraving so much in vogue in the second quarter of the eighteenth century. Then between 1740 and 1750 Lauenstein in Hanover duplicated Ravenscroft's experiments and failures, but eventually produced a really fine lead metal (Pl.41d), short-lived and worthy of a better fate. It seems that at this glass-house both lead and soda metal glasses were in production at one and the same time; some were engraved on the pontil with a lion, or, apparently less frequently, with a C for Calemberg, which I have found to be most elusive.

Nevertheless, excellent as may have been their metal, most of all to the credit of the Germans was their painstaking industrious ingenuity in decorating the glasses they had made. Not everyone will approve of the profusion with which this decoration was applied. They may dislike its intensity and regard it as a further manifestation of the German determination to impress. On the other hand, it is not easy for an Englishman of the twentieth century to form a fair judgement on foreign work of the seventeenth and eighteenth centuries; certainly the best of it, whether enamelling, painting, or decoration with the wheel, does and will rank as high artistic achievement under handicaps now easily under-estimated.

Apart from applied decoration, it came early to be realized that mere colour could attract attention and presumably quite cheaply. From about 1690 Kunckel had made opaque white glass the subject of much experiment, and the search for a competitive glass was accelerated by the rise of European porcelain, we think with less success than was achieved by our own white Bristol glass. As here, a good deal was none other than milk-glass of fair quality, often used for canister bottles (Pl.37c) and somewhat inconsiderable household articles such as mugs. There was also made in the second half of the eighteenth century a considerable quantity of well-fashioned tea-ware (Pl. 37a, b) in good enamelled and painted milk-glass. Its origin is likely to have been Bohemia, its decoration was extremely catholic, and its purpose – export, to relieve national financial and glassmaking stringencies after the Seven Years War. Some may well have been made elsewhere, for there are distinct differences in metal. The commonest examples are handleless cups and saucers, mottled with blue, and there are others with blue, purple, or green combing, or with combinations of these colours; they were nicely made. Painted decoration such as might appear on porcelain exists in styles which are foreign, or which might appeal to foreigners. The manufacture did not cease with greater prosperity, or perchance was resumed after the Napoleonic struggle, for 'black' glass cups and saucers with gilt chinoiserie were being made at Potsdam in the 1830s.

No country did in fact make so much good glass in so many different colours and shades of colour, or in so many combinations of colour, as did Germany. The ingenuities of her late eighteenth- and earlier nineteenth-century glassmasters are touched upon in Chapter VIII, and resulted *inter alia* in a wide range of hyalith glass, varicoloured and in imitation of polished natural stones. The colours were opaque, black or rather intensely deep amethyst, through all kinds of tints, whereof a palish blue was one of the favourites; very often they were veined or striated, as in a brick-red colour exactly resembling sealing-wax (Pl.48b). Translucent colours offered no difficulty, while elaborate cutting was frequently added and effectively disguised an otherwise clumsy appearance of the heavier objects. In short, the exploitation of colour was a decorative theme in itself, and of its exponents the name of Friedrich Egermann, of Bohemia, who called his glass 'Lithyalin', was in the front rank.

Somewhat preceding but also contemporary with the foregoing was the unassuming translucent painting of Kothgasser and others upon equally unassuming beakers; the combination seems to reflect the relief which must have followed the closing of the Napoleonic Wars, and it further emphasized a proper economy. This phase, never entirely extinct, fairly soon gave pride of place to another, a period of strained design, and not only so in Germany. It is hardly too much to say that the German extravagancies went furthest, at least in our eyes, not necessarily in theirs. There was the Egermann cutting itself (Pl.48a), something never attempted here, and this was transferred to glasses with other decoration, large and small vessels flashed with various colours, but very commonly with amber which might be heightened with black and gold, and rather later with plain ruby. The bowl might be windowed and illuminated with tiny vignettes in engraving or colour; topographical, floral posies, sometimes single decorative letters which spelled out a name or sentiment. Alternatively the flashing might be skilfully cut through to show in the clear glass woodland scenes, animal subjects which were generally stags, sometimes horses (Pl.44b), with or without accompaniments. Overlaid glass itself arrived in full time to display itself at our Great Exhibition in 1851, indeed flashed and engraved goblets of that very Exhibition exist. The overlaid glass was cut through to leave patterns, panels, or windows, and was itself profusely painted as well; again topographical subjects, landscapes with exotic birds, floral designs, and much else. Subsequently figure subjects were introduced on an unnecessarily heroic scale, imagery not realism, reminiscent of the front cover of a popular song-sheet.

On the whole, not too much could be done to the bowl because it had still to serve the decorator's convenience, but there was hardly any limit to the fanciful treatment of the foot; Victorian Gothic was at least fashioned to last. A lot of the glass of lesser quality was repetitive; commercial reasons required that production should be stepped up, and much of this cheaper glass was probably export goods. Eventually the individual glassmaker came to have little control over the form of glass or style of decoration, while education had not yet attempted to bring art into industry. Yet when a remaining craftsman had a free hand he could still correlate proportion and line and produce a vase or vessel which might be Victorian, but which was still a real work of art not necessarily fated to be spoiled by cutter or decorator (Pl.44d).

FOR FURTHER REFERENCE

BUCKLEY, W. *European Glass*, 1926, and *The Art of Glass*, 1929.
DILLON, E. *Glass*, 1907.
HARTSHORNE, A. *Old English Glasses*, 1897.
GLASS EXPORT and JABLONEX. *The Bohemian Glass*, Czechoslovakia, 1954.

CHAPTER VIII

GILDING THE LILY

*

1. Painting and Enamelling

FROM very early days men have painted upon glass, a simple matter in itself, the difficulty being to render the pigment permanent. Consequently there were two kinds of painting. First, where the colour was laid on with some kind of fixative and was sadly impermanent. It could be protected if shielded by a device such as another wall of glass, when it would last as long as, but little longer than its protective screen. This straightforward painting is known as 'cold painting', and it appears throughout glass history (Pl.51e). Being impermanent, it cannot be known how much the technique was used; some of it was surely the work of individual amateurs; some was not expected to last, as witness the Sunderland rolling-pins and the souvenir ware, crudely painted and splashed over with a cheap varnish, though there remain records of historic events, even at this level, such as the encounter on 15 January 1815 between *Endymion* (British, 40 24-pdrs, disabled) and *President* (U.S.A. 44-gun frigate of renown, struck); it was an episode as famous and significant then as the action in 1939 off the River Plate between the *Exeter*, *et al.*, and the pocket battleship *Graf Spee*, and, moreover, was a strikingly similar affair. More careful work in colour, as also in gold, is to be found.

Here may be mentioned two linked processes which are unlikely to concern many readers. About the sixth century what is called lustre painting, in reflective iridescent colours, appeared in Egypt, and with it could be found other colours as well called pigmental stains as anything else, for they were not surface pigments. With the lapse of the centuries their charm has probably faded, but not their desirability.

The second kind of painting required a high degree of technical knowledge, for here the paintwork was fired after being laid on, and so rendered permanent. Obviously, the colours had to fuse into the body of the vessel without the latter being affected, so that questions of materials, fluxes, and temperatures ruled the result.

It is usual to divide this fired work into enamelling or painting, the former term being used to cover the opaque or semi-opaque heavily laid work, somewhat in relief, the latter term for more transparent and smooth work, but it is impossible to draw any hard-and-fast line between the two.

As we have seen, the permanent painting of glass was practised in the third century, as in the Begram treasure; this was glass whereon, so it may be, the technique outstripped draughtsmanship, but then most of what we possess is fragmentary and more than second-hand. The art of enamelling in colours was first brought to perfection – if indeed perfection is ever attained – in Saracenic times at Damascus and Aleppo (Pl.13c), and by then design at any rate no longer lagged behind. After the incursion of Tamerlane, apart from some traces of continuity in Egypt, the technique passed to Venice, with a great change in style and for all too short a time. This has been noticed (Pl.18), as well as French (Pl.19a) and Spanish glass in the same tradition; to these countries may be added the Netherlands (Pl.35a). Here indeed was an art which must have appealed strongly to German temperament, one which had perhaps a barbaric appeal, for after the middle of the sixteenth century it was enthusiastically adopted and practised with every kind of assiduity. It was an art well suited to forest glass and not unwelcome on more polished vessels.

Convention evidently decreed that the German enamelled glasses should be dated, and for that its collectors may be grateful. The earliest record is one of 1541, but any sixteenth-century specimen is something of a prize. The enamelling maintained its vigour until about 1670, and continued into the second quarter of the eighteenth century, but by then it had lost its earlier robust character, though by no means its artistry (Pl.34b). Whereas the Italian enamel was painted on evenly, the German artists preferred to lay it on heavily, without attention to smoothness.

The quality of German work varied rather with the subject depicted, the *Reichsadlerhumpen* for instance, which are a tribute to the Emperor, being particularly well done (Pl.32a). These showed the crowned double-headed eagle displayed, its wings bearing the names and arms of the constituent States of the Empire, and the best of them also carried the figure of the Christ upon the Cross. The *Kurfurstenhumpen* were more irregular in execution, though generally worthy glasses; they showed the Emperor and the seven Electors. Glasses with the 'Ten Ages of Man' fell into the same category. There were many armorial glasses of fine quality, mostly with a string of initials to denote the owner's name and titles beside which our modern abbreviational conventions seem simplicity itself. *Apostelgläser*, presenting the Twelve Apostles each with his insignia, are too rare to warrant comment (Pl.32b). Lastly, among the aristocracy of enamelled German glasses were what may be termed guest glasses, ceremonial and individual vessels, featuring the owner in some way or other, and used, as an inscription sometimes makes plain, to compliment both host and guest, especially a first-time guest (Pl.32c). It is worth noting that on occasion it is the glass itself which is regarded as speaking, a compliment in all cases strictly uniform and unimpeachable.

Some criticism has been uttered on the quality of German enamelling. So far as the foregoing types are concerned, I would not have them altered in style or execution, for they might then lose an eminent individuality only to gain a politeness not wholly the mark of their owners. The many Guild, betrothal, and family glasses, and others with crudely comic scenes are in another category, and from their nature outside criticism. In these the drawing and colouring rarely merit praise, but it takes all sorts of glasses to fill a collector's cabinet, and many are both interesting and instructive. There was less variety with the *Fichtelgebirge* glasses, which showed a studiously conventional view of the padlocked Ochsenkopf, whence flowed four rivers. The treasures this mountain was alleged to contain were as unreal as the stags' heads which peep sym-metrically from its bright green slopes. It may be that this and other crude work was done on the glasshouse sites, the fine in such towns as Augsburg, Nuremberg, and Dresden.

The foregoing were nearly all *Humpen*, more or less cylin-drical beakers sometimes a few inches in height, more often requiring both hands to lift. *Passgläser* – banded glasses – were narrower cylindrical vessels on a pedestal foot, divided into zones by horizontal trails of glass or bands of colour. Some were very well enamelled with a playing-card, the zones of liquor having some relation to the gains or forfeits incurred in the game. Usually it is the queen or knave which is displayed on the glass (Pl.34c).

In the third quarter of the seventeenth century a competitive school of painting made its appearance, using glasses in *cristallo*. These were small and convenient in use, a low beaker on three little bun-shaped feet being a favourite model which may be assigned to Nuremberg and Lotharingia. One such example of painting, or enamelling, in white heightened with black shows the equestrian figures of two of the seven Elec-tors, Pfalz and Brandenburg, with a castle (?Juttenbuhl) on reverse inscribed *Heijelberg*; it was obviously one of a set, and likely to be quite as early as the well-known work of Johann Schaper (1621–70), who worked at Nuremberg painting land-scapes with battle scenes or ruins, and armorials, chiefly in black or sepia (Pl.34a).

Presumably earlier than Schaper was the decorator of one of the most pleasing of all glasses (Pl.35b), which is symmetri-cally enamelled in white on a very dark metal, a black-and-white affair one would naturally date to quite an early year in the seventeenth century, yet there is a Dutch conical wine of the 1670s engraved with a closely similar design. Schaper was followed by the Preisslers, father and son, who initiated a style of drawing in black and red. Others followed in the same man-ner with less and less success (Pl.34d) until a school of still more delicate painting arose in the very early nineteenth cen-tury. The Schaper tradition has been commercially revived in the twentieth.

On the Continent cheaply made and poorly enamelled glasses gradually became common after 1750; peasant glasses which had considerable popularity. Many small canister bottles, clear, white, and blue, came from mid-Europe, that is to say the Tyrol and the Swiss–German border (Pl.37c). They had conventional scrolls or foliage and some a human figure or figures, caricature-like in effect if not in intent, and there might be a sentimental or incisive motto. Having a screwed pewter top and cap, the latter usually now missing, one may think of them as spirit-flasks and remark that seemingly indistinguishable bottles are credited to Spain and America. Similarly painted tankards came from Holland and elsewhere (*Hansie in de Kelder*). Spain enamelled on both white (Pl.37d) and clear glasses, and after 1800 every glassmaking country produced its cheap decorative and souvenir ware. Our own Tyneside was no laggard in this respect and permitted itself no small artistic licence in design.

Better work included vignettes painted in bright colours on Bohemian glasses and bottles in the third quarter of the eighteenth century (Pl.36d). Conversation scenes were popular; series of designs portraying the months of the year were also in demand. The best of this rather middle-class and peasant glass is attractive and decorative, good enough to charm but not to excite admiration. It may, however, have had an influence on the later work of William and Mary Beilby, now to be mentioned in greater detail perhaps than its importance warrants.

William Beilby, I believe, worked first in a thin smoothly spread white enamel, drawing simple decorative designs of the fruiting vine and the hop and barley (Pl.36a). A fine needle was used to delineate the veining of the leaves and other details whilst the enamel was still soft. This was, maybe, an attempt to imitate the then very popular wheel-engraved 'flowered' designs. Beilby's market will have been restricted, and not much of this thin 'wash-enamel' work will be found; a single example in greyish enamel may be mentioned, even more like the engraving assumed to have been copied. Beilby went on to use a much thicker and densely white enamel

(Pl. 36c, e). The same decorative designs were used and festoons of various kinds were applied to the rims of simple glasses; a narrow circuit of gilding on the very edge of the rim is frequently to be found. This phase of Beilby's art abandoned imitation for bold and attractive representation, but it was less important than another which covered glasses of personal interest decorated and inscribed to order.

More ambitious were scenic representations of classical ruins, pastoral subjects, and a series of sports and pastimes (Pl.36e). There is a certain sameness about them, but they are scarce and esteemed by English collectors. Then there were some armorial glasses and decanters, painted in colours with great care; sometimes a signature was added. Most important of these were some goblets with the royal Arms, presumed to have been painted on the birth of the Prince of Wales in 1763. An undue enthusiasm has lifted values thereof to inordinate heights, yet it is indisputable that the Beilbys are our only English enamellers known by name. An anonymous attempt, which may have preceded Beilby because it includes the remains of a set of portrait glasses of Prince Charles Edward in colours, is less artistic, but prized for the association value and extreme rarity of the portraits (Pl.35c). By the same hand are some dram glasses of 1750–60, decorated with simple Masonic emblems in red and white only.

Michael Edkins, painter and gilder rather than enameller, worked on opaque white glass at Bristol about the same time. His decorative floral designs and figure subjects, birds, and insects deserve and receive great praise, and they multiply many times the value of the glass he employed (Pl.36b). He had unknown imitators or pupils whose work was little less proficient and it can only expertly be separated from his own, and none too assuredly. On the other side of England, one Absolon was painting and engraving simple glasses for simple people, and adding gilding to his engraving (Pl.35d).

The work of Joseph Mildner will be mentioned later, but he may have been the stimulus for another school of German painting which used a thin transparent enamel and had a decided preference for pastel tints. Among the purists in this.

style the names of Samuel Mohn, of Dresden, and his son Samuel Gottlob, and Kothgasser of Vienna, are the best known. Samuel and Gottlob were both working in the first quarter of the nineteenth century. Kothgasser had a longer career, signing and dating glasses mainly between 1814 and 1830, and his work is naturally less difficult to find. There followed lesser artists, but in general the work of all is characterized by extreme care and exactitude, extending to every detail and the decorative borderings. All these men preferred simple glasses of the small beaker type, and they produced a quite extraordinary range of subjects. Scenic representations of famous places and buildings were their mainstay, selling for quite modest sums; there were portraits, some by the Mohns being also in silhouette, while biblical, allegorical, and sentimental designs were popular. There were some delightful floral patterns. One of Kothgasser's beakers depicted an unexpectedly attractive witch astride a broomstick; another represented fish in an aquarium (Pl.37e). Playing-cards, owls in a tree, and Venus regarding herself in a mirror all added to the variety of subjects. Taken together, they are evidence of the fey side of Teutonic imagination.

A more commercially minded school of painters carried on their tradition. Floral subjects on mid-nineteenth-century overlaid glass were finely but not imaginatively done (Pl.35e). Portraiture on the later florid Bohemian vases now has its votaries, but is still hardly worthy of the pains so evidently taken. I suspect that economic considerations had transformed the artist into a hack decorator. Similar work was done in England, but by no means on the same scale. Names likely to be better known in the future include that of J. Locke, gilder and enameller of a classic design about 1840; J. T. Bott, who about 1851 emulated a Bohemian style of flowers and fruit in colour; and Erard, in the 1880s, with his chased glass decoration in gold and enamel, or silver deposit. Examples of these and many other nineteenth-century English achievements may be seen in the Borough of Stourbridge collection at the Council House.

2. Engraving

Engraving is older than painting and we have seen something
of its practice in ancient times. Egypt and Rome provided incised decoration by a hand-tool. Rome engraved and incised
glasses on the lathe, using flint or wheel, and developed this
into flat cutting. The ancients also carved glasses, but how to
draw distinctions between their wheel engraving, cutting, and
carving poses difficulties. Today, collectors recognize several
kinds of engraving:

(a) DIAMOND-POINT ENGRAVING. Executed by hand,
using a diamond or a graver (Pl.39), including calligraphic
work (Pl.38c).

(b) STIPPLING. This is somewhat similar work of a more
delicate kind, carried out in dots using perhaps a little ham-
mer, or in very fine and usually short lines. In the latter case it
approaches (a) above (Pl. 40c, d).

(c) (SURFACE) WHEEL ENGRAVING. This can be anything
from very coarse to exceedingly delicate, according to the skill
of the engraver and the type of wheel used. A stone wheel
gives a coarse effect; a copper or bronze wheel gives a sharper
cut, whose delicacy is determined by the size and quality of the
wheel; the smaller and finer this is, the more delicate the work.

(d) CARVING IN LOW RELIEF. This is effected by causing
the wheel to bite more deeply; a wider variety of wheel comes
into play, and the result is usually given a polished finish. The
finer the polish the better the work, is a general rule (Pl.43a).

(e) CARVING IN HIGH RELIEF. Again the wheel is used,
the design being made to stand up from the body of the glass
(Pl.43b). The use of other tools is not excluded, particularly
in modern practice, where hydrofluoric acid is also used to
expedite the removal of unwanted metal.

Diamond-point appears on early Venetian glass, an intricate
decorative border on bowls and dishes, and conventional
floral designs sometimes incorporating birds or animals being
found on drinking-glasses as well. It was a hazardous technique

for the frail sixteenth- to seventeenth-century Venetian glasses, and also, maybe, too laborious a task for impatient Latin craftsmen. But it had an appeal to Germans, eminent copyists by instinct. The Hall glasses (Pl.38a) of the Tyrol are engraved in Italian style, whether by Italians or German trainees cannot be said.

More individual were a few *Reichsadlerhumpen* and comparable glasses; German diamond-point work, however, was not persisted in because enamelling and wheel engraving had a still greater appeal.

The Italian decorative diamond-point work was copied in both France and England, the one known artist common to both countries being Anthony de Lysle or Lisley, to whose hand we owe identification of the rare Verzelini goblets of the late sixteenth century.

They are not separable, but it was the Rhinelanders and the Dutch who made the most of the possibilities of diamond-point, and it might be true to say that they drew upon glass as naturally as Schaper and the Mohns painted it. They produced pictures where others had only produced designs (Pl.39b). The art was not an easy one. It was one thing to engrave upon a flat surface and quite another to achieve an artistic effect on a glass bowl which had varying contours. There was, consequently, an engaging air of careless abandon in the scenes portrayed, meticulous accuracy being avoided because unattainable; the result must be assumed to have pleased the artist and his public as much as it now pleases us. Some Dutch portraiture was more sedate, and I think the less impressive for being more life-like. A different kind of accuracy found expression in the so-called 'calligraphic' glasses notable for the elaborate slender curves and flourishes which masked some motto and which might embrace the whole glass (Pl.38c). Anna Roemers Visscher (1583–1651) was the first we know of to work in this style, and incidentally the first woman artist in glass of whom we have record. Among men, van Heemskerk (1613–92) is a familiar name, but all signed work of the period is rare; it should, on all counts, be well scrutinized.

In addition to these distinctive styles, the Dutch produced

much pleasant work of a minor character in the Venetian tradition, roughly hatching in the outlined flowers and animals of convention to give body to the design. It was the easiest way, and accordingly dogmatism as to origin and handiwork is generally hazardous (Pl.39a).

Of conclusively English work there is nothing of importance until just before the middle of the eighteenth century, when the *Amen* glasses were made anonymously, and two allegorical designs by one Chapman. Francis figures one of these in his *Old English Drinking Glasses*, but neither they nor the *Amen* glasses display professional skill; their value is historical and sentimental, not artistic, and perhaps the higher for it. Other diamond-point glasses were spasmodically made; they were essentially for commemorative or presentation purposes, and until quite recent days the only series to be found consists of some mid-eighteenth-century rummers with vignette armorials, coaches, and hunting scenes; nothing came amiss. They are interesting rather than meritorious, and suffer from the inclusion of a doggerel versified sentiment in a minute and crabbed hand. Various signatures were appended, presumably those of the donors, not that of the artist.

Stippling was only successfully accomplished by the Dutch, and indeed not seriously attempted by any other nation. A few names are known, notably Frans Greenwood (1680–1761), and David Wolff, who worked between 1784 and 1795, but there must have been other similar specialists, hardly less capable, whose names remain unknown. The identification of the many stippled glasses which exist is confused by doubts and over-hasty *dicta*. The method was a simple one, the image desired being produced by a series of tiny dots punctured on the surface of the glass (Pl.40c). They provided the high-lights in the picture, the intensity being achieved by varying their closeness; the shadows and background were obtained by leaving the surface more or less alone. It must have been an assiduous business requiring great skill and patience, but the results were rewarding; the pictures seem at first sight to be breathed upon the glass, so delicate are they. Consequently collectors seek them, and signed examples are costly, but signatures should not sway a buyer unless he is sure that they are genuine.

Some artists added a few fine lines to represent some outline or to assist with a head of hair. Others used more lines and fewer dots, and some relied entirely on lines and eschewed dots altogether (Pl.40d). In such cases the result is better seen on the glass, and I do not know that the technique was any less skilful. To all intents and purposes the series ends with a few glasses by L. Adams (Pl.40b), but the present century has provided a painstaking artist who has given us fine stippling of greater intensity than that of the past.

It is significant that in the majority of cases English lead glasses from Newcastle were preferred, partly because the metal was softer and would take dots or lines with less effort, and partly because it was better fitted to emphasize the unworked shadows; indeed, the finest stippling is found on the finest glasses (Pl.40a).

Surface engraving with the wheel was anciently practised, but was then of very simple or crude description. Seeing what skill the craftsmen of the first four centuries displayed in cameo-cutting and gem-engraving, it is surprising how far surface engraving lagged behind. It can hardly be fortuitous that no single celebrated specimen of surface engraving is recorded until the early seventeenth century, and if some reason be sought, it can only be suggested that the manufacture of the essential tools, for instance the tiny wheels, had until then not been achieved.

It must be conceded that until the nineteenth century surface-wheel engraving of quality was the province of the Dutchman and the German. It was not suitable for the frail Venetian or *façon de Venise* glassware, consequently any would-be technician had to wait until there was a suitably heavy glass for him to work on. Caspar Lehmann was the earliest such, working in Prague for the Emperor Rudolf II, and signing and dating a beaker in 1605. This displays a far-advanced skill. There are two more anonymous glasses dated before the Schwanhardts, father and son, assumed the mantle of Lehmann, and, from 1622, engraved glasses at Nuremberg. They improved upon Lehmann by polishing their engraving. No less competent were their followers, Schwinger (*d.* 1683), H. W. Schmidt, and Killinger (*d.* 1726). These men used the tall, multi-knopped, multi-collared Nuremberg goblets (Pl.41a), whose relatively thin walls required a delicate hand; heavier tumblers suited to low-relief work; and bun-footed beakers. The work of this Nuremberg school is at first generally fine, and sometimes superb in its drawing as well as its execution; that of the early eighteenth century may display a flatness and lack of perspective and proportion.

In Bohemia the initiative provided by Lehmann faded out by reason of the Thirty Years War, which desolated the country. It was not until the third quarter of the seventeenth century that it again flourished in Bohemia, which by 1720–30 had outpaced Nuremberg and was herself being at least matched by Silesia. The pictorial style was abandoned in favour of formal designs composed of ribbon or strap-work, foliage, and scrolling. Flat cutting came in at the same time. The excellence of this Bohemian and Silesian work was unsurpassed; some of its portraiture was superb and closely akin to the earlier Nuremberg work, but the general characteristic was a superfluity of conventional patterns, enclosing armorials or vignette portraits, with a wealth of intricate detail and patient workmanship. Its execution was no doubt facilitated by the hard metal of the soda-lime glasses used. It should not be thought that side by side with this quality work there was not a large output of undistinguished engraving. In fact, it seems that few Bohemian and Silesian glasses escaped some form of treatment.

In the nineteenth century Bohemia in particular turned out a series of delicately engraved glasses in competition with the glass-painters of the day. The designs showed a wide range of subject; portraiture, memorial (Pl.48c), and family glass, devotional, and of course topographical glasses, being among the commonest choices. The figure and animal drawing had in many instances nothing to learn from any earlier artist and the standard of execution was generally high. The name of Anton

Simm (Pl.42c) is among the many far more familiar to continental collectors than ourselves.

From the second quarter of the eighteenth century onwards engraved glasses came from other German glassmaking centres. Brunswick, Saxony, Thuringia, Potsdam, and Zechlin were all producers of good glass, as was also a somewhat indeterminate district termed West Germany, which may mean Baden, and, rather importantly in our eyes, the Lauenstein glasshouse in Hanover (Pl.41d); all these come to mind by reason of some really fine work, though their normal production was less expensive glass, some part of it for France, Spain, and Scandinavia.

Chapter VI recorded the possible Saxon or Bohemian origin of German-type glasses engraved with the imperial Russian arms (Pl. 42a). There is a superb portrait of Elizabeth Petrovna, executed in low relief and doubtfully in Russia. Belonging to the troubled war years, these royal glasses were carelessly surface engraved and often heightened by black enamel or gilding. From their number, one assumes that the royal consumption of glassware was considerable, and, seeing the generous capacity of the bowls, the household a thirsty one.

The only serious challenge to German surface-wheel engraving came from the Dutch. Their craftsmen engraved many notable glasses from the second quarter of the eighteenth century. As in Germany, some of their work lacked skill, but much more of it had some historical or social interest. Family affairs evidently loomed large in Dutch eyes. The best-known Dutch engraver was Jacob Sang, and he and his school produced many glasses of eminent quality and appeal (Pl.70d). They chose English lead metal glasses and found no difficulty in adopting the German strap work, conventional scrolls, and floral motifs with a restraint and sense of proportion which left any main feature in due prominence. Some Dutch landscape and shipping scenes are notable for their accuracy and perspective, than which hardly anything could be more difficult on a curving surface. Some 'copper-plate' inscriptions with the wheel indicate a control few now possess with the pen. Sharp curves with the wheel were difficult indeed, so much so that in England the graver was often employed to connect the easier upstrokes and downstrokes of the lettering.

English surface engraving can hardly be called anything more than pleasant until the early nineteenth century. Such work as is found on early glasses is nearly always the work of continental engravers, and a purely English school did not arise until about 1760, when simple decorative designs were given to small wine-glasses. The trade name for this was 'flowered', though even conventional flowers were in a minority among the many designs chosen whereof the fruiting vine was an obvious and the commonest motif. A little later, portions of the design were given a high polish, as in part to most of the roses of the Jacobite glasses. The hop and barley pattern was especially effective when rendered in this fashion; it occurs in considerable variation.

Various English commemorative glasses, such as the Privateer glasses, needed greater skill, yet they cannot be ranked very highly. Not until about 1765 could any English work stand in company with that of the continental experts, and little enough of it even then. The early nineteenth century saw some improvement and a good many rummers may be found with finely executed work (Pl.42d), but it still lacked draughtsmanship and artistic inspiration.

There was a certain amount of engraving on American glass, from the latter part of the nineteenth century on. It seems to have approached English work in style and execution, but the men were so often Dutch or German that continental feeling was frequently apparent in both the glass and the engraving. Writing with only an academic knowledge of American glass, I think it must be as difficult today to distinguish between many European-made and American-made specimens as it was to separate Italian for export and the various *façons d'Italie* in the seventeenth century.

It is not easy to say when surface engraving becomes carving in low relief, but in general acceptance the latter term covers engraved work which is both deep and wide, leaving the surface of the glass with a number of concavities. Such work was polished in greater or less degree, and it required high skill to produce any sort of artistic result. Bohemians, and subsequently Silesians also, practised low relief carving towards the end of the seventeenth century. At the same time highly skilled artists were at work in Berlin, using Potsdam glasses. Martin Winter and particularly Gottfried Spiller employed themselves in both high and low relief work, as did the eminent Franz Gondelach at Cassel. Then there was Heinrich Jäger, who was undoubtedly responsible for the satirical goblet (Pl.33a) which recalls the horrid fate in 1706 of Patkul, chief mechanic of the tragic Great Northern War. The glasses used were heavy-walled goblets and beakers of small distinction in themselves and very liable to crizzling and decay, a fault so bad as to arouse surprise, for ordinarily there was no difficulty in making perfect soda metal glasses. The carving at Potsdam was deeply cut, but not always highly polished. One such glass and the odd cover, the remains of a pair of covered beakers, was elaborately engraved to commemorate our own King William III and his Queen Mary. It is a pity that so much skill should now be marred by decay and defacement of the glasses employed.

Low relief carving occurred at intervals on Bohemian glasses (Pl.43a) and came into prominence again in the nineteenth century, when amber glassware was deeply carved with stags, trees, and hounds. Though stereotyped, these and others of a like nature were naturalistic designs, and many exhibit a high degree of skill. Overlaid and flashed glass was also carved through the colour in an effective fashion, Karl Pfohl in the 1860s specializing in animal forms (Pl.44b). These later glasses of pretence were characterized by the most careful finish, with fine cutting to stem and foot, and they evidently ranked highly in the eyes of their makers, as they still rank on the Continent, and as they will eventually rank in England.

Carving in high relief was an obvious corollary of the foregoing to anyone searching for new fields to conquer. It was a laborious process, and the outstanding artists, Spiller and Gondelach, have already been mentioned. Both were Germans, working in the late seventeenth and early eighteenth century, and their glasses are prized (Pl.43b). High relief and low relief work can be found on one and the same glass; the former can also be found applied to a convex cameo medallion portrait set in a reserve on a glass already surface engraved. The cameo was attached to the bowl by some transparent adhesive, but the method was not altogether satisfactory because the cameos were apt to crack across, and also to come away entirely.

Their appearance is very different, but the technique of the modern cameo-cut French vases of Gallé and others is similar (Pl.44c). In these the vessel, whatever it might be, was overlaid with glass, or more truly lined, with one or more layers of plain or coloured metal (as with Pl.44a). The fun consisted in removing the unwanted glass so that the design, floral or scenic, would be left in high relief. A spray might stand out, with green leaves and blue flower; shading could be accomplished and a skyscape developed in the background, or lakeside scene bordered with trees. Admittedly, the colouring was more often futuristic than natural. Much of the task of removing unwanted metal could be accomplished by the use of hydrofluoric acid, but the wheel and other edged tools were needful for completion of the picture. The finished work could be polished, or made satiny, or left matt. The firm of Webb & Sons did similar but more sober work in England; the Northwoods and Woodalls (Pl.43c) are regarded as our foremost artists, and they worked in a decidedly classical style suited to Victorian taste, preferring great attention to draughtsmanship and detail and particular care in workmanship to the vagaries of French impressionism, popular as that fairly was.

3. Gilding

The possibilities of gilding seem to have been exploited less than might be expected, for hardly any decoration looks better than fine gilding on fine crystal. It had its origin in antiquity, and gold has never been out of favour. The methods of application were the same as in painting, either by a firing process or by the aid of a fixative, that is to say an adhesive. In the firing process the gilding was reasonably permanent and brilliant when burnished, but otherwise it might become slowly dulled by time, though easily restored to its original condition. In the alternative process, known as oil-gilding, the brilliance of the gold is rather better retained, but the gilding will disappear sooner or later according to the efficiency of the fixative and, of course, the extent to which it is exposed to wear. At an angle the film left by the fixative can be seen long after every speck of gilding has vanished, and it may reveal the original pattern almost in its entirety.

A third process, or it may be called an elaboration of the last, is simply protective, also as in painting, a shield of glass or foil or even paint being placed over the gilding, which in the two latter cases must be affixed to the back or inner side of the glass.

Fired gilding was used in Egypt and Syria somewhat before and also during the thirteenth and fourteenth centuries, chiefly as an adjunct to enamel work (Pl.12d). In her turn, Venice used gilding in much the same way in the sixteenth century, commonly as a broad rim-band studded by dots of enamel colour, and also beneath the radial ribs of standing bowls (Pl.14). On some goblets it is used as a background to enamel colours (Pl.18). Although fired, gilding of this kind seems not quite to have the durability of enamelling, yet on such a dish as Pl.17a, where it is on the under-surface, it has remained almost pristine. The broad rim-band or ribbon was much used by German decorators in the late sixteenth and through the seventeenth century (Pl.32). Again it was studded or 'jewelled', and with the passing of the years the joints of the gold leaf laid on became distinct, while other parts of the ribbon were worn to a transparency. England did not use gilding at this time unless on any such standing bowls as she may have made in Venetian sixteenth- to seventeenth-century style (Pl.31c); in that event oil-gilding will have been her more likely technique.

Heavier fired gilding, not just gold-leaf, was liberally used on Silesian and Zechlin glasses (Pls 42b, 41c); it has not had to last so long, but promises a more enduring life. Other districts used narrow gilt rim-bands, a continental practice little used in England and in any case not before about 1760. About 1820–30 some of our small Georgian wines were so treated, but they cannot have been popular.

In the nineteenth century both gilding and silvering were used on the delicate fancies of the transparency painters such as Kothgasser, but mainly in a bordering. Both metals were more heavily applied to the ornate glasses of display produced around the middle of the century (Pl.37e). They are inclined to dull, particularly the silvering, but can be buffed-up into their former brilliance in a few minutes.

Oil-gilding can naturally not be traced very far back, but its use becomes known, though not usually apparent, on seventeenth-century *tazze* from the Low Countries by the existence of a filmy pattern, as has already been noted. Here it may be added that there are many glasses of the later seventeenth century which show a distinctly cloudy and even a patterned zone; they have not therefore necessarily been gilded, and the cloudiness is not automatically to be attributed to long-standing liquor, for they may very well be suffering from a phenomenon known as 'sulphur bloom', an intricacy of firing of the time.

There are to be found quite a number of English wine-glasses, and some ales, belonging to the third quarter of the eighteenth century, which have oil-gilding in the simplest floral style of the Bristol gilders (Pl.45b). There are wines and goblets with the fruiting vine and ales with the hop and barley (Pl.45d), both types being well executed, pretty durable, and now rather rare. Beilby frequently used glasses made in Newcastle with very non-durable gilt rims, which it is to be assumed he gilded himself.

From about the middle of the eighteenth century it was not rare to gild the engraving on drinking-glasses, as for instance the imperial Russian goblets of Elizabeth and Catherine already mentioned, a good many English Jacobite and other glasses, and Norwegian glasses in English style. Such gilding lasted better on continental glasses than on our own, which only rarely merit any better term than 'formerly gilt'. One or two

specimens have seemed to contradict the foregoing, and they
may actually have been fired. Absolon of Yarmouth appears to
have inscribed a good many blue glasses with gold lettering,
including a number relating to the Militia and the Volunteers
in Napoleonic times; our Home Guards of the period evidently found life worth living and their units worthy of record,
but inevitably the gilded legend is all too often unreadable or
maddeningly incomplete.

The physical protection of gilding and painting dates back
to the Christian gold-glass of the third and fourth centuries,
but this seldom reaches private hands; abroad there is a production for tourists. The technique was revived in the first
quarter of the eighteenth century by Bohemians. It was precision work, two walls being used for each vessel, one fitting
exactly into the other. The inner wall projected a quarter of an
inch or so above the outer, and this projection was thicker
than the rest and cut with a flange so that it could rest upon
the outer wall. Before insertion it was ornamented with gold
leaf and etched with a needle; silver leaf and colour could be
incorporated. The joint between the rim of the outer wall and
the flange of the inner had to be an exact one; it was cemented
by some colourless adhesive and masked by a further decorative band of 'inserted gold'. Finally the complete vessel was
submitted to the wheel and cut with fairly narrow vertical
flutes from base to rim; hence the term 'many-sided' which
is frequently but erroneously applied to the little beakers
(Pl.45a) and graceful goblets made in this fashion. The base of
the beaker had a circular disc cut away from the outer
skin; another disc was given a simple ruby and gold 'insertion'
and cemented into place.

The designs chosen corresponded to those on surface-engraved glasses; hunting scenes were extremely popular,
armorials frequent, and devotional subjects varied. Designs
emblematic of the Four Seasons occur, and also of the Con-
tinents, again Four, since Australia had still to be discovered.
The weak point of the technique lay in the jointing, especially
the basal joint, and in the disfigurement which occurred if the
two skins of the vessel were not an airtight fit; in that case an

gly air-bubble would spoil the effect, and few glasses are en-
rely free from that failing. They were, and are, extremely
ffective glasses and popular abroad, if not in England.

Towards the end of the eighteenth century, Mildner pro-
uced a variant of the technique. He cut away an oval from
ne wall of a simple beaker and inserted designs in gold, silver,
r colour, or a combination thereof on the inner face of a glass
nedallion which was exactly fitted into the orifice. He worked
t Gutenbrunn between 1787 and 1807, making a large num-
er of monogram and armorial glasses, with some portraits in
olour or silhouette, and a few topographical and conversa-
ion scenes. He signed and dated his glasses on the inside with
ommendable precision. As before, the joint was masked by a
ecorative border.

4. Moulded Decoration

he very earliest glasses we have were moulded, laboriously
nd by hand. Press-moulded bowls (Pl.2d) are supposed just
o have preceded blown glass, and were given radial ribs, slen-
er or stout as the case might be, to provide greater strength
nd no doubt a pleasing appearance. Then, with the discovery
f the blowing-iron it became easy to fashion quite intricate
atterns of decoration, inscriptions, or devices, and to pro-
uce an exactly similar series of each and every kind merely by
reparing a mould and blowing the gathering of hot metal
nto it.

In early days the moulds were made in either one part or in
wo equal parts. A bowl like that of Pl.11c could be blown in a
ne-piece mould; a pattern like Pl.16a required a two-piece
nould which when separated into its two halves permitted
elivery of the object ready for use or for completion in the
rdinary way. At some time or other the two parts of the
nould became hinged. And so throughout antiquity we find a
ost of mould-blown glasses, the precision of whose decoration
epended upon that of the mould and perhaps to some extent
n the lungs of the blower.

In due course Venice used the same process; the urn-stem
of Pl.23 came from a two-piece mould, while the pedest
stems of Pl.64 required only a single-piece mould. Some type
of decoration on the bowl of a goblet or wine glass we:
formed in a single-piece mould; this is termed dip-mouldin
and is a very common and useful device much used in En:
land, France, and Belgium in the eighteenth century. It pe
mitted the fashioning of spiral fluting or ribbing simply l
giving the paraison a twist as it was withdrawn from th
mould.

From the first quarter of the nineteenth century mouldin
processes were developed, particularly in America. There
mould pattern was used for a variety of objects by a furth
blowing and manipulation at the chair, so that such divers
things as an inkwell and a decanter might owe their origin t
the same mould. By this time the three-piece mould was bein
widely used in America. Originally they were of wood, and
certain number still exist, replaced, however, by more mode
and permanent ones. Who copied whom may not be precise
known, but three-piece moulds were used in a small way
Ireland for celery vases, rummers, decanters, and especial
barrel-shaped spirit bottles (Pl.46c); one might suggest, in
very small way – judging by the rarity of the vases and rum
mers, at any rate. The well-known Irish decanters with bas
fluting, and perhaps also their mark of origin under the bas
were from one-piece moulds in the ordinary way, possibly i
sufflated (expanded) by a further blowing. The foot and ste
of the vase/ewer, Pl.52c, is from a four-piece mould.

Similarly, single-piece mould decanters seem to have bee
made in Scotland, or possibly on Tyneside; the latter distri
certainly made them in a soda metal which varied from qui
good to bad. Rather a wide range of decoration was applie
crude engraving, bright floral bands of paintwork (Pl.46b
fired gilding, flashing or part flashing, and combinatio
thereof. The stoppers were press-moulded and somewh:
pagoda-like.

The Irish product is now much more appreciated, ar
examples with the factory name or that of a factor are soug

or. Modern marked finger bowls and decanters with the lettering 'Cork Glass Company' on the base are to be seen, the
latter blown from the original moulds and quite deceptive.

Machine press-moulded glass followed, an American invention which was quickly adopted in France (Pl. 20e). This
can give extremely elaborate patterns of glass, inexcusably
costly by any other method, and the resulting vessels have an
exceptional brilliance (Pl. 20f). It was a mechanical art, but by
no means an unworthy one, for, besides the fanciful pieces, it
offered bowls and other items so sharply moulded that they
can easily enough be taken for cut glass.

5. Cut Glass

Something must be said about cut glass, a comprehensive account of which has yet to be written. Its practice in Roman and
Islamic lands has been briefly noted. In modern times it was
reintroduced by Bohemians towards the end of the seventeenth century. The art spread quickly throughout Germany,
and in due course brought German glass into countries
hitherto almost ignorant of its existence. Western Europe provided an accessible market, and the Low Countries a wealthy
one. The German export drive, as we should now term it,
took place during the earlier eighteenth century, England re-
ceiving a quota without evidence of enthusiasm, despite the
novelty. No doubt it served to put fresh ideas into the heads of
English glassmakers who themselves began to advertise cut
glass, not necessarily English however. There are these ad-
vertisements and there are documented records withal which
seem incontrovertible, yet where are the glasses? There are
indeed pre-1750 sweetmeat-glasses, yet the date of their cutting
may be decidedly uncertain. It might be put that the rarity of
1725–50 English glass both made and cut at the same time is
so extreme that unless one is prepared to postulate a virtually
complete destruction thereof, the conclusion must be that the
home market was unresponsive and the output insignificant.

In any case, the Excise Act of 1745–6 put a crippling weight tax on the contents of the glass-pot, and finance forthwith dictated a drastic reduction in the size and weight of the glasses made. Cut glass especially suffered, since the metal lost in cutting paid duty, so that the Act almost prohibited anything but very simple cutting where ornamental value compensated for duty losses, or luxury cutting where cost did not matter. The Excise of 1777 doubled the duty, which may have diminished in value through currency depreciation, and nearly halved the weight of all ordinary production lines; it also included 'enamel' glass, spelling the doom of the filigree stem, and ushered in the age of small Georgian glasses, plain or perfunctorily cut.

But the duties did not apply to Ireland. Those of 1745–6 were important enough to have induced some English glassmasters to set up furnaces in Ireland, counting freedom from duty and the too-inquisitive exciseman as full compensation for an attached prohibition of export, which difficulty may not have been so insurmountable. The Act of 1777, however, almost coincided with a grant in 1780 to Ireland of free trade wherein may be traced the influence of the quite loyal Irish Volunteer movement. This enabled Irish-made glass to go to America, and go it did, to the extent that the Irish home market became content to use cheap English dutiable glass and thus permit a greater part of its own non-dutiable production to go abroad, not only to America, but to the West Indies and to England herself.

So from 1780 until 1825, when Irish-made glass was first taxed, the success of the Irish factories was phenomenal. But the glass they produced was Irish only in name; it was really English, made in Ireland for purposes of convenience, and made by English or English-trained glassmakers upheld by English capital (Pl.47). It was by no means the first time that English glass had been made in Ireland under similar auspices, but it was the first time that the venture had reaped a due reward. Accordingly, there was nothing to prevent the same glass being made in England, if cost did not matter, and undoubtedly London in particular had a large output of luxury cut glass; how large, it is impossible to ascertain. But it does not receive the same cachet of public approval simply because so much of it is automatically dubbed Irish, with the result that a vast public has almost come to believe that only Irish glass is worth any consideration at all. Yet this is, in fact, little more than a pleasing accidental episode in all the many centuries of glassmaking.

The styles of cutting changed with the years, and a volume of illustrations would be necessary to figure the patterns evolved, yet still leave the story imprecise. It may be possible to declare that a certain specimen is Irish, but risky to decide upon a Dublin, Cork, Waterford, or other origin. It verges on the impossible to assign English cut work; a London or Midland origin is more likely than any other. There is much misdating of the later cut glass. Good Irish and better English work was still being turned out after 1840, but it passes for late Georgian glass, and indeed differentiation may be most difficult.

Following precedents, the Dutch had already adopted, and I think improved on, the German cut work. In the early 1760s they were importing glasses from Newcastle and faceting the stem and bowl base in as good a manner as anyone; the bowl itself was reserved for engraving or had already been engraved. These were a special, not a production line. When Irish flat cutting came in, the Dutch did it equally well on a tinted soda glass which could, and does, easily pass for the mythical bluish Waterford. The rectangular, triangular, and polygonal bottles they made for travelling cases, and very luxurious they could be, are still fairly frequently seen and well worth attention.

Something has already been said as to the prevalence of cutting in eighteenth-century Germany. It was elaborate and suited current taste, but was unimaginative. That particular quality began to appear when, after another peace-making in 1815, Bohemia developed some fine cut work on goblets and beakers, though it may not be to English taste; the French Baccarat factory was not far behind, and the metal of both was superlative. Both productions, however, lacked the lustrous quality of the late eighteenth-century lead glass of Britain, the styles of which overflowed into the following century. Soon, however, economic considerations appear to have dictated a simplification, or maybe demand increased without the requisite skills, and the glass-cutters contented themselves too easily with different arrangements and varieties of flutes and diamonds. German example certainly tempted mid-century manufacturers into extreme exuberance, the technical efficiency of which was remarkable and a feature of the 1851 Exhibition. The phase passed and a certain seeming austerity which by no means spelled simplicity became apparent in the third quarter of the century; it was marked by a long series of wines and goblets the stems of which were given knoppings cut to square, rectangular, or other shapes, not a curve remaining. The exactitude of the cutting was admirable and by no means the simple affair.

This twentieth century has seen something approaching systematic reproduction of early cut glass, yclept Irish. The deceptive pieces are not without merit, but their production must be deplored. Wisdom will discount fairy stories about *trouvailles* from Irish castles and ancient manors and dictate close examination, particularly when sets of candlesticks, wall-lights, and chandeliers are in question. None the less, there exists really fine Irish-cut glass in Ireland, though it is not necessarily for sale.

6. *Other Decorative Techniques*

Attempts to replace the wheel and to engrave glasses by the aid of hydrofluoric acid cannot be said to have been made before the end of the eighteenth century at the earliest; a record that acid was used by Heinrich Schwanhardt may be corroborated by the existence of a single unsigned panel dated 1686, and something was accomplished on flat glass from about 1700, but the Frenchman, Marcassus de Puymarin, was the first known to experiment with drinking glasses. We have his publication, but not his glasses. There were subsequently German exponents of the art, and eventually English ones, commercially minded. Very little is known of these men or their work; I will only say that it comes off best on rummers with wide cylindrical bowls (Pl.48d) and decanters, now known to be English. They have the word *Patent* acid-etched on the pontil. Late work included portraits of English notabilities such as Disraeli; they were not high art, and rank as honest souvenir ware, but more ambitious attempts have met with less success. It may be added that some of this kind of work looks harsh and the 'etching' rough; it seems that the decoration is susceptible to scratching and may be removed to some extent without much trouble. Glasses of the kind were not truly acid-etched, but possibly decorated by some form of printing process.

At some time in the third quarter of the seventeenth century a now extremely rare technique came into being whereby a glass could be decorated with a scenic representation in vari-coloured glass pastes, the whole being cemented to the bowl. It must have been a troublesome business and the upshot a dust-catching and vulnerable excrescence, however attractive in a mint state. Plate 49c is an example of the work, the subject being a winged Eve in the Garden of Eden with the serpent coiled round her body. A comparable specimen from the Muhsam collection was regarded as Nuremberg work; the glass, however, was not manifestly German, and possibly Lotharingian might be a fair attribution.

In the third quarter of the eighteenth century, James Tassie was producing miniature portraits in an opaque white glass paste, a soft, heavily leaded, potash metal; he also engraved coloured glass gems, as others also quickly did. Subsequently the Frenchman, Desprez, produced fine cameo portraits equally in a white porcellaneous material, and by the very early nineteenth century was enclosing them in crystal glass, where they took on a silvery appearance. Many of these portraits were set in shaped plaques of glass and framed to hang, but they also came to be inserted in the sides of beakers (Pl.51b), cream-jugs, scent-bottles, and decanters, and eventually in paper-weights. Our Apsley Pellatt of the Falcon glasshouse,

Southwark, interested himself deeply in the process, which he termed *crystallo-ceramie* and less euphoniously *cameo incrustation*. The French *sulfures* or *sulphides* seem to be more convenient appellations. Pellatt took out a patent in 1819 and left some account of his work. This, however, is not easily recognizable, for very little of it was signed, or rather marked. The scent-bottle (Pl.51d) might easily have enclosed a sulphide, but is in fact engraved, with the head of William IV, and inscribed 'Pellatt and Co Patent'. Desprez of Paris, on the other hand, signed many portraits of royal and prominent people, some less familiar now than then; Andrieu followed in his footsteps and Gorringe in Pellatt's, represented by a few well-executed cameo-scapes of sporting instances set into decanters and other vessels. There were other executants.

There was the added work, well repaid and offering no special technical difficulty, of covering the incrustations with gold or brilliant enamel colour. The Baccarat factory specialized in armorials, crests, and monograms, and set them in gold and colour in table-ware and even in complete services (Pl. 30c), luxury goods patronized, for instance, by Tsar Alexander I, who presented such a service to Prince Czwertinski on his marriage to Madame Narishkine, his (the Tsar's) once much-favoured friend. A wide market existed for beakers and shrines (Pl.49b) with silvery cameos representing the Christ or the Madonna and Child; some were finely done; others more indifferently than they need have been to satisfy a welcoming indigent public. In recent years sulphides have enjoyed a favour long denied them.

It was a short step from crystallo-ceramie to the enclosure of designs composed wholly of coloured pastes within a more or less hemispherical crystal prison, and in most eyes a greater success was achieved; moreover, the two styles could be effectively combined.

So we can admire or decry a quite bewildering array of most decorative paper-weights (Pl.50) and other utility items such as door-handles and vases; drinking glasses exist, chiefly small tumblers wherein scattered canes are embellished with simple engraving to form a floral decoration (Pl.5oh). The basis of one main type of weight was a series of canes arranged with care in some sort of pattern, or haphazardly; their styles can be called close millefiori or spaced, patterned, or scrambled. The other type of weight included flowers, natural or more often imaginary, vegetables, moths, snakes, and so on.

It was a French triumph of ingenuity, and its success was immediate. Novel, attractive, and even useful, the new paper-weights could hardly fail, yet even Victorian letter-writers needed but one or two, and it has been reserved for a third generation to make their collection almost a scientific pursuit with, some may think, too little discrimination. We know of three factories which were concerned. That of St Louis was very early in the field, for I have had an obviously immature specimen with the marking SL and date 45. Progress was rapid, for there are St Louis vases dated in the same year. Baccarat was making and dating millefiori weights in 1846, and doubtless Clichy was turning out its own models, though it did not date any. The hallmark of a Clichy millefiori weight is a 'Clichy Rose', usually pink and green, and once noted it is never forgotten; it could also appear in white, much more rarely in blue or yellow. In addition, a 'C' has equal significance, or, if you are fortunate, the whole word *Clichy* in capitals. By 1849 the era of dated weights was over.

Despite the foregoing, it is Italy which is credited with initiating paper-weights, at the hand of one Pierre Bigaglia, a small and rather crude cube being signed PB 1845. Bigaglia was exhibiting in May 1845, with commendation, and if indeed the initiator, it is strange that the possibilities were not realized and followed up. There are little items of glass millefiori with canes showing a tiny gondola, used for necklaces and pendants. Was the gondola the ancestor of the small private zoo which distinguishes the millefiori of Baccarat? The weights regarded as Italian are rather poor things, partly on account of the soda metal of which they were made; a rather frequent use of avanturine was a characteristic.

Competitive English attempts at paper-weight making (Pl.5o) have never been accepted as equalling French work.

Contemporary weights were made at Birmingham, by Bacchus, and by the Islington Glass Works, the latter using, on occasion at least, the marking IGW and a large cane displaying a horse. On the whole the colours were pallid; pastel shades by Bacchus, something brighter by Islington. The output was far smaller and the designs uninspired, yet there is something to be said for the best of our work, which could equal the exactitude of the foreigner, even if not his colouring, and there is not much to be said for the worst of the work of any country. Having once rather derided English weights, I for one begin to admire their chaste colours.

More suitable than paper-weights for the document-ridden days we now endure are the door-stops of bottle-glass into which some factories inserted silvery-looking flowers and bubbles. They go back at least as far as 1829–44, when one J. Kilner, ancestor of the modern preserving-bottle firm, of Whitwood Mere near Wakefield, was producing such things at his glasshouse and marking some of them beneath the base. Nowadays quite a collection of tropical blooms are used as well, but such objects cannot be taken seriously. Of recent years paper-weights have been made in Scotland, some with a PY marking being not without merit, others unlikely to interest collectors.

It remains to say that paper-weight collecting has become a solemn affair. The subject has been well documented, yet much remains to be done before the valuation of varieties is much more than a matter of chance and habit. It is indeed a matter of surprise that a French weight should have been publicly sold and bought for nearly as much as the most costly English glass.

In the middle of the nineteenth century a curious process was evolved. A double-walled vessel was blown rather on the lines of a thermos flask, and through an orifice in the base the interior was treated with a solution of silver nitrate, the hole sealed with a disc of cardboard or the like, and a bright silvery vase, for instance, would result. The solution could be coloured to choice, if desired. Much thin cheap rubbish was made, but also quite striking goblets and vases could be produced. The outside could be flashed with colour, which was then cut away to leave flutes, ovals, or other devices as a silver background. Engraving also stood out well. Plate 49d shows a heavy amethyst-flashed scent-bottle with spiral cutting, and a green-flashed goblet is known engraved with the arms of Thomas Farncombe, Lord Mayor of London 1849–50, both by Varnish & Co. The circular disc may be impressed with the lettering HALE THOMSONS PATENT LONDON, this firm being the patentee, or an otherwise similar disc with the above name VARNISH & CO, a licensee. Some cylindrical palm cups are marked ELFIN, gilt inside, and there are other English pieces of good quality, but the great majority of specimens are of the cheapest description and the silvering sadly liable to deterioration.

One further system of decoration is as old as glasses themselves. I refer to applied work where spots, blobs, trails, or shaped (or shapeless) patches of glass were applied to an otherwise finished vessel. The coloured Egyptian sand-core glasses have zigzag circuits and festoons applied to and marvered into the surface. Clear Roman period glasses might have spots of blue glass applied and allowed partly to merge into the walls; Arab glass had queerly shaped patches laid on, vaguely like a fingered starfish and maybe in a differently coloured metal. Trailing is as old as blown glass, vertical and heavy, zigzag or herringbone-wise and lighter, or horizontal and then often thread-like and called stringing. In this department the 'snake-thread' glasses of the Rhineland, c. 200, are among a collector's dreams. Besides these items, body cordons, applied masks and other prunts, loops and rings, vermiform collars, gadrooning of various kinds, the trailed and dentate 'ears' or wings on Venice-style glasses, our own English 'nipt diamond waies' and cable trailing, all these are among the extraneous devices used to adorn the lily or to mask its imperfections.

It is not applied work, but the Roman trick of nipping the sides of a little globular bottle may be mentioned here; it was intended to be decorative, not part and parcel of the design of the glass, such as thumb-pressing the walls of a beaker or the scalloping of a bowl rim.

It would require a long chapter and more knowledge than the author possesses to deal with the later nineteenth-century developments, and the processes by which glass of graded colours and new surface effects can be made (Pl.52a, b). Some of it is likely to be emphemeral, in a utilitarian age; some also is most attractive, both to the eye and touch, and has high decorative value. The same may be said of the quite modern American, French, Czechoslovakian, Swedish, and Viennese glass. English makers perforce competed in an almost international search for novelty, but catalogues, price-lists, and illustrations of our modern output are hard to come by. Perhaps it was the repeal of the Excise Act in 1845, perhaps it was the wealth and solidity of the early Victorian era which swayed some English glassmasters at the Exhibition of 1851 towards weight, size, and elaboration, and in a variety of supposedly antique styles as well as in some modern continental ones – Bohemian, for instance.

It was, however, an unnatural phase, and it brought its own remedy. A reversion to simplicity rewarded those manufacturers who found it possible to relate design to the exigencies of commercial production, and who did, in fact, import modern Art into modern Industry.

There is much in all this glass, continental or English, which is worth attention. It may or may not appeal, yet it is foolish to condemn an article merely because it is modern or novel. Nobody will deny that, among all peoples, appreciation of inherent art is quickest in the French. This cultured nation has found it worth while to maintain a museum devoted to contemporary workmanship, partly, no doubt, to encourage the manufacturer, partly to educate the people. Paris has therefore a series of the chosen work of modern makers, including glassmakers, and a collection which is already documentary. It is a noteworthy event that the Stourbridge Town Council has now a first-class collection of Victorian glass, largely of the second and third quarters of the century and including its more adventurous sallies. A study of this will do much to establish the best Victorian glass as the equal of anything of its time, and that is high praise. The collection is based on the bequest of the late Mr Wm Richardson's private accumulation, supplemented by loan and other specimens. It would be a still more noteworthy event if some other English museum, preferably in London, could find the means and space to do likewise in some degree, and having done so to continue into present times; it would not then be difficult to keep it up to date in the future and so assure posterity of a documentary collection for which it will be more than grateful.

FOR FURTHER REFERENCE

6. BERGSTROM, E. H. *Old Glass Paperweights*, 1948.
2, 6. BUCKLEY, F. *History of Old English Glass*, 1925.
1, 2. BUCKLEY, W. *European Glass*, 1926.
2. BUCKLEY, W. *Art of Glass*, 1929.
2. BUCKLEY, W. *Diamond Engraved Glasses of the Sixteenth Century*, 1929.
2. BUCKLEY, W. Monographs on Greenwood, Schoumann, and Wolff, 1931, 1935.
6. IMBERT, R., and AMIC, Y. *French Crystal Paperweights*, Paris, 1948.
1–6. HONEY, W. B. *Glass*. Victoria and Albert Museum Handbook, 1946.
4–6. JANNEAU, G. *Modern Glass*, 1931.
4–6. McKEARIN, G. S. and H. *American Glass*, New York, 1941.
4–6. McKEARIN, G. S. and H. *Two Hundred Years of American Blown Glass*, New York, 1950.
4–6. PELLATT, A. *Curiosities of Glassmaking*, 1849.
1–6. THORPE, W. A. *English Glass*, 2nd edition 1949.
1–6. THORPE, W. A. *History of English and Irish Glass*, 1929.
4–6. WESTROPP, M. S. DUDLEY. *Irish Glass*, 1920.

CHAPTER IX

GLASSMAKING IN ENGLAND

*

1. The Pioneers

ALTHOUGH one may suggest that glass may have been made in a few places in earlier days, the documentary history of English glass begins with a record of one Laurence Vitrearius – *sc*. Laurence the (?window-)glassmaker – coming from Normandy about 1226 and settling at Dyers Cross, near Pickhurst, with such success that in a few years he was making glass for the Abbey at Westminster (*c.* 1240).

Granted that he had to go somewhere, the question arises – why to Pickhurst? Today this is a tiny hamlet a mile or so from Chiddingfold, lost in sparsely populated forest country, halfway between Guildford and Petworth. It is difficult to assess the relative importance of these places in medieval times, but neither can have been much more than a village. Pickhurst lies on the western outskirts of the ancient forest of Anderida, some ten miles as the crow flies from the Roman Stane Street running from Chichester to London, but – in the thirteenth century – what miles and across what country! That a foreigner intent on making glass in England should then have arrived here without some inside information seems unlikely; that he should also have hit upon Pickhurst by chance or search seems almost incredible, and so I shall infer that glass-workers, indigenous or otherwise, had already established themselves in the Chiddingfold area. Dyers Cross is shown by Winbolt as a road fork, a few hundred yards south and west of Pickhurst.

There Laurence worked, apparently with more than one furnace, and there he prospered. He was succeeded by his son William, now 'le Verrir', who may have laid more emphasis on the firm's vessel glass. He too was successful, and it was partly due to him that Chiddingfold received a Royal Charter in 1300.

Whether success bred apathy or whether other circumstances supervened, we do not know, but half a century later the Schurterres had captured the Wealden industry. This implies no more than that they were the most important makers, for individualism was by no means dead and as late as 1586 one Ogniabene Luteri, apparently in turn a Carré man, a Verzelini man, and self-employed, is on record as in trouble over his fuel supply. Our John le Alemayne now appears, rather as factor it seems than actual glassmaker, to take his part in an industry which was still based on the production of window glass and whose vessel glass was still simple and severely utilitarian. In their turn the Schurterres had to meet the competition of the Peytowe family (1435), and the industry was still active if not necessarily progressive in the first half of the sixteenth century.

Until now, each new arrival had probably succeeded by virtue of greater technical knowledge. During the third quarter of the sixteenth century (1549–75) still better equipped glassmakers reached England, Protestant Lorrainers headed by Carré, including Hennezel, Thisac, Thietry, and Houx, and Catholic Venetians represented by Giacomo Verzelini. Carré's was the moving hand and he obtained a licence in 1567. He followed tradition, and policy also, so far as to set up furnaces in the Alfold area of Surrey, but broke new ground in establishing a glasshouse in London itself, where he intended to produce quality drinking-glasses in *cristallo*. It was the obvious thing to do. Alfold, and for that matter Chiddingfold, was then more uneconomically situated from a transport point of view than almost any part of Britain today. Proper supervision must have been very difficult, and the Spanish *barilla*, if and when used, could only be imported by sea. Any transport of materials or finished products to or from Wealden sites in the depths of Surrey and Sussex, over roads and tracks which were always hazardous and often impassable for wheeled vehicles, was necessarily tedious and expensive. It was an ambitious and yet sensible scheme, and Carré had the honour of establishing modern glassmaking in England.

But the success of so doing was not to be his, perhaps with justice, for his relations with his business associates seem open to criticism. His intervention alarmed the older Wealden glassmakers and there were forceful protests from the Wealden ironworkers who also had claims upon the available fuel. Change is always resisted in rural England and strangers suspect. Whether justly or otherwise, the importunity of the ironworkers largely prevailed, and so Carré's Lorrainers dispersed, with or without men of the older tradition, first to the woods of Hampshire (Buckholt – *à bouque haut*), then on to Gloucestershire (Forest of Dean and Woodchester), to Blore Park near Eccleshall, and Stourbridge in Worcestershire, to Cheswardine in Shropshire, and eventually to Newcastle-on-Tyne. It may be mentioned that this was not entirely a one way traffic for it is on record that as early as 1380 a John Glazewryth (John the Glassmaker) went from Staffordshire to Chiddingfold under a contract for nine years with Joan, widow of John Schurterre, to manage her glasshouse. It is permissible to infer that the industry was more widely established in England than we know, and at earlier dates.

Most of the places mentioned lie in districts where coal is found or easily obtained, and their choice cannot have been entirely fortuitous. That some popular or particular resentment was the immediate cause of this migration is likely enough; that it was the deciding factor is much less certain. There can, indeed, hardly have been any decisive shortage in 1567, and what the glassmakers used was the lop and top, suitable for nothing but firewood. The Edict forbidding the use of timber as fuel did not appear until 1615, by which time not only were glassmakers established in coal-bearing areas, but new furnaces had been designed (1611). The only possible conclusion is that the glassmakers were aware of the advantages of coal fuel long before the authorities, and had made their dispositions accordingly. State edicts are liable to lag behind events. A correspondent kindly quotes Dr Hudig as authority for saying that coal was in use in the Low Countries in 1627. It may have been in use still earlier and before we in England adopted it, for the Wealden men dispersed without noticeable protest, well before the Edict, and if the glassmakers of Maastricht, Antwerp, and Liège had already pressed their local deposits into service, Carré's Lorrainers and others would have been aware of it and ready enough to follow suit.

Some of the newer Surrey–Sussex furnaces carried on working until the end, but the initiative had passed elsewhere, and if anybody suffered it may have been less the glassmakers than the ironworkers themselves who had so strongly raised the issue. They would have been well advised to follow the lead given to them. They had already been prohibited from using wood as fuel in certain parts of the country (1558), and this ordinance may have disposed them to quarrel with the glassmakers. The building of more Sussex ironworks was prohibited in 1584, but it was a long time before ironworkers as a whole took kindly to the idea of mineral fuel.

It is not quite certain whether Carré saw his *cristallo* glasshouse in Crutched Friars in full production. He probably saw it started about 1567, with the help of the Lorraine men, and was so disappointed with the result that he enlisted Venetian workers instead. They arrived in June 1571, but Carré died eleven months later and Verzelini reigned in his stead.

It is no disparagement to say that Verzelini reaped where Carré had sown. There were still pitfalls in plenty for the most welcome of manufacturers, and Verzelini was a stranger, unknown to his customers-to-be, and suspect by the strong group of English merchants whose business was the importation of glass from abroad. The connexion is unproven, but when in September 1575 the Crutched Friars glasshouse was in full operation and was destroyed by fire, Verzelini demonstrated his own opinion by promptly seeking protection from the Privy Council. The London glass merchants protested with equal promptness but less success, for on 15 December of that year Verzelini secured a royal licence giving him the sole right to make Venice glasses in England for twenty-one years. It further prohibited the importation, by anyone, of foreign glass, thereby assuring him freedom from outside competition, and affording the country a timely period during which it could assimilate a knowledge of fine glassmaking.

This licence and his own qualities determined Verzelini's success. He avoided Carré's mistake of trying to make different kinds of glass at one and the same time in London and remotest Surrey, and his late opponents, who after all were only concerned with selling, will have done as they were to do a century later, that is, patronize the home manufacturer as soon as he could provide the goods they wanted. If Verzelini made any mistake, it was one which affected his successors rather than himself. He seems not to have moved with the times in the matter of coal fuel, and under the circumstances then ruling it is not easy to see that he could have done so. His twenty-one-year licence was apparently determined on his retirement in 1592. He took with him the respect of the community, and a fortune to match.

Sir Jerome Bowes took over the men and obtained a new licence, more extensive than the old one in that it included the sole right to import Venice and Murano glasses if he so wished, or a limited obligation to do so if he did not so wish. It was, however, operative for twelve years only, and an annual rent was exacted. A soldier by profession, Bowes had small knowledge of glass, and probably did little more than pay his way. His glasses would naturally be in line with those of his predecessor, and the one known example of his regime, the Barbara Potter glass, is also reputedly engraved by de Lysle but possesses a stem practically identical with that of Pl. 38a (see p. 104). Bowes' licence expired in 1604 but seems to have been temporarily renewed in 1606, and other somewhat ineffective grants were made before the Edict of 1615 opened a new chapter in the history of English glass.

Between Laurence and Carré more than three centuries had elapsed, and it might be thought that some specimens of that long period would have survived. If they have, they have not been recognized, unless it be one or two trivialities of almost timeless glass. But from sites in the Surrey-Sussex Weald a great number of fragments have been collected; mostly it is window glass, but there are the bases of drinking-vessels and he necks of little bottles. Very many of the fragments are too small, and sometimes too affected by long burial, to be of any guidance. All these relics have been recovered from the old glasshouse sites, the earlier ones compactly set around Chiddingfold, and the later ones more scattered and lying east and south-east rather nearer Stane Street. Some of the sites seem to have been in use more or less continuously over the centuries. Dating accordingly becomes difficult, and the matter is further complicated by the possible finding of cullet brought in, say, from London, on the return journey of whatever transport was used, presumably chiefly pack animals. The location of ost sites and their excavation, the recovery of the fragments, and the arrival at any deductions, all this is indeed a labour of love, and disappointingly unrewarding.

There are records, too, of a furnace at Woodchester, after the exodus from the Weald, and the finds there have been published,* some items being probably fortuitous. Something has been done by practical men towards reconstructing certain of the fragments found, rather unconvincingly I think. The actual reconstructions have become rare. Plate 31a records an early *verre de fougère* glass of as imperfect a metal as can be imagined, having a hollow-blown high-kicked foot and a bowl whose shape could only be guessed at from the possession of its base alone. It is now known to be a later fourth-century Gallic glass, rather thinly blown, with a sheared rim and of a coarse bubbly greenish metal, only half translucent, with many tiny flaws or impurities which look like black flecks. They seem to originate in the larger surface bubbles which have burst. The illustration is retained because it serves to show what I personally imagine was to be expected in the medieval period here or elsewhere, provincially made glass sufficing for any peasant's cider or home-brewed.

To summarize the Wealden production, we have first and foremost its types of window glass. Of vessel glass there is the earlier coarse metal which Winbolt describes as milky-green and semi-opaque. But there is also a later type of metal of the Carré period, to which too much praise can hardly be given.

* *The Woodchester Glasshouse:* J. Stuart Daniels. 1950

The fragments betray excellent workmanship, the metal is homogeneous and free from bubbles, while its texture and finish is surprisingly good. Its counterpart is found in a number of *bénitiers* (Pl.31b) attributed to Antwerp, and of the same period, and if Carré's Surrey glass was as similar in style to his Antwerp glass as it was in metal, distinction between the two must be very difficult indeed. This particular metal is by no means a *cristallo*. Its colour varies with thickness and the range of bluish and greenish tints is wide. Latterly it was a rather deep blue-green, not too unlike that found in the southern Spanish coastal glass of relative and later date. In fact, the whole range of tints recalls the varying colours of seventeenth-to eighteenth-century Spanish glass. The Weald has also provided fragments of crystal glass, something like early Mohammedan crystal, but whether they were made on the sites is uncertain.

In view of the brevity and mischances of the Carré regime in London, little is to be expected and nothing is known. All we can guess is that his styles would have been Altarist and not Venetian, and they quite likely matched examples of his Antwerp production whatever that may have been, and if his crystal was as attractive as his *verre de fougère* its absence is certainly to be deplored.

With Verzelini we fare better. His was a high-class production, in so far as we know it, in the Venetian tradition, and eight glasses can now be ascribed to him, some with rather more confidence than others. They are dated from 1577 to 1590, a perfect specimen of 1578 having been discovered a few years ago. Their metal seems not to be the equal of that which Carré is likely to have made, being of much darker tone. All are engraved with the diamond-point and in much the same style, almost certainly by one Anthony de Lysle hailing from France, and but for his work it is doubtful whether the glasses would ever have been recognized as English at all. As mentioned, only a single specimen of the Bowes period is known, engraved, and dated 1602 by de Lysle. This glass has a strong affinity to the *tazza* at Pl.38, regarded as work of the Hall glasshouse in the Tyrol.

It is a meagre tally for so distinctive and important an output over almost forty years, and it ought not to be regarded as a complete one. One would say that if so many commemorative pieces have survived there ought to be other, unspectacular, glasses remaining; some might be small and strong, such as salt cellars, others large and safeguarded by their size then, and later by a lack of use, i.e. bowls and *tazze*. On the Continent many more glasses of the period have survived despite an equal fragility or a greater clumsiness. The conditions for survival were probably more favourable in England than elsewhere, and her people no more careless than foreigners.

No doubt the matter is primarily one of recognition, and we are apt to think in terms of drinking-glasses only. These were in fact not only a relatively small part of Verzelini's output but the more vulnerable part. The table of a wealthy nobleman needed more than goblets. It needed, and possessed, a much larger proportion of bowls, stands, and dishes than is called for today, and how far this is true may be learned from the Kenilworth Castle inventory of glass belonging to the Earl of Leicester in 1588. Thorpe quotes it, and there are at least three times as many bowls and dishes as there are drinking glasses. Not all of them were necessarily for the dining table, but many were, and Pl.31c represents the type of bowl which Verzelini and Bowes may very well have supplied, and also Mansell. It can be traced from Venice in the early 1500s to England in the late seventeenth century, with connecting links.

Many fragments of high-class work have been found, particularly the stems of drinking glasses, and while it may be impossible to allot any certain dating, or to distinguish between what was made here and what may have been imported, they have this significance that they tell us to think of good English sixteenth-century glass as a definite *façon*, more that of the Low Countries than of Venice. It is no use at all searching for something outstandingly different. We may in time come to recognize certain small points as indicative of English make, but the general appearance will remain conventionally Venetian.

2. Mansell

Bowes, the soldier, was succeeded by Mansell, the sailor. Not quite at once, because two or three other licences were current when the coal-compelling Edict was issued, only Bowes being placated by an annuity he did not live long to enjoy. It was to Sir Edward Zouche and his partners that a new and comprehensive patent was issued, in effect conditional upon his using coal fuel, since the drafting prohibited wood. And it was an already augmented and prosperous Zouche Board that Sir Robert Mansell joined in 1615. Three years later he had bought out his fellow partners and was in full control.

The story of Mansell's career has been recorded elsewhere in such detail that repetition is superfluous. Suffice it to say that he was what we now call a financier, but he was, and indeed had to be, an organizer of no common order as well, and during the forty years of his domination he transformed an unstable and scattered art into a genuine industry. His was a harsh monopoly, the sort of thing now regarded with so much abhorrence. It did indeed bear hardly upon the small man, even though a discreet pirate may have had his opportunities. The alleged sins of the State being visited upon its favoured nominee, Mansell had to meet opposition both legal and illegal, and sabotage as well. The situation was regularized in characteristic fashion when the Government cancelled a re-drawn monopolistic patent granted only the year before, and replaced it by equally effective Letters Patent in 1624. The point is that at that time, and under the conditions of seventeenth-century society, only a harsh monopoly could build up a coherent industry capable of competing on terms with Italy and the Low Countries. The importation of Venice glasses was intermittently prohibited, and they were always dutiable, despite constant representations from the Venetian ambassador. A few favoured persons received special permits to import for their private use, and no doubt some unscrupulous people disregarded the regulations altogether and smuggled foreign glasses into the country, but Mansell had not much to fear.

We can easily infer that glass in quantity, if not of quality, was now recognized as so essential a commodity that we could not afford to rely upon a foreign production which might cease entirely in times of trouble, and which was certain to be expensive even in times of peace, lacking home competition. Mansell must therefore be regarded as the individual who, for no unimportant monetary consideration, was privileged to pull the essential chestnuts out of the foreign furnaces, for the ultimate benefit of the community. Carré and Verzelini had shown how it could be done. Mansell developed his plan on the largest scale, and whatever criticism is levelled against him ought more properly to be levelled against the Government which empowered him, for good and sound reasons of state, to act as he did.

There is no evidence that Mansell made his own fortune in the process. On the contrary, it is likely that he conferred far greater benefits upon the industry, and indirectly upon the country, than ever the industry conferred upon him. It is an experience not unknown to many subsequent financiers and organizers in other walks of life.

Mansell's disability was, naturally enough, the same as that of Bowes, a lack of knowledge of glass itself, and so he was largely in the hands of his workmen. After some years of disappointments with a series of Venetians of whom Miotti, in 1619, was the best, he procured a company of Altarists from Mantua. These men included Da Costa and Dagnia, in 1630, and later on a few even more highly qualified Murano men joined him, among them Brunoro and Mazzola, in 1637. His first concern was of course to arrange for supplies of coal to serve his Broad Street furnaces. This he brought by sea from the then independent Kingdom of Scotland, an arrangement so suggestive to Scottish ship-masters that they were easily induced to raise their charges from 14s to 24s per ton, a figure which presumably included the cost of the coal but which was nevertheless prohibitive. It fell to Lady Mansell, in the temporary absence of her husband on an expedition against Mediterranean pirates, to counter the pirates nearer home by resorting to the coal of Tyneside. It is a measure of the progress that the Tyne has since made, that this expedient was regarded as a surprising one in 1621, and it is a reason for gratitude to the much-abused monopolist. A glass enamelled by Beilby of Newcastle in the third quarter of the next century with the simple wording *And The Coal Trade* may reflect something of the close connexion between glass and coal.

Scottish glassmakers at Wemyss in Fifeshire were a further source of trouble, filching his workmen and generally exploiting their nuisance value until Mansell bought them out, lock stock, and barrel, in 1627. There is nothing to show that the suborned workers liked the climate of Scotland any better than that of London, but they would, as always, go anywhere for a large enough bribe, and with the old mental reservation to leave as soon as they thought fit. Theirs was a monopoly of skill, and they proved it to be just as vicious as any other kind of monopoly, more easily exploitable and less easily checked. It remains a major problem today, perhaps as obnoxious as any our society has encountered in the past.

That Mansell continued so long in business proves that he learned as time went on, not only about glass but also about the foibles of his workmen. It is moreover complete evidence of his business acumen. That his output was important is shown by his control of glasshouses from Purbeck to Fifeshire, and from Milford Haven to Lynn. It is demonstrated by his trade lists and by the fact that he was able to export his wares. He initiated (wine) bottle manufacture, developed medicine bottles (if indeed age-old simplicities are capable of development), and mirrors, and he did not disdain to make beads, no less old than medicines and more welcome. I trace a certain criticism regarding the artistry of his glass, something incapable of proof or disproof because of the lack of evidence. Of course, it cannot be expected that he troubled himself much with questions of art. People wanted glass, not art, and they wanted it in all sorts of shapes and sizes, and Mansell was there to supply them. I suspect that if we had a representative range of his manufactures it would not be very different from that which America made in the first half of the nineteenth century; different of aspect perhaps, but designed or similar purposes. Particularly in a nobleman's household o the requirements of the kitchen need to be satisfied before he banqueting hall can be properly served, and in minor de- rees that applies to lesser folk.

A small output of high-quality Mansell drinking-vessels eed not be excluded. The skill was there, the metal was there, nd there also was the market. So also must the glasses have een, however much or little they interested the financial nagnate responsible for them. Unfortunately they are not here ow, or else we cannot recognize them. Plate 53a shows one of he very few good glasses likely to be of Mansell origin, and s preservation is doubtless due to the fact that it is a chalice ollowing a contemporary silver style, and made, so one sup- oses, to replace a silver one melted down to sustain one side r other in the Civil War. It displays uncommon dexterity in nanufacture, good design, and beauty of line if not of appear- nce, but that is because the bowl is double-blown, the walls nclosing a now dulled silver foil, with a pontil mark at the ottom thereof. The metal is not recognizable either as Vene- an or Netherlandish and it is tinged on the foot with an irid- scence not due to burial or decomposition.

It is not clear when Mansell's monopoly lapsed, but it is cer- in that the Civil War and the Commonwealth regime seri- usly affected trade and business, his among the rest. The conoclastic proclivities of ignorant, if sincere, men may well e in part responsible for the absence of examples of Mansell's etter work; his utility output had to meet the greater hazard f day-to-day usage. There are those today who delight in the estruction of what they do not comprehend, and it is too nuch to suppose that men were any less prejudiced 300 years go. I follow Thorpe in thinking that about 1650 there was a eversion to older practice, with scattered glassmakers blow- ng glass where and how they could, if not within the letter of ne law at least without disturbance by it. In other words, the nonopoly dissolved through natural causes; it had done its york and needed no retaining. Sir Robert's bolt was shot and e died in 1656.

Complete Mansell glasses other than medicine phials are, as

stated, virtually unknown, and we have to guess at their forms. His list is non-descriptive, but from other sources we know that he made cylindrical beakers ('beer-glasses'), some probably with trailed horizontal cordons round the walls. He may reasonably be suspected of having made serpent-stemmed and winged wine-glasses in Italo-Netherlandish styles. He may have used filigree or *lattimo* ornament, and there is no reason why he should not have experimented with colour (see Pl.53b).

Of fragments there must be many which will have come from one or other of his glasshouses; they are scattered in various museums and collections, and rarely are the circumstances of their provenance at all precise; even if otherwise their lesson is likely to remain obscure. Generally speaking it is the stem which survives, and we do find a number of the mould-blown lion-mask stems such as Verzelini used and some strong hollow cigar-like stems which were late (Pl.53c, d). Mansell must have used both types and variations of both types. Rightly or wrongly, one particularly associate him with the second of these forms; the masked urn stem was essentially polite continental work and accordingly well received anywhere. Some of these may have been Mansell or post-Mansell work; most will not, for, as we shall see, there was a considerable business in the importation of continental glass in the later 1660s and possibly earlier.

3. *The Glass Sellers Company*

Those glass-merchants who gave Verzelini so much trouble may or may not be identifiable with the Glaziers and Painters of Glass, now the Company of Glaziers, whose history goes back to 1328 and whose first charter was granted by Charles in 1638. The Company denies the soft impeachment, but be that as it may, there is evidence that a glazier might sell glass just as a hosier might sell hose, and it does not seem at all improbable that some glaziers were also glass-merchants. As Company, it had never been either rich or influential, and iffered much from unauthorized competition. The Glass ellers Company as such comes into view in 1637 with a pro-st against the alleged badness of Mansell's glass, probably in oncert with the Glaziers Company.

The Restoration of 1660 was wisely and widely welcomed ecause the people had discovered that progress was impossible nder a party which ruled by the boot, and whose supporters ere in the main characterized by ignorance and stupidity. A enial blackguard may be a pleasanter ruler than an intolerant ore. That Cromwell raised the power and influence of Eng-nd to as high a relative point as she had ever reached in her istory meant little to the peasant who had to deal with his ntentious and – can it be doubted – his frequently hypo-ritical and unlovable troopers. It meant still less to the trader hose trade was lost or bridled. A democracy of the seven-enth century had triumphed over a monarchical tyranny, hich was good. But an eternal dictatorship appealed to no-ody, so Charles was invited back to his throne, and a standing rmy has never since been welcome to Englishmen.

With Charles back, a new spirit was immediately apparent, nd nowhere was this more decisively exhibited than in the ts and sciences. England, far behind the Continent in such aatters by reason of her late dissensions, had a further twenty ears of leeway to make up. A charter to, and a quickening of irit among, the Glass Sellers was one of the results. Imbued ith the prevailing enthusiasm, their policy became construc-ve and helpful, and until the end of the century the Company xercised a control which was none the less real for being dis-reetly disguised. It shows the strides the industry had made aat the Company, as a seller, could in effect dictate what the aanufacturer should make. It chose wisely, and could afford ractical encouragement, and of course it relieved the actual lassmakers of much anxiety by offering a ready market and steady market for their wares.

It was as much to run with the now fashionable scientific ound as to hunt the profitable hare that George Villiers, econd Duke of Buckingham, usurped the position which Iansell had held. He was perhaps drawn into the affair by one

John de la Cam, who persuaded the Duke to finance a schem
for making 'rock-crystal' glass, and of course to procure th
necessary patent. The Duke obligingly complied and for th
next fourteen years (1660–74) he had a finger in every pie con
taining glass. Naturally he knew nothing about the mystery
glass itself, and when people who did know, Clifford an
Powlden, and Thomas Tilson, also obtained licences – but no
patents – to make particular kinds of glass, the Duke enliste
them in his own service and turned their licences into patent
to their mutual advantage. It was the same when John Bellin
ham proposed to make mirrors by a secret process. The Duk
gave him a handsome salary, put him in charge of the Vaux
hall plate glasshouse, and secured the patent for himself.

Whether these transactions were profitable we do not knov
Very likely the Duke was equally ignorant, and content th
things should go on as they were in the habit of doing, pro
vided that nobody troubled him unduly. He had plenty
other duties, and pleasures, to occupy his thoughts. I think w
may infer that the Glass Sellers quietly stepped into the breac
which would have been caused by the Duke's absences and i
attentions, and guided the various managers in the way the
should go. The Company men, as retailers, assumed they be
knew what the public wanted, and when they could not g
their ideals realized, they were courageous enough to find an e
perimentalist, and wealthy enough to back him, as we shall se

We know very little about the Duke's glass, except that it wa
good glass as things then went, and that it could be extreme
thinly blown, though not that it was all like that. Of existin
specimens, the 'Royal Oak' goblet of 1663, commemoratin
the marriage of Charles II and Catherine of Braganza, is th
most famous. There is the 'Exeter' flute with a bust portrait
Charles II and the sprouting oak stump, and there is th
'Scudamore' flute, with the Royal arms and those of the Scud
more family. These three historic specimens date from th
1660s, and with them it may not be unfair to include the u
engraved glasses about to be mentioned and to say that
may have come from the Duke's Greenwich glasshous
though of absolute proof there is none.

These further glasses lack the individuality of the engraved ones specified above, but they have the importance which attaches to a collection of undisturbed relics. They came to light in 1949 when an ancient English home was abandoned after, at the least, three centuries of occupation. They are significant because some thirty of them throw light on what was used in England in high circles during the sixth and seventh decades of the seventeenth century, and a presumptive English, and therefore Buckingham, origin, is fortified by the presence of three indubitable sealed Ravenscroft posset-pots. All but these three were well made in thin soda metal; a very large wavy-edged *tazza*, unhappily since destroyed (Pl.55a); a large plain one and a set of ten smaller with saucer trays; three possets (as Pl.54b) doubtless replaced by the three sealed ones in the new perfected lead metal (Pl.55d, e); and last but not least a rummer-like goblet with short spiked gadroons beneath a body cordon (Pl.55b), an approach to which appears in Greene's first order to Morelli in 1667. There were further two plates in rather heavier soda metal and ten light wines in two sizes (Pl.59a). The latter should be compared with the small French wine in Pl.20a; it should be added that quite a series of comparable glasses has been found in England, some similarly moulded, others plain (Pl.59). Others have come from Scotland, Italy, France, and reputedly Liège, and among the lot several examples have shown a positive, though not a heavy, reaction when tested for the presence of lead.

It is fair to date an increased demand for glass to the early 660s, and one which outran supply. At least, the prohibition on foreign glass had lapsed or been lifted, and we find the foresaid John Greene, a prominent member of the Company, following the lead of a competitor and corresponding with Alessio Morelli of Murano (1667–73), directing what should be made and in what manner and fashion. We are fortunate in that Greene's letters, or some of them, have been preserved, and with them a large number of drawings, many lettered, some duplicated or waste, and life-size up to a point. No sizes were given, and since the same design was sometimes ordered for beer, French wine, and sack, it seems that the relative heights were a matter of common knowledge or common sense. Here, perhaps, we have an early indication that suites of drinking glasses were coming into fashion, with the large beer-glasses predominating, maybe in place of tumblers for water. Plate 56c shows a glass much more often seen in soda metal than in lead, and it is found in very stable form in just such sizes as would have met Greene's requirements. It was made both in Holland and in England and well illustrates the general run of pattern which Greene continually ordered similarly Pl.59d illustrates a continental glass 5 inches high which resembles a sack glass. Some of Greene's designs will be found in various text-books, and the value of the series is that it reflects the popular English demand of the day.

Greene seems to have been a timid and anxious buyer, not without his simple subterfuges; Morelli with the order in his pocket maybe a little casual or inattentive. He may have found his orders less explicit than Greene imagined, and his inter pretation left somewhat to be desired, or so Greene thought and plaintively wrote. There were, too, considerable break ages in transit, which need surprise nobody acquainted with the thinly-blown ware of the period. Any trader could easily compose the letters of both parties, though perhaps less politely, and in any case no great harm was done, for Greene came back for more, until the forward policy of the Company revolutionized the supply position.

Granted that something more substantial than the fragile glasses of Murano and Greenwich was required, it became a matter of experiment, or, as we now call it, research. Beside the vision which the Company possessed, and the finance which also was at its disposal, a suitable director of the enter prise was also needed.

The man selected, or who came forward at need, was the aforesaid George Ravenscroft, a man of intelligence and scientific attainments, and of sufficiently independent mind and means to accept guidance but not direction. It was a good and timely choice. Dr Merret had translated Neri's *Art of Glass* in 1662 and had given Englishmen a much-wanted guide of which Ravenscroft will have made full use, and from which he may have drawn his inspiration to include oxide of lead in the batch.

In 1673 Ravenscroft built a glasshouse in the Savoy and shortly afterwards applied for a patent. It was granted in May 1674, by which time the Duke's patents were expiring and Ravenscroft and the Company had come to terms. There was a second glasshouse, primarily an experimental plant, at Henley-on-Thames, a location which must have had something more than isolation to recommend it, but one seemingly ill-suited from a fuel point of view. It was at this house that another Da Costa was working in 1675. Ravenscroft knew what was particularly wanted, a metal which would resemble rock crystal, combine strength with clarity, and yet have the tractability of glass. One may suppose that his first experiments were on long-familiar lines, and they gave him a crystal-like metal which was certainly thick and probably clear, but it was subject to surface decomposition. Plate 54c shows such a specimen, and a smaller example has also been seen. It is free of any trace of lead, and its mere existence suggests that decomposition, or 'crizzling' as it is called and may be spelled, was a progressive disease. Its form was derived with considerable exactitude from the little Egyptian jug of Chapter 1.

Before long Ravenscroft thought of introducing oxide of lead into the batch and the crizzling problem was reduced, but not overcome. Further experimental work on the proportions of the mixture led him to think that success had been achieved, and in June 1676 the Glass Sellers Company announced that earlier faults had been remedied and that future supplies would be satisfactory. It seems that a small plain disc of glass was pressed on to the supposedly perfect glasses to distinguish the old from the new. This was a few months before May 1677, when the now-famous raven's head seal superseded the plain one, and a fresh three-year agreement was executed between Ravenscroft and the Company, providing for a supply of the perfect glasses to, and their purchase by, the Company. One specimen at least is known with what has been taken for the plain seal, a large jug of far from perfect metal and of rather unattractive shape. It clearly dates to the early years of

lead crystal, but none the less is engraved with the persona
coat of arms of Catherine of Braganza, as a widow. The chang
of status occurred in February 1685; no doubt an existent jug
was used.

Shortly after the execution of the 1677 agreement, and
rather unaccountably unless possibly influenced by the Titu
Oates furore, Ravenscroft gave the necessary six month
notice to determine it. In the absence of some unrecorded
gentleman's agreement whereby Hawly Bishopp carried or
work in Ravenscroft's name at the Savoy – and that would be
the least surprising alternative – we might conclude that the
glasshouse ceased work altogether until Ravenscroft's paten
expired and Bishopp could legitimately take over. The deter
mination of the agreement need not have meant that Ravens
croft, or Bishopp as his deputy, did not go on as before
though no longer by obligation, making the much-wanted
glasses, at least until Ravenscroft's death in May 1681, which
practically coincided with the expiry of the patent.

The satisfaction demonstrated by the use of the seal wa
premature, for half the sealed glasses are crizzled in some de
gree, as are a number of specimens of the Hawly Bishopp
reign which ensued. It seems to me that the seal was therefor
quietly dropped. As this is written, fourteen specimens with
the raven's head seal are known, and two stem fragments
Logically, the perfect sealed glasses ought to outnumber the
imperfect ones, but rarities in glass are insensitive to logic
While some attempts will have been retained for observation
one imagines that hopeless failures will have been destroyed
It is understood that some imperfect unsealed glasses were
eventually graciously permitted to go abroad, and it is the fac
that some crizzled goblets with considerable lead content and
with engraving of historical English interest have been found
on the Continent. There are lead glasses which sweat profusely
that is to say they cloud over with a semi-sticky moisture. I
can be washed, but will return, and it may well be an inter
mediate stage in the progressive glass disease, which can also
affect non-lead glasses just as seriously.

Looked at as a whole, I think that Ravenscroft succeeded

1. EGYPTIAN GLASSES in *pâté de verre*, conventionally 500 B.C.
(a) *Oenochoe*, white body, purple decoration. (b) *Oenochoe*, purple brown with 'palm leaf' decoration. (c) *Amphora*, lapis lazuli blue, pale blue and yellow decoration. (d) *Alabastron*, as (c)

2. ROMAN GLASS, 1st to 4th century

(a) Thin clear-glass beaker. (b) Footed wine cup in greenish glass. (c)
Small blue mould-blown bottle. (d) Ice-green press-moulded drinking
bowl. (e) Amber drinking bowl, grooved and finished on the wheel. (f)
Vase in near-clear glass, stringing and zigzags in dark green. (g) Flask
mould-blown *unguentarium*. (h) Small purple white-marbled bottle

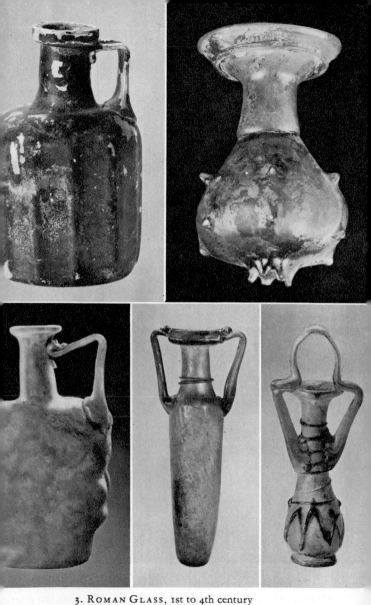

3. ROMAN GLASS, 1st to 4th century

(a) Many-sided mould-blown bottle. (b) Dropping-bottle, simulating a cactus, in yellowish glass. (c) Janus bottle, greenish glass. (d) Closely wry-en *unguentarium*, greenish glass. (e) Handled and looped *unguentarium*, inging in dark green

4. ROMAN GLASS, 1st to 4th century
(a) Mosaic bowl. Ray Winfield Smith Coll. (b) Miniature bucket (?), greenish metal. (c) *Amphora*, brilliant green metal. (d) Plate, with rim grips. (e) Vase, with zones of incised horizontal lines. (f) Footed beaker, delicate looped trailing. Perhaps Western (Gallic), 3rd cent.

5. GALLIC GLASS, 1st to 4th century

(a) Ewer, trailed handle. Amiens. (b) Ewer, Medusa mask. Amiens. (c)
Frontinus bottle, marked FRON. Seine area. (d) Palm cup, spiked kick in
base. Rhine area

6. GALLIC GLASS

(a) Cinerary urn, nine grooved horizontal circuits. 2nd cent. (b) Handle
beaker, olive-green. 2nd to 3rd cent. (c) Shallow dish, basal cordon, applie
foot rim. 2nd to 3rd cent. (d) Cup, ribbed, near-clear metal. Ashmolea
museum. Merovingian. (e) Claw beaker, from Lyminge. Lewes Cast
museum. *c.* 450

7. GLASS OF THE 5th TO 8th CENTURY

Amphora, mould-blown, in amber and green. 5th to 6th cent. (b)
nethystine flat oval flask. 8th cent. or after. (c) Bottle, with strong trailed
coration; blue-green. 4th to 5th cent. (d) *Amphora* in amber and blue,
bed. 4th to 5th cent. (e) Jug, mould-blown. 8th cent.

8. GLASS OF THE 5th TO 8th CENTURY

(a) Large *amphora* or water pitcher, blue on green. Syria, 6th to 7th cen[t.]
(b) Tripod *unguentarium*, blue on greenish. Syria, 5th to 8th cent. (c) Drink-ing bowl, clear bluish metal, excavated at Faversham. 7th to 8th cent.

9. ISLAMIC AND EARLY GERMAN GLASS

Trailed bottle, amber on amber. Islamic, 6th cent. (b) *Unguentarium* with cage or grill, set on horseback; amber and blue on amber. Islamic, h to 8th cent. (c) Small drinking or other bowl of granular glass. German, 10th to 12th cent. or Iraqi, 9th cent. (d) *Maigelein*, with smooth black crustation. German, 15th cent.

10. ISLAMIC GLASS, 8th to 10th century
(a) Mould-blown bottle with bulbed neck. Islamic, 8th to 10th cent. (
Ring beaker, blue on greenish. Syria, 8th to 9th cent. (c) Small wheel-c
bottle. Islamic, 8th to 9th cent. (d) Facet-cut bottle. Islamic, 9th to 10
cent.

11. Islamic Glass, 10th to 13th century
Parti-coloured mould-blown bottle in amber and blue. 10th cent. (b)
ould-blown ewer. 10th cent. (c) Shallow mould-blown bowl in rich blue
ass. 12th to 13th cent. (d) Sprinkler bottle, green on pale amber. 12th
nt.

12. SYRIAN AND ISLAMIC GLASSES

(a) Thin-walled 'snake thread' dropping bottle. Syria, 3rd to 5th cent.
Heavy-walled dropping bottle, with trailing finished to simulate carv
aquatic birds. (?) Syria, 5th to 6th cent. (c) Damascus sprinkler bottle, b
enamel device at base of neck and decorative body band in red colo
End of 13th cent. (d) Beaker, banded red and gold. 14th cent.

13. GLASS MADE IN IRAN OR FOR THE IRANIAN MARKET
(a) Sprinkler bottle in ivory white glass. 12th cent. (b) Wine bottle, green and red, with nail-shaped stopper. Perhaps 14th cent. (c) Standing bowl, Aleppo *'rotreliefierte'* type. *c.* 1260

14. SCALE-GILT AND JEWELLED VENETIAN BOWLS
(a) First half of the 16th cent. (b) Second half of the 16th cent.

15. VENETIAN GLASS

(a) Ewer, masked handle simulating gold. *c.* 160b. (b) Crackle-glass vase. 5th to 17th cent. (c) Wine cup, gilt and jewelled rim, blue foot. 15th to 5th cent. (d) Phial of Syrian 11th to 12th century type, in green, 'exca- ated in Finsbury'. (e) Goblet, lion-mask stem. 16th to 17th cent.

16. VENETIAN GLASS

(a) Bowl of a goblet-vase, from a two-piece mould. 16th cent. (b) Covered vase, in *latticinio* glass. 16th to 17th cent. (c) (d) (e) Wines of the 17th cent.

17. VENETIAN GLASS

(a) Salver, etched gilt and gemmed border. Early 17th cent. (b) *Netzglas* wine. 17th cent. (c) Wine, double-blown bowl, tubular stem with white ribbing. First half 17th cent. (d) Footed beaker, *latticinio* glass with colour. c. 1850

18. VENETIAN GLASS

(a) Flared beaker, with the Fugger arms in coloured enamel partly on gold ground. Set in an ancient copper foot for stability. Dated 1584. (b) Standing bowl in *schmelzglas*. Second half 16th cent.

19. FRENCH GLASS

) Marriage goblet enamelled in colours, with DE BON ♥ LE VOUS
ONNE and Latin biblical quotation. 16th cent. (b) Ewer. Normandy, *c.*
760. (c) Ewer, near-quatrefoil knop, crizzled glass. Normandy, *c.* 1680

20. FRENCH GLASS

(a) Wine, hollow pedestal stem, moulded flutes beneath honeycombing. Early 18th cent. (b) *Tonnelet*, splashed blue, red, and white. Early 17th cent. (c) Cordial, English lead glass for export to Normandy. Mid 18th cent. (d) Shallow bowl and cover, pinkish crizzled. Burgundy 18th cent. (e) Bowl and cover, press-moulded and stamped BACCARAT. Second quarter 19th cent. (f) Small oval bowl and cover, press-moulded. Modern

21. SPANISH GLASS

(a) *Cantaro*. Catalonia, 18th cent. (b) Handled vase, plume-prunted, pale green metal. Granada, mid 17th cent. (c) Vase, pale amber brown, floral trail. Perhaps Castile, early 17th cent. (d) *Porron*, white spirals. Catalonia, c. 1800

22. SPANISH AND LOTHARINGIAN GLASS

(a) *Nuppenbecher*, deep green metal. Rhineland, *c.* 1500. (b) Bowl on silver pattern foot, pendant rings. Liège, 16th cent. (c) Wine, lipped bowl, slender stem. Catalonia, 18th cent. (d) Shaker, deep green, pinched trails. Spain or Liège, late 17th cent. (e) Wine, brown glass, pendant rings, coil foot. Rhineland, *c.* 1600. (f) *Stangenglas*, spirally trailed. Rhineland 16th to 17th cent. (g) *Jarrita*, sea-green, shell-prunted. Granada, mid 17th cent.

23. RHINELAND AND ANTWERP GLASS

(a) Beaker, Lotharingian. Later 16th cent. (b) 'Unbreakable' beaker. Lotharingian. Dated 1663. (c) Goblet, ribbed and horizontally strung, lion-mask stem. Perhaps Dutch, 16th cent. (d) Goblet-vase, part in crackle glass. Neptune masks on bowl and stem. Antwerp, 16th cent.

24. GLASS OF THE LOW COUNTRIES, 16th to 17th centuries
(a) Goblet, the knop moulded and *semé d'or*. Liège. (b) Tall wine. Antwerp
(c) Goblet, with 'beech-nut' moulding. Amsterdam. (d) Goblet-vase
mould-blown bowl showing pair of opposed lions. Antwerp

25. GLASS OF THE LOW COUNTRIES

(a) Cup and cover, blue-green glass. Liège, 17th cent. (b) Beaker, decorated in blue and white. Liège, *c*. 1650. (c) Puzzle jug. Liège, *c*. 1700. (d) Cylindrical goblet, lacking cover. Probably Antwerp, late 16th cent. (e) Wine. Antwerp, late 17th cent. (f) Tiered *tazza*. Liège, mid 18th cent.

26. GLASS OF THE LOW COUNTRIES

(a) Trick glass, perhaps Spanish Netherlands. Early 17th cent. (b) (c) (d)
Wines. Belgian, 17th cent.

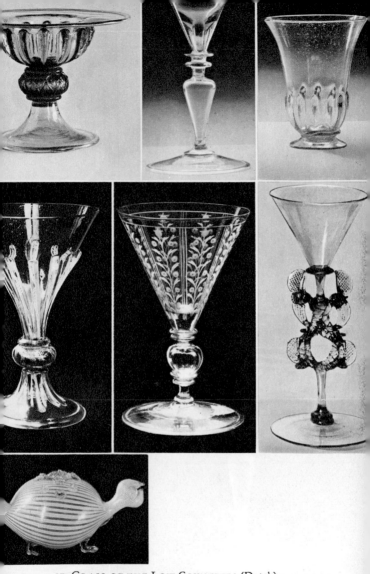

27. GLASS OF THE LOW COUNTRIES (Dutch)

(a) Salt, dark metal, knop *semé d'or*. Late 16th cent. (b) Cordial glass,
receptive bowl, dark metal. Late 16th cent. (c) Jelly or dram glass. Late
17th cent. (d) Wine, applied ribbing to bowl and foot. Early 17th cent. (e)
Wine, quatrefoil knop, panels of like engraving. Late 17th cent. (f) Wine,
pale green metal, convoluted stem. Later 17th cent. (g) *Bouquetière*. Holland or Liège, *c.* 1650

28. GLASS OF THE LOW COUNTRIES

(a) Thin-walled beaker of international form. Holland, 17th cent. (b)
Small 'hour-glass' ewer in *latticinio* glass. Antwerp, early 17th cent. (c)
Tazza, stepped and ribbed bowl. Belgian, 17th cent. (d) Goblet, with
spiked gadrooning, one quatrefoil, and one pear knop. Liège, *c.* 1680

29. NORWEGIAN GLASS

(a) Air twist wine, engraved, gilt, and inscribed. Hurdals Verk, c. 1780.
(b) Wine, with monogram of Christian VII. German, or in German style,
c. 1780. (c) Colour twist wine, with the 'Norwegian Cartouche'. Hurdals
Verk, 1779. (d) Marriage goblet for Christian VII and Caroline Matilda of
England, engraved and signed *Villas Vinter*. Nøstetangen, 1766. (e)
Zirat flaske, dated 1832. *Kunstindustimuseet*. Gjøvik Verk (1809–43)

30. SWEDISH AND RUSSIAN GLASS

(a) Beaker, crizzled, initialled *CF fait A°* 1706. (b) Goblet, with monogram of Elizabeth Petrovna of Russia. Mid 18th cent. (c) Case bottle, with monogram of Alexander I of Russia, 1805–25. (d) Wine, the wall enclosing armorials in gold and colours. Baccarat, *c.* 1820. (e) Vase, overlaid with colour; incised mark and date, for Nicholas II, 1909

31. GLASS OF INDECISIVE ORIGIN

Peasant goblet in *verre de fougère*, sheared rim and double-blown foot.
rhaps 15th to 16th cent. (b) *Bénitier*, probably by Carré of Antwerp and
ndon. Third quarter of 16th cent. (c) Standing bowl, the rim with blue
cuits and formerly gilt, foot rim overlaid with blue. Presumed English,
e 16th to 17th cent.

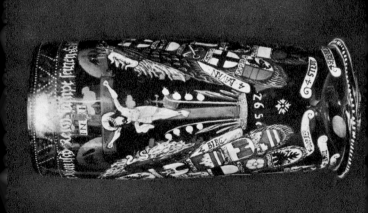

33. GERMAN ENGRAVED GLASS
(a) Satirical goblet and cover, by Heinrich Jäger, 1707. (b) Polish Eagle with bearded head in beak; *Nosce te Ipsum.* (c) Swedish Lion and Bee: *Non nimium Securg* (abb.). (d) Engraved goblet, green bowl and foot; showing Christ appearing to Mary Magdalene at Gethsemane; symbolic figures on reverse. Nuremburg, *c.* 1720. (e) Faceted goblet and cover, crizzled; alternate ruby and gold and ruby spirals. Bohemia, late 17th cent.

34. GERMAN ENAMELLED AND PAINTED GLASS

(a) Bun-footed beaker, painted by Schaper with armorials. Landscape and ruins on reverse. Mid 17th cent. (b) *Humpen* and cover, enamelled with the arms of Frederick Augustus, King of Poland and Elector of Saxony, 1740. (c) *Passglas*, dated 1723. (d) Beaker, painted in black. 18th cent.

35. ENAMELLED AND PAINTED GLASS

(a) Marriage beaker, enamelled in colours and dated. Holland, 1598. (b)
Goblet, very dark metal enamelled in white. Holland, c. 1600. (c) Wine,
enamelled in blue, red, and white, with portrait of Prince Charles Edward,
c. 1760. (d) Rummer, painted in white and colour; SUCCESS TO FARMING,
by Absolon, c. 1805. (e) Footed beaker, overlaid white and painted in
colours. Bohemia, c. 1850

36. PAINTED GLASS

(a) Ale, with wash-enamel decoration by Beilby, Gp x. (b) Bristol opaque
white vase and cover, painted by Edkins or his school. Third quarter of
the 18th cent. (c) Wine, with vine border in white enamel by Beilby, Gp
(d) Bohemian scent bottle, with enamel decoration in colours. Third qua
ter 18th cent. (e) Wine, with fox-hunting scene by Beilby in white ename
Gp x.

37. PAINTED GLASS

(a) Cup and saucer in blue-speckled milk-glass. German or Dutch, 18th cent. (b) Cup and saucer, black and yellow decoration. 18th cent. (See chap. VII). (c) Canister bottle, painted in colours. Central European, c. '75. (d) Tumbler, good milk-glass, enamelled in colours VIVA CARLOS I REY DE ESPANA. (e) Beaker, 'Fish in an aquarium', attributed to othgasser. c. 1820

38. DIAMOND-ENGRAVED GLASSES

(a) (b) A *tazza*. Tyrol or English, late 16th cent. (c) Wine, with caligraphic motto *Nequid nimis* (sic), [Never too much]. Dutch, late 17th cen(
(d) Oval bottle, silver mounts. Low Countries, second half 17th cent. (
Wine, *Die State van Hollandt* with armorial Lion on reverse. Dutch, *c.* 16

39. DIAMOND-ENGRAVED GLASSES

(a) Bowl, with monsters and floral repeat. Dutch, 16th to 17th cent. (b) Roemer, with fishing scene. Lotharingian, etched in Holland, early 17th cent. (c) Wine, with conventional floral repeat. Italian or Dutch, 17th cent.

40. STIPPLED GLASSES (English, with Dutch engraving)
(a) Baluster goblet; signed *F. Greenwood* in script, undated. (b) Goblet,
faceted stem, signed *Adams fecit*, c. 1806. (c) Wine, stippled in dots, probably by Wolff. Late 18th cent. (d) Goblet, stippled in line: arms and
ordination of Adriaan Wittert in 1765, artist unknown

41. GERMAN SURFACE-ENGRAVED GLASSES

(a) Nuremberg goblet, with continuous landscape scene, *c.* 1720. (b) Potsdam goblet, with arms of George I as Elector of Hanover and (reverse)
King of England, *c.* 1715. (c) Zechlin goblet, gilt. (See Chap. XI), *c.* 1742.
(d) Lauenstein goblet and cover, with the arms of the Emperor Francis I,
glass of lead, *c.* 1760

42. SURFACE-ENGRAVED GLASSES

(a) Engraved and gilded goblet, monogram of Catherine the Great. (?
Saxon, c. 1765. (b) Silesian goblet, c. 1755. (c) Beaker, engraved by Anto
Simm. Bohemian, c. 1835. (d) Square-footed Rummer, with arms of th
burgh of Leith, on reverse a variant of the royal Scottish arms, c. 1800

43. Engraving in Low and High Relief

(a) Beaker, David and Goliath, in low relief. Bohemian, 1st half 18th cent.
(b) Goblet and cover, carved in high relief. Silesian, *c.* 1740. (c) Vase,
'Syrena', overlaid opaque white and cameo-cut; signed *Geo. Woodall*.
Stourbridge, late 19th to early 20th cent. (d) Vase, overlaid and cameo-cut;
Webb and Son, as (c)

44. DECORATED OVERLAID AND FLASHED GLASS

(a) Three-layer vase, blue over clear on opaque white, painted black and gold, panelling in black, gold, and blue. Bohemian, *c.* 1850. (b) Goblet and cover, ruby-flashed, carved through and gilt, perhaps by Pfohl. Bohemia, *c.* 1870. (c) Vase, overlaid and cameo-cut; signed *de Vez*. Modern French. (d) Vase, royal blue on opaque white, painted and gilt. English, *c.* 1860

45. GILDED AND SILVERED GLASSES

(a) Bohemian beaker with 'inserted gold' decoration, *c.* 1740. (b) Barrel tumbler, engraved and gilt; *Let Farming Flourish*, attributed to Absolon of Yarmouth, *c.* 1810. (c) English ale, gilt hop and barley decoration, *c.* 1760. (d) English goblet, gilt rim and fruiting vine, *c.* 1765. (e) Wine, deep green glass, gilt. Probably Bristol, *c.* 1770

46. MOULDED GLASS. ENGLISH CUT GLASS

(a) Flat flask, amethyst moulded with American Eagle. Masonic emblem
McKearin, G. U.S.A. 1825–30. (b) Half-pint decanter, painted in colour
press-moulded stopper, soda metal. Tyneside, early 19th cent. (
Barrel-shaped spirit bottle and stopper from a three-part mould. Iris
c. 1830. (d) Ice pail, cut vertical flutes, prismatic circuits and rim blaze
English, c. 1820. (e) Urn and cover. English, as (c)

47. IRISH CUT GLASS

a) Piggin and Stand, slanting pillar cutting, *c.* 1825. (b) Oval bowl with
ars, and domed cover, cut relief diamonds, *c.* 1780. (c) Ginger jar, cover
nd stand, cut flutes, prisms, and husk circuit, as (b). (d) Semi-ship decan-
r, target stopper, husk-cut rings, *c.* 1790. (e) Bowl, cover and stand, cut
ink diamonds, as (b). (f) Water jug, *c.* 1800

48. HYALITH GLASS AND OTHER DECORATIVE TECHNIQUES
(a) Hyalith beaker, marbled turquoise and gilt, by Egermann. N. Bohemia
c. 1840. (b) Hyalith beaker in 'sealing wax' red, gilt band. N. Bohemia, as
(a). (c) Engraved 'silhouette' beaker, Napoleon at St Helena. Perhaps
Vienna, c. 1821. (d) Acid-etched rummer, bluish lead glass. English, as (a)

49. OTHER DECORATIVE TECHNIQUES

(a) Figure of St Peter in coloured *pâté de verre*. Nevers, 17th cent. (b) Shrine, with inset *cristallo-ceramie* decoration. Paris, *c.* 1830–40. (c) Wine, with modelled scene in coloured pastes, Eve in the Garden of Eden. Rhineland, later 17th cent. (d) Hollow blown scent, amethyst over clear, cut through to show silvered interior; stamped, Varnish & Co. Patent London. *c.* 1851

50. PAPERWEIGHTS AND MILLEFIORI GLASS, mid 19th century
(a) Close concentric circles of like canes, enclosing a similar mushroo[m]
Bacchus Birmingham. (b) Close millefiori set round a central florette. (c)
Spaced florettes and cameo canes, 1847 Baccarat. (d) Fruit weight, [on]
opaque white *latticinio* basket. St Louis. (e) Overlaid blue, with mushroo[m]
of concentric canes, Clichy. (f) Crown weight, radiating bicoloured a[nd]
white twists. St Louis. (g) Goblet, millefiori foot and panels to bow[l]
Baccarat. (h) Goblet, engraved sprays with millefiori blossom. Baccarat.

. Various (a) Opaque white handled bowl. English, late 17th or early
th cent. (b) Tumbler, inset sulphide, the heads of Napoleon and Jose-
ine. Baccarat, *c.* 1820. (c) Monteith bowl. English, 3rd quarter 18th cent.
Cut scent and stopper, engraved head of William IV and PELLATT &
PATENT. 2nd quarter 19th cent. (e) Opaque white bowl, cold-painted
colours. English, early 19th cent.

52. MODERN GLASS

(a) Modern French vase in tinted glass. Lalique. (b) Satin glass spill va
in shaded blue and silver. English, late 19th cent. (c) Victorian raspberr
red vase, mounted as an ewer. Attributed to Birmingham, 1840–50

53. ENGLISH 17th-CENTURY GLASS

(a) Chalice, double-blown bowl with silver foil inserted. Mansell period, 1642. (b) Goblet, lion-mask stem and deep emerald bowl. Antwerp or London. (c) Strong hollow cigar-shaped stem. Mansell period, excavated London. (d) Hollow lion-mask stem, as (c)

54. ENGLISH 17th-CENTURY GLASS

(a) Wine, a close approach to one of Greene's patterns, attributed to Morelli of Venice, *c.* 1670. (b) Posset pot. Perhaps Venetian, for the English market, as (a). (c) Jug in soda metal, heavily crizzled. Early Ravenscroft period, *c.* 1674. (d) Goblet, distinct traces of lead, probably from the use of lead cullet. Presumed English, for the Dutch market, *c.* 1700

55. ENGLISH 17th-CENTURY GLASS

) Wavy-rimmed *tazza*, dished and radially ribbed, soda metal, *c.* 1665–70.
) Goblet with cordon and spiked gadrooning; soda metal. Before 1670.
) One of a set of three, perhaps altar vessels; lead metal, *c.* 1680–5. (d)
adrooned posset pot, with the raven's head seal. 1677. (e) Ribbed posset
ot, as (d)

56. ENGLISH 17th-CENTURY GLASS

(a) A Greene pattern in uncrizzled glass of lead, presumably by Raven
croft, c. 1675. (b) Flute, with horizontal blue milled trails, glass of lead
c. 1680. (c) Quatrefoil-knopped wine, glass of lead, as (b). (d) Wine
crizzled glass of lead, c. 1680–2

57. SOME TYPES OF DECORATION to English 18th-century wines (a) Moulded ribbing. (b) Moulded wide fluting. (c) Diamond and/or honey-comb moulding. (d) Leaf or petal moulding (?). (e) Scale cutting. (f) Panel moulding

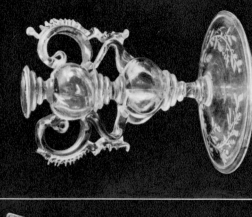

(a) Large goblet, glass of lead, in Netherlands style, c.1685s. (b) The stem and foot of a quatrefoil-knopped and winged goblet. Glass of lead. Hawly Bishopp period, c.1681. (c) Quatrefoil-knopped goblet, crizzled glass of lead. Arms of the Province of Utrecht. Hawly Bishopp period, as (b)

59. GLASSES OF THE LATER 17th CENTURY

(a) Wine, with flutes rising into 4 rows of honeycombing; hollow stem, found in England; soda metal. Third quarter 17th cent. (b) Wine, plain stepped bowl; stem, date, and metal as (a). (c) Biberon, quatrefoil knop, solid handle; soda metal, as (a). (d) Wine, in *netzglas*, probably for Sack. Dutch or Venetian, *c*. 1665–75. (e) Goblet, hollow bobbin stem, glass of lead, *c*. 1690–5. (f) Candlestick, light horny metal; glass of lead. Not after 168₅. (g) Wine, with spiked gadrooning and winged knop; glass of lead. Late 17th cent. (h) Wine, pinched flammiform gadrooning, glass of lead. Conventionally late 17th cent.

60. FURTHER TYPES OF BOWL, RIM, AND FOOT

(a) Bowl moulded with wide fluting: dentated rim: foot, pressed radial grooves. (b) Overstrung foot (enlarged). (c) Folded rim: milled thistle foot. (d) Tavern dram with corrugated bowl

See also

i Faint fluting, pls 88a, 89d ii Wrythen bowl, pl. 93i iii Part-wrythen bowl, pl. 94d iv Swirled ribbing, pl. 94a v Flammiform gadrooning, pl. 94b vi Plain gadrooning, pl. 93a vii Sunk gadrooning: as vi, but no horizontal ridge viii Lynn bowl, pl. 88d

61. BALUSTER GLASSES (Group 1)
(a) Goblet with cipher of George I. (b) Goblet with cipher (T 5 E) for
Prince Thomas Emanuel, Count of Soissons, 1702–29 etc. (c) Wine. (d)
Cordial

62. BALUSTER AND MOULDED PEDESTAL STEMS. (Groups I, II)
(a) Goblet, bowl base protruded into an acorn, over mushroom knop,
1700. (b) Goblet, with annulated knop; soda metal, c. 1705. (c) Giant goblet, knop over 8-sided pedestal. (?) c. 1700. (d) Wine, solid bowl base, c
cone drop knop, c. 1710. (e) Cordial, solid bowl base, on slender baluste
c. 1720. (f) Wine, 4-sided pedestal, (?) provincial and late 17th cent. (
Wine, 8-sided pedestal, *Richard Wright, Lynn,* 1746; soda metal

63. MOULDED PEDESTAL STEMS (Group II)

(a) Wine, hand-forged stem. (b) Wine, thistle bowl. (c) Wine. (d) Wine, engraved in diamond point with the arms of the Province of Utrecht, trolling players on reverse

64. MOULDED PEDESTAL STEMS (Group II)

(a) Wine. (b) Sweetmeat, dentated rim. (c) Wine, engraved with the arms of the Seven Provinces. (d) Champagne. (e) Covered goblet or sweetmeat

65. MOULDED PEDESTAL STEMS AND BALUSTROID GLASSES
(Groups II, III)

(a) Champagne, deeply wrythen pedestal stem, *c.* 1755. (b) Cordial, slender
[4?]-sided stem, *c.* 1760. (c) Candlestick, with (true) 4-sided pedestal, *c.* 1730.
[(d?)] (e) Front and reverse of Jacobite wine, *c.* 1715(?). (f) Wine. Mid 18th
[ce]nt. (g) Wine, light lead metal, as (f). (h) Jacobite wine, (?) Centenary of
[th?]e Boscobel Oak, 4 Sept. 1651. (i) Wine, soda metal, 17th and 18th cent.

66. BALUSTROID STEMS (Group III)
(a) Low champagne. (b) Trinket glass (?) with folded and spired rim. (
Wine. (d) Wine. (e) Wine (with base knop)

67. BALUSTROID STEMS (Group III)
(a) Wine. (b) Wine. (c) Champagne. (d) Ale

68. BALUSTROID STEMS (Group III)
(a) Wine. (b) Ale. (c) Wine. (d) Goblet. (e) Toastmaster's glass. (f) Wine, plain gadrooning

69. BALUSTROID GLASSES AND LIGHT (NEWCASTLE)
BALUSTERS (Groups III, IV)

(a) Giant regimental goblet, equestrian figure of William III on reverse.
Gp III. Mid 18th cent. (b) Wine, with arms of Rotterdam, allegorical figures on reverse. Gp IV, as (a). (c) Wine, cylinder stem. Gp III, c. 1730. (d)
Wine, tapered baluster. Gp III, c. 1735. (e) Wine, in near-stipple diamond
point, signed *F à Schürman* 1757. Gp IV

70. LIGHT (NEWCASTLE) BALUSTERS (Group IV)
(a) Candlestick, domed and terraced foot, *c.* 1735. (b) Wine, slender i
verted baluster, *c.* 1745. (c) Wine, engraved with the arms of the Admiral
of the United Provinces. (d) Betrothal or marriage glass ('I love but one'
Dutch engraving, probably by Sang

71. LIGHT (NEWCASTLE) BALUSTERS (Group IV)
(a) Wine. Dutch engraving. (b) Wine. (c) Wine. (d) Goblet

72. LIGHT (NEWCASTLE) BALUSTERS (Group IV)
(a) Wine, with teared cushioned knop; Jacobite multi-petalled rose and
'empty bud'. (b) Wine, with teared mushroom knop. (c) Wine, Dutch
engraved, 'Het Welvaaren Van De Leepelaer' (knops at base). (d) Wine,
familiar Newcastle stem type, but in soda metal, *c.* 1750

73. LIGHT (NEWCASTLE) BALUSTERS (Group IV)

) A *Salus Patriae* goblet showing warship, *c.* 1730. (b) Wine, slender
arless stem with familiar knopping, probably of the 1750s. (c) Gin glass,
ith knopping in lieu of stem, *c.* 1748. (d) Bobbin-stemmed wine, as (c)

74. LIGHT (NEWCASTLE) BALUSTERS AND COMPOSITE STEMS
(a) Jacobite wine with Rose and single bud. Before 1741. Gp IV. (b) Wine
inset trumpet bowl. Gp IV, c. 1735. (c) Goblet, stem with opaque white
twist over plain section. Gp V, c. 1765. (d) Candlestick, shaft with air twist
section over a moulded pedestal. Gp V, c. 1755

75. COMPOSITE STEMS (Group v)
(a) Wine, short plain section over long air twist, *c.* 1750. (b) Wine, as (a).
(c) Wine, long air twist over a short plain section, *c.* 1755. (d) Champagne,
as (c), but no base knop, *c.* 1760

76. COMPOSITE STEMS

(a) Wine, Dutch-engraved. Gp v. (b) Wine, opposed air twist baluster the weld in the annulated knop where twist is lost, *c.* 1760. (c) Wine Dutch-engraving; with coat of Holland. Gp v. (d) Wine, Dutch-engraving. Gp v

77. PLAIN STRAIGHT STEMS (Group VI)

(a) 'Williamite' cordial, Irish. (b) Newcastle wine. (c) Wine, panel-moulded bowl and foot. (d) Election goblet, *Succefs to Sir Francis Knollys*, 1761. (e) Toasting glass

78. PLAIN STEMS. HOLLOW STEMS. (Groups VI, VIII)
(a) Dram, with oversewn foot. Gp VI, mid 18th cent. (b) Wine, sauce
topped bowl, domed and folded foot. Gp VI, as (a). (c) Wine, bowl an
foot honeycomb moulded. Gp VI, as (a). (d) Ale, with plain gadroonin
Gp VI, as (a). (e) Wine, tapered stem, collaring above and below. Gp v
as (a). (f) Trumpet wine in soda metal; engraved *Rich^d. Spurgeon*, 1746. (
Wine, engraved and polished vine. Gp VIII, *c.* 1750

79. AIR TWIST STEMS (Group VII)

(a) Wine. (b) Wine. (c) Jacobite wine, with two-budded Rose, Star and 'Redeat' on bowl: Oak Society. (d) Jacobite semi-cordial, with two-budded Rose, and 'Redi' with twin oak-leaves on foot. (e) Cordial

80. AIR TWIST STEMS (Group VII)
(a) Jacobite 'Audentior Ibo' wine. (b) Wine, with the arms of the City of Norwich. (c) Wine, probably of Newcastle origin. (d) Wine, saucer-topped bowl

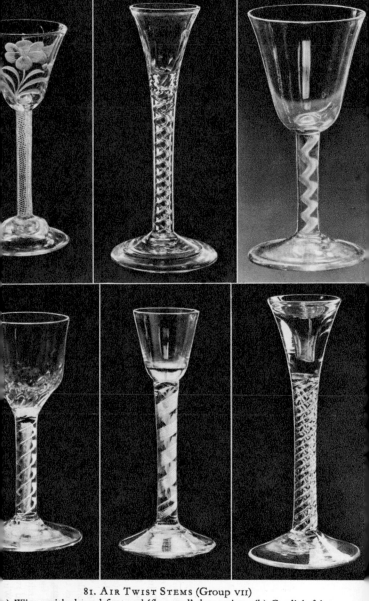

81. AIR TWIST STEMS (Group VII)

(a) Wine, with domed foot and 'flowered' decoration. (b) Cordial, faint-
fluted bowl and folded foot. (c) Small goblet. (d) Wine, bowl honeycomb
moulded at base. (e) Cordial. (f) Toastmaster's glass

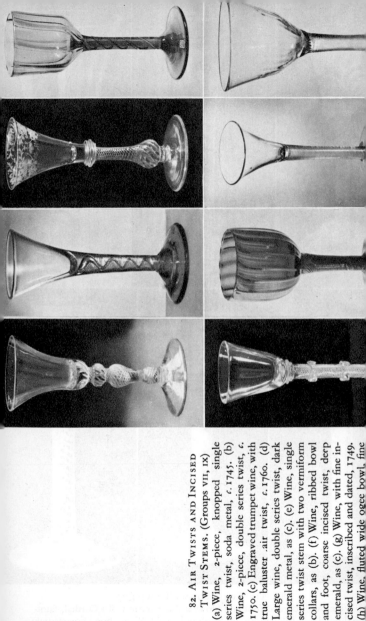

82. AIR TWISTS AND INCISED
TWIST STEMS. (Groups VII, IX)

(a) Wine, 2-piece, knopped single series twist, soda metal, c. 1745. (b) Wine, 2-piece, double series twist, c. 1750. (c) Engraved trumpet wine, with true baluster .air twist, c. 1760. (d) Large wine, double series twist, dark emerald metal, as (c). (e) Wine, single series twist stem with two vermiform collars, as (b). (f) Wine, ribbed bowl and foot, coarse incised twist, deep emerald, as (c). (g) Wine, with fine incised twist, inscribed and dated, 1749. (h) Wine, fluted wide ogee bowl, fine

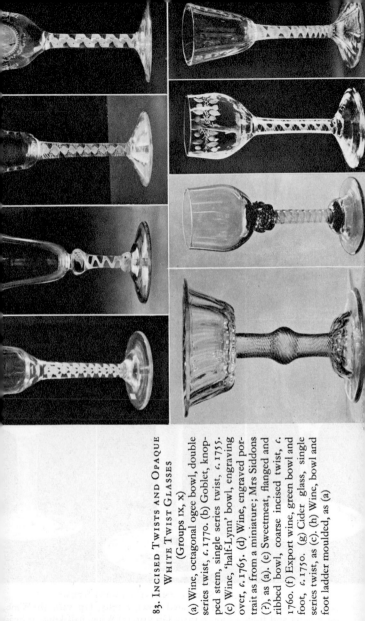

83. INCISED TWISTS AND OPAQUE WHITE TWIST GLASSES

(Groups IX, X)

(a) Wine, octagonal ogee bowl, double series twist, c. 1770. (b) Goblet, knopped stem, single series twist, c. 1755. (c) Wine, 'half-Lynn' bowl, engraving over, c. 1765. (d) Wine, engraved portrait as from a miniature; Mrs Siddons (?), as (a). (e) Sweetmeat, flanged and ribbed bowl, coarse incised twist, c. 1760. (f) Export wine, green bowl and foot, c. 1750. (g) Cider glass, single series twist, as (c). (h) Wine, bowl and foot ladder moulded, as (a)

84. HOLLOW STEMS. INCISED TWIST STEMS
(a) Sweetmeat, flanged and dentated bowl, *c.* 1765, Gp VIII. (b) Wine, ogee bowl and folded foot, *c.* 1750, Gp VIII. (c) Wine, half-knop at head of stem, incised twist, as (a), Gp IX. (d) Wine, coarse incised twist, as (b), Gp IX. (e) Wine, fine incised twist, as (a), Gp IX

85. OPAQUE TWIST STEMS (Group x)

a) Wine, knopped stem, multiple spiral opaque twist, *c.* 1760. (b) Wine,
nopped stem, twist rising into bowl base, *c.* 1755. (c) Jacobite wine, with
Rose and two buds: soda metal. (d) Champagne, folded rim. (e) Frigate or
Privateer glass *Success to the Lyon Privateer*. (f) Wine

(a) Pr of Spiral Tapes or Threads/Single Close Multi-ply Spiral Band: *also* 1, 3, 4, or 8 *do*. Threads: Pr of *do*. Bands: Pr of Solid Spiral Bands. (b) Multiple Spiral Twist

 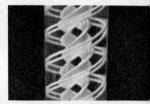

(c) Gauze/Pr of Corkscrews: *also* Gauze with Core: Twin Corkscrews. (d) Pr of Multi-ply Spiral Tapes/Pr of 2-5 ply Spiral Bands: *also* Four *do* Tapes: Four 2-3 ply Spiral Bands

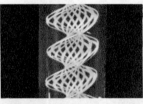 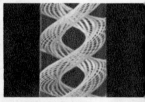

(e) Lace Twist. (f) Pr of Spiral Gauzes: *also* Three Spiral Gauzes

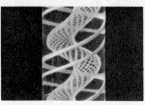 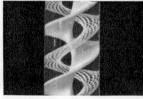

(g) Spiral Gauze and a Single 2-ply Spiral Band: *also do* and a 3-, 4-, or 5-ply Spiral Band. (h) Spiral Gauze and a Corkscrew

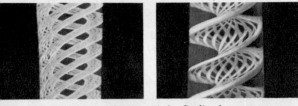

(a) Four Spiral Gauzes. (b) Lace Twist Outlined

(c) Multi-ply Corkscrew: *also* Pr of *do*. (d) Spiral Cable: *also* Pr of *do*: Vertical Cable

(e) Spiral Gauze with Core: *also* Pr of *do*. (f) Pair of Multi-ply Spiral 'U' Bands

(g) Corkscrew/Single 6-10 ply Spiral Band: *also* Pr of 6-10 ply Spiral Bands. (h) Vertical Column/Four Corkscrews/Single 10-20 ply Spiral Band: *also* Vertical Thread: Screwed Vertical Column

88. OPAQUE TWIST STEMS (Group x)
(a) Wine, with opalescent stem. (b) Dram, terraced foot. (c) Champagne
with plain gadrooning. (d) Lynn (or Norwich) wine, with three horizontal
ridges. (e) Ale, ribbed bowl and foot. (f) Ratafia

89. MIXED TWIST STEMS (Group XI) 1760–70

(a) Wine, single series white and air twist. (b) Wine, double series air/white twist. (c) Wine, double series white and colour/white twist. (d) Wine, double series air and white colour twist

90. MIXED TWIST AND FACETED STEM GLASSES
(Groups XI, XII)

(a) Goblet, stem cut six vertical flutes, petalled foot, *c*. 1790. (b) Goblet baluster type, with later foreign decoration: the glass before 1740. (Flute wine, over gauze/pr air spirals. Last quarter 18th cent. (d) Dra with green and exceptional white twist formation, *c*. 1765. (e) Sauce topped wine, opaque white. Corkscrew/M.S.A.T., as (d)

91. FACETED STEMS (Group XII)

(a) Wine. (b) Wine. (c) Wine with scalloped firing foot. (d) Ale, engraved with hops and barley. (e) Goblet, with English engraving. (f) 'Britannia' wine, commemorating the Treaty of Paris, 1763

92. JACOBITE GLASSES

(a) Disguised glass, with Rose, two buds, butterfly, and grub. Gp VII. (...)
(c) Front and Reverse of Mourning glass, with Forget-me-nots. Gp VI(...)
(d) Wine, with Rose and two buds, Oakleaf, and *Fiat* on bowl; Prince o(...)
Wales plumes on foot. Gp VI. (e) Wine, with Rose and single bud. Gp X(...)
(f) A later wine. (See Chap. x). Gp XII

93. OTHER RUDIMENTARY STEMS (Group XIII)

Dwarf ale, with plain gadrooning. (b) Dram, thistle foot. (c) Jelly, ...nged rim. (d) Jelly. (e) Jelly. (f) Jelly. (g) Jelly. (h) Jelly. (i) Dwarf ale.

94. OTHER RUDIMENTARY STEMS (Group XIII)

(a) Dwarf ale. (b) Dwarf ale. (c) Dwarf ale. (d) Dwarf ale, part wrythe
(e) Geo. wine, wide fluting. (f) 'Thistle' dram. (g) Geo. ale. (h) Rumm
wide fluting. (i) Rummer

95. OTHER RUDIMENTARY STEMS (Group XIII)

Geo. wine. (b) Dram. (c) Geo. wine. (d) Tavern dram. (e) Dwarf ale,
ceptive bowl. (f) Rummer, hollow domed and square foot. (g) Rummer,
lid domed and square foot. (h) Rummer. (i) Rummer, vertical ribbing.

96. Other Rudimentary Stems (Group XIII)

(a) Jelly, bowl set directly on a high rounded dome. Perhaps near 170[
(b) Jelly, diamond moulded. Second quarter 18th cent. (c) Small jelly
miniature loving cup, folded foot. Perhaps before 1700. (d) Monteith
heavily ribbed or corrugated bowl, petalled foot. Third quarter 18th cen
(e) Monteith, plain. Irish, as (d). (f) Monteith, notched rim and rib
domed star pattern foot. Early 19th cent. (g) Posset glass. Mid 18th cen
(h) Dwarf ale on moulded hexagonal pedestal foot. Early 19th cent. (
Dwarf ale on domed octagonal foot, as (h)

arly in making a perfect metal. Plate 56a shows such a glass in he manner of Greene; it corresponds with a broken example a greenish soda metal in the London Museum, and with an-ther in a private collection, brilliantly clear, also in soda lass. Plate 56a is presumably the 'flint crystalline' of the Woburn Abbey bills under an early trade description; it is a lear link between Greene and Ravenscroft and a light-weight lass. The metal is thin, and for that reason may not have satis-ed the Company. What I think Ravenscroft found so diffi-ult was to make a thick, strong glass of equally perfect metal. They may have looked well enough on emerging from the nnealing oven – hence the optimistic seal – but in time a good nany of them developed the old troublous fault in some egree.

If the proportions of the salts and the lead were correctly elated, as eventually they were, a perfect glass would result. Otherwise crizzling may have been apt to occur more often in eavy glasses than in light ones, even though at any moment a an experimental period mere chance might produce an occa-onal pot of perfect metal. It is a notable fact that, two genera-ons later, the Lauenstein glasshouse in Hanover, the first we now of to make lead glass on the Continent, had exactly the ame trouble which Ravenscroft experienced.

Bishopp officially took over the Savoy glasshouse in Feb-uary 1682, and had his own agreement with the Company. If nything was still wanting, either in the metal itself or the ower to repeat it at will, the credit of the discovery must be is. It is quite likely to be his in any case. Ravenscroft had ade the initial and essential discovery, but I cannot help inking that it was Bishopp who rounded it off. In so doing think he modified the thickness, clarity, and the inherent mpidity of the metal, but that is something incapable of roof; whether or no, there is a tendency to attribute lightly izzled glasses of thinner metal to Bishopp. By May 1682, owever, uncertainty begins to disappear, for the new flint asses, as they were called, were in full production, and mem-ers of the Company were selling them to the public at prices f six shillings a dozen for light or 'single flint' glasses, and

twelve shillings a dozen for 'double flint', i.e. strong one
reputedly made of two gatherings of the metal. The price
soon came down.

Apart from the sealed specimens, it is often not possible to
be certain whether Ravenscroft or Bishopp was the maker
But we are now beginning to have some confidence in ou
power to recognize the unsealed and uncrizzled work of thes
men, for the perfect Ravenscroft metal has a character and
marked quality of limpidity which can pretty well be held ii
mind when once known, but cannot be described. The year
1674–81 were years of trial and error, and the glass of thi
period is often termed 'experimental lead'. On the whole i
was utility glass, jugs, *tazze*, bowls, and other items, witl
stemmed drinking glasses in a minority (Pl.58a, b). It onl
remains to add that the new metal was thought significan
enough to find an export market, and good enough for th
continental experts to engrave, or at least to try out experi
mentally.

Apart from the two seals mentioned, there is a fragmen
bearing the letter S, supposed to signify the Salisbury Cour
glasshouse, and a complete posset-pot, in soda metal, fron
Ham House, displaying a female figure using a bow, conjectur
ally the mark of Bowles & Lillington of Southwark. Ther
may have been others, but all sealing was short-lived becaus
found to be superfluous – a discovery we must regret. Only o
wine bottles and a very few tankards, before and also lon
after the period under review, was sealing common, some
times signifying the owner, sometimes the wine merchan
The practice persisted into the nineteenth century and was als
not uncommon on the Continent and further used there t
mark spa-water bottles.

By 1685 the new lead metal was being made almost as
matter of course, and the Glass Sellers Company could cor
gratulate itself on a forward policy which had indeed returne
it dividends beyond all expectation. English glass had bee
brought to the notice of the world and given an individualit
it was to retain for 150 years. Yet although the world too
notice and was even complimentary about the new metal,

oes not appear that the world adopted it, much less copied
ur styles of vessel. Its novelty and qualities brought scattered
rders, and in the fullness of time a limited market for special
urposes, for instance as most suitable for the Dutch en-
ravers. Later on, a certain export market was secured, but
here was no question at all of our capturing the world's
narkets at a single swoop, as some have rather seemed to sug-
est. The natural prejudices and differing tastes of continental
lassmakers effectively prevented any such thing, and reason-
bly enough. They, too, could make good glass. Equally, the
elebrity of lead metal should not lead us to suppose that
oda metal was abandoned (Pl.54d). Lead glass was preferred
y all our manufacturers whose business it was to make fine-
uality glasses, but there are similar types to be found in a
oda metal which can be very good indeed and which is often
ot recognized as soda metal at all (Pl.62b). Throughout the
ghteenth century and later, for utility glass and cheap glass,
oda metal continued to be used, particularly in the North. It
resents an almost untouched field for the collector, and in-
estigation will bring out some interesting results.

With 1685 a new era in English glass began, and it is from
hat date that most collections commence. Something of the
nnumerable types and fashions produced will be described in
ubsequent chapters.

FOR FURTHER REFERENCE

UCKLEY, W. *European Glass*, 1926.

The Art of Glass, 1929.

Diamond Engraved Glasses of the Sixteenth Century, 1929.

ARTSHORNE, A. *Old English Glasses*, 1897.

ERCIVAL, McIVER. *The Glass Collector*, 1918.

OWELL, H. J. *Glassmaking in England*, 1923.

HORPE, W. A. *English Glass*, 1935 (2nd edition 1949), and *History of English and Irish Glass*, 1929.

The Glass Sellers' Bills at Woburn Abbey. Transactions of the Society of Glass Technology, Vol. 22, 1938.

INBOLT, S. E. *Wealden Glass*, 1935.

CHAPTER X

JACOBITE GLASS

*

NOBODY who writes about English glass can escape a mention of our Jacobite glasses. Scores of articles have been compiled on this difficult theme, and a wealth of sentiment lavished upon the romantic adventures of Bonnie Prince Charlie, to the extent that a glass collector unfamiliar with our eighteenth century history might get an entirely fanciful idea of it.

With apologies to those who know, let it first be said that the term Jacobean is attributable only to objects of the reign of James I; that the epithet Jacobin refers to those who favoured the anti-monarchical ideas of the French Revolution; and that a Jacobite is a partisan of James II or his descendants. We commonly extend this last term to cover propaganda and objects sympathetic to the Stuart cause.

Let it also be said that seldom has a claimant to a throne had fewer real adherents than the so-called James III, James Francis Edward, the Old Pretender or, perhaps more fairly Claimant. And few of royal blood can ever have done more to antagonize what supporters he had, or less to draw new ones to his side. His attempts in 1708 and 1719 barely merit the word. In 1715 insular prejudice and faded memories of the religious question offered a real opportunity. The threat was rising in the West, but ill-judgement, ill-luck, and resolute action by George's Government countered the danger; subsidiary risings in Scotland and the North failed dismally, and are now chiefly remembered for Sheriffmuir, where

> A battle there was that I saw, man.
> And we ran, and they ran,
> And they ran, and we ran,
> And we ran, and they ran awa', man!

nd for the dramatic rescue of her condemned husband from
ne Tower by the Countess of Nithsdale. Prince Charles Edward, born in 1720, inherited a hopeless cause, and if anything
n our island story is certain, it is that no power on earth could
nen have replaced a Stuart permanently on the English throne.

Abroad, the Papacy, Spain, and particularly Louis XV of
rance were either anti-Protestant or anti-Hanoverian or both,
nd ready enough to exploit the nuisance value of Jacobitism
or their own ends, but none was prepared to risk backing it
ith any real strength.

At home, experience had already shown that any movement
n Ireland was anti-English and anti-Protestant rather than pro-
tuart. The resources of that island were in any case too pitiful
nd its determination too uncertain for it to be much more
nan a benevolent hindrance. The idea that the Scots wanted a
tuart and not a Hanoverian is pure fantasy. The majority of
nose who dwelt in Scotland were anti-Catholic, and while a
oodly number were sufficiently anti-Union to move them to
ne Stuart side, the desires of most were those of the common
an: peace and a stable government. The Highlanders, a race
part which in the seventeenth century was regarded as a race
f hereditary cattle-thieving savages, cared neither for Stuart
or Hanoverian. Their loyalties were exclusively to their chief-
ins, who had never bowed to kingly authority in the past
nd had not the smallest intention of doing so in the future.
heir upholding of the Stuart cause arose primarily out of clan
alousies, and neither those who espoused it nor those who
ood aloof or opposed it had more than a perfunctory interest
the ultimate fortunes of the Claimants.

And, since it was the English throne which was being
ught, it is not too much to say that success depended on
e English Jacobites. It would seem that James misled him-
lf as to the real state of affairs, or was misled by over-
nthusiastic or unscrupulous agents. It was characteristic of
m to expect all and provide nothing, not even intelligent
ason. Louis, it appears, was more realistic.

As it was, in both the major attempts the English Jacobites
iled the cause. In 1715 they may be said to have had some

chance of success, but their leadership failed. In 1745, outsi
a small body of sincere and loyal men, the Stuarts had r
reliable supporters. What cards they had they played badl
The attempt was made without due warning, almost in d
fiance of Louis' advice, and headed by an impatient and in
experienced young man of twenty-five, whose natural hope
may easily have misled him. Indeed, many of his Englis
Catholic supporters may have been in a like case. After a
these dining and wining fox-hunting squires enjoyed the
freedom and maybe their estates in a period of increasing pro
perity. It was one thing – and in England a very commo
thing – to rail at King and ministers in security, and quite an
other to implement an over-stated antagonism by rising
armed support of a House they might have suspected had n
backing from the people at large. They had not been for
warned; many could not rise for reasons geographical, an
others held back. But justice does bring the thought that the
might quickly have taken up arms had Louis been rash enoug
to land French troops in Stuart support, but then only to repe
not to further the invader and his *protégé*.

Once committed, Charles needed to be fool indeed n
quickly to have realized how insecure his backing was, ho
selfish most of his immediate adherents, and how uncertain h
more distant friends. If he was forlorn and apprehensive in th
days of his reign in Edinburgh, all the reasons stood besi
him. It must have been with deep foreboding that Stua
obstinacy and princely intuition were permitted to overri
sound advice, to order action to replace festivity, and to con
mence the march which ended ingloriously at Derby. Yet it m
have been as good an alternative as offered in a hopeless case

Yet even after the 'Forty-five', our English Catholic squir
may have deceived themselves and possibly others equally u
realistic. They might still inveigh against the wickedness of t
usurper; they might find it exhilarating to play at treason;
drink toasts to the 'King over the Water'; to organize the
clubs and their coteries, and generally to plot and plan with a
assiduity which might have seemed real enough to themselv
but which did not disturb the Government. Nor, apparentl

id it encourage Prince Charles, for a further attempt believed
o have been projected for 1750 was never launched, and
isely so.

Something of all this human history appears on our glasses,
nd to facilitate an understanding of what follows it is neces-
ary to explain the 'Jacobite theory', which is here entirely
cast. The standard Jacobite glasses are engraved with a very
able Rose, having either one or two buds. They are commonly known as Rose glasses. Other emblems may be present,
nd of these the principal are a Thistle, an Oak Leaf, a Star,
nd the word *Fiat*. Portraits and latin tags are among devices
f a more specialized nature and self-explanatory; more
bscure symbolism exists, and not all is yet fully understood.

All is based on the Rose, and years ago this was best ex-
lained as follows: the large Rose was alleged to stand for
ames Francis Edward, the Old Pretender or Claimant. Of the
wo buds, the larger one on the dexter side (the left as the glass
faced) is about to open, and this was said to represent Prince
harles Edward, the Young Pretender or Claimant. The other
ud, on the sinister side (the right as the glass is faced), is un-
pened, and this was said to stand for Prince Henry Benedict,
e younger son. Glasses with the two-budded Rose precede
ost of those with the single bud, and the disappearance of
ne bud was said to coincide with the acceptance by Henry of
Cardinalship of the Church of Rome in 1747, whereafter he
as no longer considered a possible heir to the English throne,
nd eliminated from English glass.

Subsequent writers have generally subscribed to this theory,
ome I think without much conviction. Among the obvious
fficulties is the existence of a few single-budded Roses (Pl.
4a) which are earlier than any two-budded Roses and which
ate from Prince Charles' legal infancy. There are also very
any two-budded Roses which patently date long after 1747,
e year Henry became a cardinal. It had then to be conjec-
red that the engraver was carelessly working in the old
adition, putting two buds where only one was permissible,
t also nobody seems to have remarked that it is invariably
e larger Charles Edward bud which is missing and not the

small unopened Henry bud. There are other difficulties, and i
short the theory is untenable, and another has to be formulate
in its place.

The late Rev. J. G. Knowles once enunciated the basic sol
tion in a paper read to the now defunct Arundel Society
Manchester, but he carried his exposition to no distance.
recent years Capt. W. Horridge, to whom I was indebted f
the hint which threw an entirely new light on what had alread
become a widely open question, has been responsible for
pamphlet containing his own conclusions, based on a wid
knowledge of Jacobite glass and Jacobite history. His accou
and explanation of the subsidiary Jacobite emblems diverg
rather considerably from the story given here, but there is an
I think, must be, unanimity on the basic proposition. That
the important fact, the truth of which is surely vouched for l
its simplicity. It is this.

The Rose did *not* represent James Francis Edward. It repr
sented the Crown of England, just as it did on the counte
Jacobite glasses of the Hanoverian Georges. The one si
claimed it and the other possessed it, but it was the sam
Crown and to all intents and purposes the same Rose. Th
traditional connexion needs no stressing when there is a 'Ro
and Crown' in half the villages of England.

The earliest standard form of Jacobite engraving show
the Rose with a single unopened bud on the sinister side (F
74a). For a short time this bud represented the Old Pretende
and so far Horridge agrees. But in 1741 (when twenty-one) h
son Charles Edward came of age and either then, or mo
probably in 1745, when the Prince became personally know
to his supporters, he was deemed worthy of inclusion in tl
emblematic design. By this time Jacobite hopes were natural
running high and on the whole the types of the glasses us
support the later date. It was then necessary to distinguish b
tween father and son, so the former was represented by an e
pectant opening bud on the senior dexter side, and the latt
took up the position and emblem his father had previous
enjoyed on the sinister side. For the engraver it meant mere
the addition of the dexter opening bud.

It is to be particularly noted that Henry was not represented in any way at all, either on the Rose glasses or on any other type of Jacobite glass, save only in some instances on the *Amen* glasses, and then by afterthought as it were. This accords perfectly with his unimportance in the eyes of even the most zealous Jacobite.

From 1741, let us say, there was no change in the Rose and buds design for a quarter of a century. Then in 1766 James Francis Edward died, and properly to mark the change it was only necessary to omit the dexter bud, leaving the design as it had been on its inception. Further comment is needless. The crudities of the old theory vanish, and we are left, not only with a straightforward explanation, but with a new factor which will help to determine the date of quite a number of interior-twist and particularly facet stem glasses. The rule is often – but not always – broken in cases where the thistle and rose form a wreath round a portrait of Prince Charles.

That is my explanation. Horridge thinks that on the two-budded Roses the larger bud always represented Charles; that the smaller one still represented James; and that such glasses were favoured by the many Jacobites who considered that Charles, not James, was the real hope of the Cause. He further credits the equally common single-budded Roses to those who still regarded James as the rightful king. I have to dissent, partly because such a state of affairs suggests impolitic comparisons, if not differences, but chiefly because it offers no explanation of those numerous single-budded Rose glasses obviously made after the death of James. If the larger bud represented Charles, how is it there are no late Rose glasses with that bud alone?

Given that explanation, some account of other Jacobite glasses can be proceeded with. The half-century which included the risings of 1715 and 1745 and the other abortive attempts, and which concluded with the battle of Culloden Moor in 1746, is marked by comparatively few Jacobite glasses. There are some early memorial specimens imprisoning a coin of Charles II or James II, and very occasional individual records and disguised glasses. One of these is a soda glass of

good quality which might just be *c.* 1715 and must be befor
1735; it is privately engraved with the legend *A Halth t*
I...ms and there is a blackbird (so I judge it) on the revers
(Pl.65d, e). The soubriquet referred to James by virtue of hi
swarthy countenance. There is, however, but the one stabl
type of engraved glass exclusively of the first period. It has al
ready been referred to as being engraved with the first single
budded Rose. It never has any additional emblems and is ver
easily recognized, being a wine with a small waisted bowl,
multi-knopped stem with tears, and a domed and folded foot
It is not a common type, and seems to be still rarer unengraved
It cannot be later than 1745, or presumably there would b
two buds, and it could date back to the early 1730s.

Until fairly recently, the *Amen* glasses, of which not les
than two dozen genuine specimens are on record, were re
garded as the earliest stable type, and as having been mad
between 1720 and 1725 to commemorate the birth of one o
other of the two Princes. This was an assumption wrongl
based on the wording *To the Increase of the Royal Familie* foun
on a few specimens, for the word 'increase' refers to th
power, status, and influence of the House of Stuart, not to it
numerical strength. It has, however, been shown that (as fa
as the engraving is concerned) not one of the *Amen* glasse
could be earlier than 1735, and that all were almost certainl
post-1740. I am now convinced that the whole series is post
Culloden.

An *Amen* glass is one engraved in diamond-point with
royal crown, the cipher IR direct and reversed, incorporatin
the figure 8, together with (as a rule) either two or four verse
of the Jacobite anthem, concluding with the word 'Amen'
They are essentially private glasses, expressions of persona
loyalty to James the King and Charles Edward the Prince c
Wales (both directly referred to in the anthem), and sometime
also to Prince Henry by particular mention, presumably out c
politeness. A few are dated: the Dunvegan Castle glass t
1747, the Mesham and the Drummond Castle glasses both t
1749. Some very dangerous forgeries were put into circulatio
in the 1930s. Of them all, the Dunvegan Castle most intimatel

recalls the times, with its dedication on the foot to *The Faithful Palinurus*; only remarking that Palinurus was the pilot of Aeneas, I will leave it to curious readers to fathom the historic story. Another recent discovery has been the 'Laird of Lennox-love' glass, a re-discovery really; its history recalls La Belle Stuart. Add the Traquair specimen inscribed *Prosperity to the Family of Traquair*, and we have three outstandingly personal reminders of the Jacobite endeavour.

It is very unlikely that any glass bearing the word *Fiat* is of pre-Culloden date. *Fiat* has been stated to be the peculiar Word of the Cycle Club, founded in 1710, reconstituted in 1724, but only glass-conscious (so far as we know) in the time of Sir Watkin Williams-Wynn the Second, from 1745 onwards. But the *Fiat* is far too often and too differently found for it to be peculiar to the Cycle Club, and it is best regarded as a general eighteenth-century Jacobite slogan, suggestive of enterprise but still quite non-committal (Pl.92d). Such glasses are frequently seen, are a collector's favourite, and are there-fore fairly expensive. They are well enough, though there are a few good forgeries, and a heterogeneous collection of so-imagined reproductions. For no obvious reason the Word also comes on the *Hic Vir Hic Est* glasses and on the *Turno Tempus Erit* wines I have seen. Both these types are extremely rare.

After two centuries it seems clear enough to us that the battle of Culloden Moor, the ignominious flight of the Prince, and the subsequent penetration and pacification of the High-lands, together spelled final doom to Stuart hopes. Con-temporary Jacobites, however, seem to have thought other-wise. Whether they were stimulated by defeat in the past or by hopes for the future, preparations were reputedly made for a further attempt, said to have been expected in 1750. Judging by the earlier attempts, 'preparations' is too strong a word. There is no evidence that the Claimants took any factual steps whatever, and indeed that side of it all rested wholly with Louis XV; on the other hand, there was undoubtedly much underground activity of a wordy sort among the English Jacobites.

It is to the two decades after Culloden that so many of our Rose glasses, all our *Fiats*, and all our Portrait (Pls. 80a, 35c) and Motto glasses (Pl. 79d) belong. These last are rare. The best portrait-glasses are those showing the Prince in profile. His full-face portraits with the label *Audentior Ibo* are relatively common, often crude, and they need examining with some care. There are also reproductions which should not deceive.

Not a few Jacobite clubs sprang up, among them the 'Hunt' clubs such as the Caerwys, the Tarporley, and the Friendly which hid their rather vaporous Jacobitism behind a *façade* of dining and drinking. Their history is obscure, but they have bequeathed us a glass or two. More important was the Oak Society, to which there seems reason to attribute a few glasses with the word *Redeat* (Pl. 79c). In Scotland there were Rose glasses inscribed *Success To The Society*, which meant The Society of Jesus. Such glasses are both later and rarer.

But what could not be achieved after Fontenoy, could certainly not be accomplished after Aix-la-Chapelle. The Government knew well enough that the bark of all these clubs and coteries was much worse than their bite. It permitted them to play at being traitor until monotony begat indifference. A third forgetful generation soon grew up.

Something must now be said about the other emblems commonly employed. Of these the most important is the Thistle which was the Scottish counterpart of the Rose. It represents the Scottish Crown, and may be provided either with one or two buds, but it has no set form. Examples are considerably scarcer than the Rose glasses. It may appear on a glass which has also a Rose and bud, and in one stable type is engraved rising from the same stem as the Rose, which is then multipetalled and in profile, with but the single sinister bud. On my theory the latter glasses date after the death of James in 1766, most of them, perhaps all, have a white twist stem.

The Star is found on a number of mid-century and later glasses (Pl. 79c), some of which carry the *Fiat*. It signifies the aim, the object, the guiding principle of Jacobitism, and so expresses loyalty and perseverance.

The Oak Leaf is at least as often seen as the Star. There is something very English about the oak, and, as its leaf was then used on no recognizably Scottish glass that I know of, it may have come to mean Restoration to the English throne, a train of thought derived from the Boscobel Oak of Charles II and the oak-twigs he wore on his return to London in 1660. Usually the leaf is single and isolated on the reverse of a Rose glass, but twin leaves are known, as on the foot of a *Redi* glass (Pl.79d), and there are a few instances where the use of oak-leaves has a mourning significance, as on what are known as disguised Jacobite glasses. The Stricken Oak is in rather a different category. It stands for the unlucky House of Stuart, and may show a young sapling beneath, as in the *Revirescit* glasses, or two sprouting leaves; less often it is flanked by two saplings, representing the recognized heirs. Finally there is the Boscobel Oak itself with the head of Charles II showing through. As a memorial it requires something more, such as the triple Crowns of the Kingdom threaded on the branches; otherwise it may represent nothing more factious than the local 'Royal Oak'. Plate 65h illustrates an exceptional example where Charles is shown as the trunk of the oak, with candle in hand, symbolizing the Church as the mainstay of the Kingdom. Horridge regards both the Star and Oak Leaf as referring to Charles personally. Anything from that quarter merits attention, but I prefer the idea of Restoration wherever possible.

An extremely rare emblem is the Compass, apparently a special Jacobite club device, and generally taken to be that of the Cycle Club or some affiliated body. It appears on a few globular-bodied decanters. Then there is the Forget-me-not, an emblem whose importance has escaped adequate recognition; it is used conversely to denote mourning for James Francis Edward (Pl.92b, c), for on those specimens seen the larger rosebud has been lacking.

Less decisive is the Daffodil, which has nothing to do with Wales, but I now think it must be regarded as an emblem of mourning, comparable to the Forget-me-not. It is known to have been used thus on private glasses. It occurs on a few 'disguised' wines provided with oak leaves rising from a common stem, with a grub or grubs on stalk or leaf and with one, or two, really lifelike hovering butterflies; it may be termed a Daffodil-*cum*-Oak glass. A few Rose-*cum*-Oak glasses show the same grub on the stem and the same butterflies. One of them, a most significant specimen, has been elaborated and has the Forget-me-not in the place usually occupied by the larger dexter rosebud, and to me it is proof that the larger bud represented James.

In a variant Rose glass, the smaller bud is actually severed from the Rose; an allied glass has the Rose and buds, a cater-pillar (not a grub) on the stalk, a cobweb between the Rose and the larger bud, and a fly hovering over.

An explanation of such glasses as these (Pl.92a), long sought, has been given me by a Scotsman from a Scotsman, and as it seemed entirely satisfactory to those two gentlemen, whose delight in old glass was supplemented by a real knowledge of Scottish lore and tradition, and moreover vouched for by others who knew the tradition without understanding glass, it will surely serve for the rest of us. In any case, it has no competitor, for certain it is that the disguised glasses in question do *not*, as Grant Francis postulated, signify the decay of the Jacobite movement; no Jacobite would want to proclaim the failure of his own cause. Very shortly the explanation is this; it is a firmly held belief or tradition that when a Scotsman dies 'furth of Scotland' his soul returns to his native country instantaneously, and in the early days that was assumed to be underground. The representation of this belief offered obvious difficulty, and the selection of an emblematic grub is no more absurd than any other I can myself conjure up. Here, then, is the best solution yet offered, and dubious or curious readers may like to know that the belief is the theme of that familiar song *The Bonny Bonny Banks of Loch Lomond* only it should, apparently, read *Binnorie* in order to rhyme. It was in fact the lament of a Scotsman under sentence of death in Carlisle jail for cattle-thieving; it will be remembered that he was to take the 'low road' and yet be in Scotland before his fiancée, to whom he was permitted to say good-bye.

In another very small group of Jacobite glasses there is a Rose with a single bud which has the peculiarity of being without a centre, in fact an 'empty bud' (Pl.72a). The glasses selected seem early on the whole, but there is at least one exception. They smack of the North Country, as does the engraving, for the Rose is multi-petalled and in profile. I have no explanation to offer.

There is a large group of otherwise simple Rose glasses, which whether with one bud or two, have on the reverse an indeterminate insect which resembles a moth more than a butterfly, and which is very different from the lifelike insects on the disguised glasses. On later glasses (Pl.92e) this ugly insect becomes quite a presentable bee. Grant Francis wrote of the 'hope' and 'despair' motifs supposedly to be inferred and also of the 'Return of the Soul', to which phrase he attributed a different meaning to that given above. Granted that the 'decay-of-the-movement' theory can comfortably be abandoned, there seems to be a possibility that Rose glasses with these stereotyped winged insects might conceivably represent the 'Return of the Soul' as sensibly as the 'grub' glasses, though one might ask whose Soul, when the glass is a two-budded one. Horridge regards the butterfly-moth on a Rose glass as a symbol of the individual Jacobite owner-user; a reconciliation of the two ideas seems possible.

Besides those mentioned, other flowers have had a certain Jacobite significance attached to them. Mostly I think they are decorative, but there is a saucer-topped bowl on an air-twist stem which took a band of engraving very well, and there certainly is a set form of floral work not infrequently found on it, which shows the Rose and bud, the Carnation (or Pink if preferred) and Honeysuckle. A theory has been put forward that the Carnation stood for *Carolus* and the Honeysuckle for *Henricus*. But we have already seen that Henry did not come into Jacobite calculations at all, and he had been a cardinal for years before these glasses were made, so that even on the old theory he ought not to be represented. If, then, the decorative idea is unacceptable, some other theory must be sought. There are other ingenuities, too, such as translating the Passion-flower (if and when it is such a flower) as *Princeps*. The Sun-flower has also been given unexplained distinction, unless it can be claimed as an emblem for Louis XV, which seems highly improbable.

It does remain true that certain combinations of flowers do appear with surprising stability on many different kinds of glasses. Besides the design referred to above, a combination of the lily-of-the-valley, the honeysuckle, and a large rosebud is frequent. The lily appears alone, and so quite often does the rosebud. I would not like to assert that these emblems do not carry some significance, but it does not have to be Jacobite.

Strangely enough, one entirely reputable type of Jacobite Rose glass has been – rather illogically, in any case – rejected by collectors because it is assumed to be of Dutch, or at least of continental origin. It appears to have been accepted that there was a party in the Low Countries which held Jacobite leanings, exactly why is nowhere explained. There is no evidence that James had any following or popularity in France, where he was Louis' honoured guest, and any idea that the Protestant Dutch upheld his pretensions to a throne their own William of Orange had mounted seems outside all reason. The real reason why these glasses are labelled foreign is that they are made of soda metal (Pl.85c), and bygone English collectors somehow became persuaded that because the Continent used soda metal, therefore soda metal glasses were continental. The error still lingers.

Actually, these despised Jacobites were made on Tyneside, engraved on Tyneside, and no doubt sold there too. They tally in form and twist exactly with recognized English lead glasses, and the engraving tallies too, in every detail. The soda glasses are cheaper, and usually (but not necessarily) an inferior production, but they are indubitable English Jacobite glasses for all that, and it is only fair that proper recognition should be accorded them.

A few words must be added about late Jacobite glasses and glasses in the Jacobite tradition. One finds the style of the Rose and single bud engraved in a descending scale, from a well-executed design down to a crude form in which the bud is hardly distinguishable from a leaf (Pl.92f), or else is entirely non-existent. Cut and polished work is often incorporated, especially on the facet-stemmed series of glasses, and with it comes the bee. The best of these are quite definitely true Jacobite glasses (Pl.92e). Just how far some others are late Jacobites, how far some are simply inexpensive Jacobites for those who could not pay for better work, and how far some are in fact purely decorative but decadent examples in the older Jacobite tradition, must be a matter of personal opinion. No rule can be laid down, but I am inclined to think that any Rose and bud engraved in the stylized form, however crudely, has at least some claim to inclusion in the Jacobite family. It must be admitted, however, that some are very poor relations indeed.

With a new appreciation of the significance of the Rose as emblematic of the Crown of England, all the inconsequences of the old theory vanish, and that holds whatever interpretation is given of the minor emblems. Collectors will realize that problems still remain for solution, but whether solved or not, these and all other Jacobite glasses will never lack their devotees, if only on account of their sentimental and historical appeal.

FOR FURTHER REFERENCE

FRANCIS, GRANT R. *Old English Drinking Glasses,* 1926.
HARTSHORNE, A. *Old English Glasses,* 1897.
HORRIDGE, W. *Bulletin No. 56 of the Circle of Glass Collectors.*

CHAPTER XI

COMMEMORATIVE GLASS

*

A T the very beginning of this book the debt which civilization owes to glass was emphasized and, as if in acknowledgement, civilization has continuously made use of its glasses to commemorate its people, their sentiments and conventions, hopes and deeds.

Naturally, the record we inherit is an imperfect one, but during those periods when glass was abundant it is sufficiently ample, and even continuous, to suggest that it perpetuated most important events and people. If human nature has changed at all during the past thirty-five centuries, it has not modified man's urge to transmit his name to posterity by one means or another. The schoolboy who carves his name on desk or panel has the desire in common with any would-be world conqueror to leave his name behind, perhaps knowing subconsciously how fleeting must be his importance.

History in Glass began appropriately enough with our very earliest specimens, when Thothmes III had his name recorded on three glasses, fifteen centuries before the birth of Christ. There was much greater scope after the invention of glass-blowing, and we find Roman cups displaying chariot races or gladiatorial combats, generally with the names of the contestants, as in the Colchester-found *Crescens Ave – Hierax Vale* specimen. Strangely, half the known glasses of this kind were found in England, which suggests that our enthusiasm for competitive sports is of very ancient standing. Comparable glasses (*Take the Victory*) were given as prizes. By the fourth century there were also glasses inscribed with such legends as *Bibe Vivas Multis Annis*, a little more explicit than the English *Success to*, the German *Vivat*, and the Dutch *Het Welvaaren*, but the underlying idea was the same. There was the very personal

gilt glass of the cemeteries, not all of a religious nature, and
not least there was – destroyed at Strasbourg in 1870 – the cage
cup with the name of the Emperor Maximianus, who was
assassinated in 310.

Later, the names and titles of various Mamluk and other
potentates were recorded on the finely enamelled medieval
Islamic glass, and very occasionally (taking advantage of the
opportunity) the name of the humble artificer as well. Glasses
are also known with inscriptions which, however, are not only
meaningless but in imaginary characters. The bowl in Pl.13c
has a bold interior circuit in pseudo-Kufic characters, so need-
lessly that one can only conclude that neither decorator could
write nor owner read. Of the later Middle Ages it has been
mentioned that few glasses now exist, but just enough commemorative specimens remain, such as the fifteenth-century
Berovieri marriage cups, to make it quite certain that more
were made.

During the sixteenth century examples became commoner,
particularly armorial glasses from Italy, the Low Countries,
and Germany. By the end of the century these must have been
very popular, if not universal among those whose birth was
lofty or whose wealth was great (Pl.18a); to judge by the
glasses which have survived, their good taste avoided undue
ostentation. There were also social glasses of the period, including marriage and betrothal glasses from France (Pl.19a)
and from England, including some of her Verzelini glasses.

Commemorative glasses became increasingly frequent during the seventeenth century, and actual historical events were
first recorded, including events of English history. But England was decidedly behind the Continent in this respect, and it
was not until the final years of the century that she could,
thanks to the Ravenscroft revolution, challenge the lead of the
Low Countries and Germany. Then, however, she made
amends in full and, throughout the eighteenth century, historical, political, and social happenings of all kinds were
recorded on her glass, ranging from events of world-wide
importance to social matters now hardly understood, and to
personal records never intended to interest the world at large.

Their name is legion; in execution they naturally varied with the competence of the engraver, and in meaning from the simple and straightforward to the obscurely allegorical and sentimental.

Most commemorative glass was wheel-engraved, and it came chiefly from Holland, Germany, and England, the countries in which wheel-engraving particularly flourished. The designs could of course be traced by other methods. Diamond-point engraving, stippling, enamelling, cold painting, and gilding were alternative devices. Glasses could be blown into a prepared mould, in the old Roman and Venetian fashion, and in the nineteenth century they could be press-moulded. A few glasses, such as coin-glasses and casts of notable men, required no subsequent decoration at all.

Taking a bird's-eye view of this commemorative glass as a whole, it can be divided into certain well-defined categories, although there are glasses which might fall into more than one class, and a few whose true import is not now clear. There are so many glasses of historical or social interest, covering such a wide range of human thought and effort, that a perfect analysis is impossible, and no particular importance need be attached to the classification given here. It should be understood that not every inscribed glass is contemporary with the event. Most are, or very nearly so, but some may be much later, such as centenary glasses. The table does not go behind the sixteenth century, and many of the examples mentioned will be found illustrated in our standard text-books. The schedule includes many foreign glasses. Continental records often appear on English glasses (Pl.61b); the reverse is seldom the case.

A CLASSIFICATION
OF COMMEMORATIVE GLASS

1. *Records of Public Congratulation or Appreciation*

A. SPECIFIC ROYALTIES, ON ACCESSION, MARRIAGE, JUBILEE, OR DEATH

All English sovereigns from Charles II. The Emperors Leopold I, Joseph I, Francis I: Maria Theresa: Elizabeth Petrovna

Catherine the Great, Alexander I of Russia: Augustus II and III, Kings of Poland. Frederick William I and Frederick the Great, of Prussia: Ferdinand IV, King of Naples and Sicily. Cosmo III, Grand Duke of Tuscany. Very many minor rulers, such as electors, landgraves, princes, bishops, and counts.

B. PARTICULAR COUNTRIES OR RULING HOUSES

The United Netherlands, the Seven Provinces, the Province of Utrecht. The Cape of Good Hope. The Houses of Hanover, Nassau. *Reichsadlerhumpen.*

C. ESTABLISHED AUTHORITIES OR INSTITUTIONS

George and Liberty and other glasses of our Hanoverian dynasty. *King and Constitution. Prosperity to the Church of England. Success to the British Fleet. Salus Patriae* glasses. *Kurfurstengläser. V.O.C.* glasses.

D. SPECIFIC SAILORS, SOLDIERS, STATESMEN, AND PUBLIC FIGURES, ON THEIR ACHIEVEMENTS OR DEATH

Admiral van Tromp. George Walker of Derry. 'Amèn' glasses and portrait glasses of the Young Pretender. The Duke of Cumberland. The King of Prussia. Dean Swift. George Washington. Admiral Keppel. Hendrik Hooft. Lord Nelson. The Duke of Wellington. Napoleon III. Disraeli. Jenny Lind. Lord Roberts.

E. BATTLES ON SEA OR LAND

Siege of Landau. Capture of Gibraltar. Defence of Gibraltar. Quiberon Bay. Camperdown. Dogger Bank. Trafalgar. Peninsular battles and Waterloo. The *Endymion* and the *President.*

F. TREATIES OF PEACE

Ryswick. Utrecht. Aix-la-Chapelle. Treaty of Paris (Britannia glasses). Amiens. Second Treaty of Paris.

G. HISTORICAL EVENTS

The Restoration. 'Union' (of 1801) glasses. Repeal of the Test Act. Reform Bill.

H. MYTHOLOGICAL

Diana and Actaeon. Perseus and Andromeda.

2. *Similar Records of a more Restricted or Semi-private Nature*

A. PUBLIC WORKS

Hereford Cathedral. Sunderland Bridge. The Great Exhibition of 1851. Glasgow University. Alexandra Palace. Very many German and Bohemian churches, town halls, and institutions.

B. SPECIFIC MEN OF WAR

't Welvaaren Van de Leepelaer. Success to the Renown. Prince George – Admiral Digby. Privateer glasses.

C. SPECIFIC REGIMENTS

Londonderry Fusiliers. First Regiment. Loyal Colchester Volunteers. Argyllshire Militia. Many Irish Volunteer units.

D. CITIES, TOWNS, AND VILLAGES

Norwich, Newcastle, Utrecht, Dresden, Nuremberg. Scenic representations: Rialto, Baden, Wiesbaden, Map beakers. *La Pucelle de Gand.*

E. CITY COMPANIES, GUILDS, CORPORATIONS

Turners. Goldsmiths. Stationers. Weavers. Dutch East India Company. Various German trade guilds.

F. CLUBS AND ASSOCIATIONS

Masonic Lodges. *The Gore Inn Club. The Sober Club. The Black Face o't.*

3. *Records of Political or Controversial Import*

A. PARTY OR FACTION

Jacobite and Williamite glasses. 'Orange' glasses. Queen Caroline – *God and my Right. The King and the Friends of His Majesty's American Loyalists.* Carlos III. *Liberty and American Independence.*

B. MOVEMENTS AND AGITATIONS

The Friendly Hunt and other Jacobite Club glasses. *The Sea Serjeants.* Admiral Byng glasses. The Dundee Martyrs. *No Excise Rights of Man. Liberty and Wilkes. Sir Francis Burdett liberated 1810.*

c. Parliamentary Elections

Liberty and Clavering For Ever. Sir I. Pole For Ever. Success to Sir Francis Knollys.

d. Of Derision

Napoleonic cartoons and St Helena 'silhouette' glasses. 'Bute' glasses (?).

4. *Records of Social and Private Interest*

a. Individual Ownership

(a) Personal Armorial glasses of many persons from Royalty downwards.
(b) Cipher, Crest, and Monogram glasses of the same.
(c) College and other wine bottles with impressed seals.

b. Friendship

(a) Allegorical. *Concordia* and billing doves. David and Jonathan. *Amicitia* and clasped hands. Conversation scenes.
(b) Gift Glasses.
> *Brid^t Alderson to Ann Brooks.*
> *Elizabeth Lumby, the gift of her Mother 1860*
> *A Present from Ramsgate.*
> Souvenir rolling-pins, mugs, and tankards.
(c) Formal Presentation Glasses.
> *Arch^d Govan, Clerk to the Lord Drumore, 1754.*
(d) Portrait Glasses.
> Silhouette and medallion portrait glasses.

c. Family Occasions

(a) Births and Christenings.
> *Charlotte Hayward Born March the 9, 1774.*
(b) Coming of Age.
> *Prosperity to the House of Downing ... to commemorate the coming of age of David Pennant Esqr.*
(c) Betrothal.
> *Aux Bonnes Etrennes. Ik Bemin Maar Een.*
> Allegorical and sentimental scenes.

(d) Marriage.

> The 'Dier' glass. *'T Goed Success Van 't Huywelyk.*
> *Floreat die Ruhr fahrt* and respective arms.
> *S.I. to Mr Hutchinson – Stony Gill 1764* and a verse.
> Allegories.

(e) Anniversaries.

> *Zilver Bruiloss Feest.*

(f) Death.

> Hearts and initials on a sarcophagus (plague glass).
> Memorial portraits. Mourning glasses.

D. RECREATION

(a) Sport.

> Cock-fighting. Lion, Stag, Fox, Bear, and Chamois
> hunting. Coursing. Steeplechasing. Skating. Yachting
> Shooting. Fishing.

(b) Games of Chance.

> Cards. Dice beakers. Gambling scenes.

(c) Travel.

> Coach and Four. Riding. Ballooning. Railroads.

E. PROPERTY AND POSSESSIONS

(a) Real Estate.

> Farms. Homesteads. Vineyards. Windmills.
> Alnwick Castle.

(b) Animals.

> Racehorses – *Blink Bonny, 1857.* Prize Bulls.
> Foxhounds. Greyhound – *Master McGrath, 1868, 1869
> & 1871.*

(c) Ships.

> *Success of Boston. William & Mary.*

F. COMMERCE AND BUSINESS

(a) Good Luck glasses.

> *Vivat Negotiae. Success to Irish Navigation and Trade. Speed
> the Plough. Let Farming Flourish.*

(b) Specific Trades or Firms.

> Whaling. Agriculture. Inns. The Linen Trade. The Hop
> Trade. The Coal Trade. *Success to the Swordmakers.
> Cowan & Co.* with the Leith and Scottish Arms.

(c) Memorials of Trade or Work.
>> Launch of the *Nelson*. *Up to Sowerby Bridge* (canal). Lock Gates. Mills. The York Coach.

G. SENTIMENT AND CONVIVIALITY

(a) Extolling liquor.
>> Bacchus glasses. *Take a Dram Old Boy.*

(b) Toasts.
>> *Families, Friends, and Favourites. No Grumbling.*
>> *Au Premier Plaisir. Le Vin Guerit la Tristesse.*

(c) Religious or Philosophical.
>> *Apostelgläser.* Eve in the Garden of Eden. Christ appearing to Mary in the Garden of Gethsemane. Madonna and Child. St Christopher. St Hubert. Samson and the Lion. Ten Ages glasses. The Twelve Months. The Four Continents. The Four Seasons.

(d) Cryptic and Double Entendre.
>> *Maat Houd Staat* with Daedalus and Icarus.
>> *I elevate what I consume.*

(e) Comic.
>> *Hansie in de Kelder* glasses. Strolling Players. Crude Love and Drinking scenes.

(f) Allegorical.
>> *Aurea Libertas* with escaping bird. Conversation scenes.

(g) Repeats of Drawings.
>> Aesop's Fables.

(h) Mottoes.
>> *It is to Wine that Prudence Opposes herself.*
>> *Nequid Nimis* (sic).

A great many of these commemorative glasses are recognizable at sight and offer no problem. Others, however, require to be 'read' before they have any meaning for collectors of the twentieth century. Here is the description of an English mid-eighteenth-century glass, engraved in Holland. Behind a rounded hill the sun is rising. On either side, in the foreground, stands a drummer and a trumpeter. Above the hill is a pair of crossed naked swords, and round the rim runs an inscription in Dutch. At first sight it looks rather like some elaborately sentimental picture of a dawn or sunset. But that leaves no obvious reason for the crossed swords, and no particular reason for drummer or trumpeter. Taken as an allegory, however, it is apparent that the engraving represented some important change in fortune. A translation of the inscription *Den Goeden Oorlogh* (The Fortunate War) confirms this, and reference to history makes it possible to say that the glass (Pl.73d) is a Dutch commemorative of the Peace of Aix-la-Chapelle in 1748.

In another case an elaborately engraved Zechlin glass bears a representation of an army parade at Busau, together with armorials and the inscriptions *Séjour Agréable* and *Vive l'Armée Prussienne*. That appears odd, because Franco-Prussian relations have not been conspicuous for their cordiality. Again history comes to the rescue. For a short while during the War of the Austrian Succession, France and Prussia were allied against Maria Theresa and of course England, whose attitude was automatically anti-French. Some rather complicated manoeuvres culminated in the battle of Czaslau in May 1742. The *Séjour Agréable* at Busau or Brusau, which places lay on the line of march, a few miles from Zwittau on the Bohemian-Moravian border, must have occurred between January and May 1742. The armorials are those of Von Oppen, of Silesia, Saxony, and Anhalt, and the glass (Pl.41c) was doubtless a present from a French officer to his temporary host and ally.

Now, no particular intelligence is required to read glasses like this. A little imagination is necessary, and quite often some book of reference. The point is that old glasses were not decorated with unexpected designs without reason. Outside purely formal or decorative engraving the design had a definite meaning. It is a part of glass-knowledge to realize on sight when there is a meaning, and an omniscient connoisseur would know what is its purpose.

That, however, needs a degree of knowledge which nobody has yet reached, or is soon likely to reach. It would entail an impeccable memory and scholarship in a score of the sciences. To mention but a few, one would need acquaintance with languages, especially Latin, Dutch, and German, and with their contemporary usages and script, together with a capacity to make allowances for an artist's errors in transcription. Mythology is another requirement. History, especially of the seventeenth and eighteenth centuries, is essential, and this means not only facts and names and dates, but also an appreciation of seventeenth- and eighteenth-century thought, manners, and customs. Topography and continental geography, as it used to be, is needful. We speak learnedly today of Netherlandish glasses, without troubling to consider whether we cannot be more precise. Frontier changes and political supremacies have continually to be kept in mind. Heraldry is constantly in question, with errors and omissions in the armorials to be reckoned with. Coats of arms and also Orders and insignia will require identification, and continental heraldry is more diverse than our own with even small towns boasting a coat of arms. Various emblems carry a meaning, or may have a meaning entrusted to them in a particular case. Allusions which were no doubt clear enough in the past now require interpretation. As an instance, there is the Bate rummer engraved with a cat playing the bagpipes, with the legend *Honour and Friendship*. Nobody has discovered its meaning, and the two lines of approach I have found leave it still in doubt. The design bears a strong likeness to a French copper-plate engraving illustrating Aesop's fable of the wolf and the kid. Judging by another glass which is similarly but more lengthily inscribed and which mentions the Dee, the legend seems to be adapted, or perhaps wrongly rendered, from a song printed in Hogg's *Jacobite Relics*, in which the refrain is:

> Let Honour and Friendship Unite
> And Flourish on Both Sides the Tweed

In another case we have a goblet with the Jacobite Rose and two buds on one side, and the inscription *Lyster And The Honest Freeholders* on the reverse. Perhaps one should have known, but much inquiry failed to elicit the significance of the 'Honest Freeholders', and only a chance reading of Macaulay showed that the phrase meant 'loyal and sincere electors'. Lyster himself was the feudal-minded and feudal-living Shropshire squire of Rowton Castle, a Tory and a Jacobite, who sat almost continuously in the House for forty years. That suggests the very antithesis of democracy, yet he kept open house once a week for his country supporters, and his London tradesmen thought enough of him to meet his coach and six, and to escort him from Hampstead to his London house at Bow. When he died, in 1765, somebody neatly epitomized him and his electors in this glass. It may be noted that it has a faceted stem and, in 1765, still two buds to the Rose.

One could recite instances where whole pages of history come to life in the elucidation of an engraved design. Plate 30a shows a Scandinavian glass signed *C F fait A° 1706*, i.e. Cristoffer Fransysk, the clue a small badge rather than a full armorial, set on a plinth and lettered VRIT MATURE. The boy of six is Charles Frederick Duke of Holstein, shown taking up the arms and apparel of his deceased father. After vicissitudes he married Anna, daughter of Peter the Great and Empress of Russia to be. In 1742 their son Charles Peter Ulrich was recognized as Anna Pavlovna's heir, and married Catherine of Anhalt-Zerbst. Charles Peter became Tsar in 1761 on his mother's death, but survived an extreme unpopularity for only a matter of months, so things were apt to go in Russia, and Catherine (the Great) reigned in his stead, 1762–96. But our Charles Frederick, next in the line of the royal house of Sweden, failed for reasons politic to ascend that throne, or Sweden and Russia might have been linked in the person of his unlucky son Charles Peter with unguessable results to the history of Europe. That is an example of a serious historical sequence read from a glass unforeseeingly engraved two and a half centuries ago.

In case all this may tend to discourage any enthusiast for commemorative glass, he may find consolation in the fact that access to a good reference library will smooth out most of the difficulties. The interpretation is almost always perfectly simple, once the clue is discovered, and a little experience and a certain imagination will carry him a long way. Where highly specialized knowledge is called for, as for instance in the reading of archaic German or obscure continental heraldry, it may be possible to find an expert who will assist in what can be a troublesome and time-devouring task. It is hardly necessary to add that one should not expect such help to be gratuitously given.

There is indeed hardly any limit to the curiosities and whimsicalities of History in Glass, and it will be found an absorbing subject, with not a few prizes for an imaginative collector. Purists, who regard any sort of extrinsic decoration on glass with regret, will not be interested, and there is something to be said for that point of view. Collectors who are concerned only with glass forms will not need to be interested. But those whose imagination is touched by the human interest of specimens which speak of men and deeds and customs, now enshrined in or even forgotten by history, will find a field of never-ending interest in commemorative glass.

FOR FURTHER REFERENCE

BATE, P. *English Table Glass,* 1905.

BLES, J. *Rare English Glasses of Seventeenth and Eighteenth Centuries,* 1926.

CHURCHILL, ARTHUR, LTD. *History in Glass,* 1937.

PART TWO

ENGLISH GLASSES OF
THE EIGHTEENTH CENTURY

*

NOMENCLATURE AND
CLASSIFICATION

*

With the closing years of the seventeenth century, a state of affairs is found matched only in the heyday of Roman production. Every manufacturing country was making as much glass as it could, with Britain, thanks to Ravenscroft's discovery, coming rapidly to the fore, and providing an article which in some respects was superior to all alternatives.

I am inclined to rank the combination of strength and clarity in front of all else. Strength meant durability, and durability meant economy, as anyone knows who has bought cheap modern glass. Clarity, however, was still a relative term. It did not mean the hard crystal-like brilliance of the glass today. It meant even translucency, an absence of heightened tints where the metal was thicker. Our English lead glass for the better part of a century was not at all crystal-like. It might have a faint greenish or, more often, a blackish tone, but these were uniform throughout the glass, and are now regarded as a merit, not a demerit. Any sort of a yellowish or amethyst cast is, on the other hand, looked on with disfavour by collectors, because such tints were accidental and unstable.

The lead metal had a softness of look which was very pleasing, and a further intrinsic softness which some continental engravers found very convenient. It had, as well, a quite new and lustrous quality, a power to diffuse light. As time went on, manufacturers eliminated the earlier greenish and blackish tints, but the metal retained its soft appearance, while its light-diffusing quality was exploited by suitable cutting. In due course a certain hardness of look did eventuate, notably on ovoid goblets with a plain stem and foot; it may have been due to some small change in the metal formula such as a more economical use of lead.

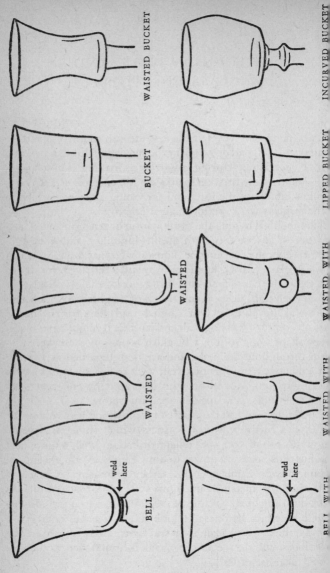

WAISTED BUCKET

INCURVED BUCKET

BUCKET

LIPPED BUCKET

WAISTED

WAISTED WITH

WAISTED

WAISTED WITH

weld
here

BELL

weld
here

BELL WITH

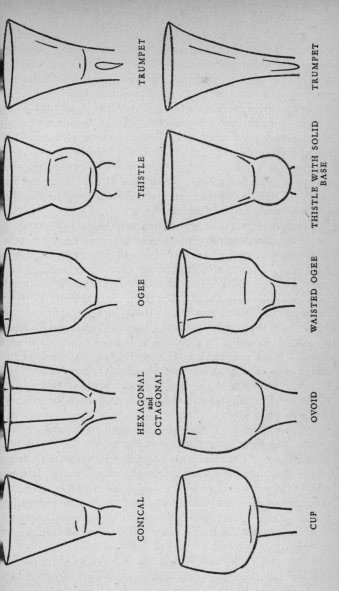

TRUMPET

THISTLE

OGEE

HEXAGONAL and OCTAGONAL

CONICAL

TRUMPET

THISTLE WITH SOLID BASE

WAISTED OGEE

OVOID

CUP

At the end of the seventeenth century, London was leading
the way in the use of lead metal, with eleven glasshouses de
voted to its manufacture. Bristol and Stourbridge followed
distantly, with four and five such houses respectively, no
necessarily of as great capacity. Newcastle had but one, al
though probably an important one. As will be seen, the Tyne
side area turned out some notable glasses, but it also made
great quantities of utility glass in the cheaper soda metal, fo
the poorer, or more frugal, people of the North. That does no
mean that every lead glass was good, or that every soda glas
was poor. The latter metal could be, and was, fashioned into
glasses of fine quality, and some of them can easily be mistaken
for their more frequent lead brethren.

A little coloured glass was made from the very beginning o
lead glass, blue, opaque white, and amethyst certainly. A rathe
bright roemer-type green was in use by the air twist period
it gradually became darker until the nineteenth century saw a
green which, in thick glass, seemed almost black. Bristol made
dark blue and opaque white glass from the middle of the eight
eenth century. There was a paler blue in both soda and lead
metal from the northern centres, and milk-glass from nearl
all. Amethyst and ruby glass mostly belong to the nineteenth
century, but a true red-ink 'Kunckel' glass was made at Bir
mingham by Mayer Oppenheim about 1755, and I have seen a
specimen which could be nothing else. With all this, on th
whole the English did not, and still do not, care for coloured
drinking-glasses.

Other writers have dealt so fully with eighteenth-centur
glasses and their history that it is not proposed to repeat i
brief what every student must needs read elsewhere in detail
There does, however, seem room for a more precise classifica
tion of the various types of drinking glass made, based on th
structure of the stem, with bowl and foot variations regarded
as subsidiary. There are in fact families, genera, and species o
drinking glasses, the last possessing no inconsiderable numbe
of varieties.

There is also a crying need for a uniform terminology
Authors have used the same word to describe different things

and different words to describe the same thing, for it is none too easy to be faithful even to one's own phraseology. It should be easy to visualize a glass from a description, and then to sketch it, but how seldom that is possible at present will be learned by referring to lists and catalogues which appear in print. It matters very little what terminology is employed, provided it is generally accepted and steadfastly observed.

The following, then, is a list of the types of eighteenth-century (1690–1830) drinking glasses. The stem is presumed to be of normal length and thickness unless otherwise stated. The figures of capacity are in liquid measure and represent normal expectation. The basis of comparison is the ordinary 6-inch wine-glass of the mid eighteenth century, with round funnel or ogee bowl of a size one might describe as for port.

Ale: capacity 3 to 4 oz; with long and relatively narrow bowl (Pls 36a, 67d).

Short Ale: the same, but stem shortened.

Dwarf Ale: the same, but stem very short, rudimentary, or absent (Pl.94).

Giant Ale: over 12 in. in height with appropriate capacity.

Georgian Ale: 4 to 5 oz; a Georgian wine (*q.v.*) with long bowl (Pl.94g).

Beaker: capacity variable; predecessor of the tumbler; with or without foot rim (Pls 28a, 34d).

Champagne: 6 oz; a wine or small goblet; bowl width equal to or greater than its depth (Pls 67, 75d, 88c).

Low Champagne: 4 oz; the same, but stem shortened (Pl.66a).

Cordial: 1 oz; a small bowl on a rather tall and extra-stout stem (Pls 61, 77, 79).

Short Cordial: 1 oz to 1½ oz; the same, but stem shortened to normal length.

Semi-Cordial: the same, but stem of normal length and thickness (Pl.79d).

Cup (and Saucer): up to 4 oz; with or without a handle (Pl.37).

Dram (or Spirit) Glass: up to 3 oz; bowl variable; stem very short, rudimentary, or absent (Pls 88b, 93b).

Georgian Dram: up to 2 oz; a small edition of the Georgian wine (*q.v.*) (Pls 60d, 94f).

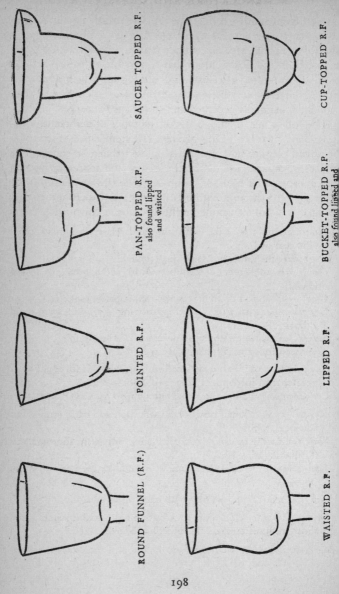

SAUCER TOPPED R.F.

CUP-TOPPED R.F.

PAN-TOPPED R.F.
also found lipped
and waisted

BUCKET-TOPPED R.F.
also found lipped and

POINTED R.F.

LIPPED R.F.

ROUND FUNNEL (R.F.)

WAISTED R.F.

198

FOOT FORMS

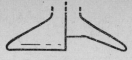

PLAIN CONICAL

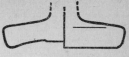

FIRING

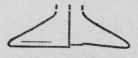

SOLID CONICAL

BEEHIVE

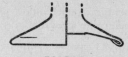

FOLDED

PEDESTAL

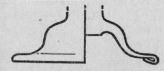

DOMED AND FOLDED

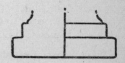

STEPPED SQUARE FOOT

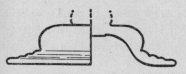

DOMED AND TERRACED

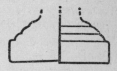

TERRACE-DOMED
SOLID SQUARE FOOT

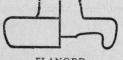

FLANGED

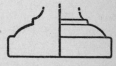

DOMED SQUARE FOOT

Gin: a miniature wine-glass (Pl.73c).

Goblet: 4 oz and over; bowl large in relation to stem height (Pl.91).
Giant Goblet: over 10 in. in height.
Mammoth Goblet: over 12 in. in height.

Loving Cup: 8 oz and upwards; a short-stemmed goblet or standing vase with a pair of handles, with or without(?) a cover.

Mead Glass: a goblet with stem rudimentary or absent; not after *c.* 1760. The term is insecure.

Mug: capacity variable; a tumbler with handle.

Posset Glass: 2 oz to 3 oz; a glass of jelly type with a pair of handles and a spout (Pl.96).
Posset Pot: up to 15 oz; a low cylindrical vessel with a pair of handles and a spout, and (originally) with a cover (Pl.54).

Ratafia (or Flute Cordial): capacity 1 oz to 1½ oz; with long and very narrow bowl (Pl.88).

Rummer: 4 oz and over; a goblet with short stem; only after *c.*1770 (Pls 94, 95).
Giant Rummer: over 10 in. in height.
Mammoth Rummer: over 12 in. in height.

Tankard: capacity variable; a footed mug.

Toasting Glass: 2 oz to 4 oz; a wine or small goblet on a tall and exceptionally slender stem (Pl.77).

Toastmaster Glass: ½ oz to ¾ oz; a cordial or dram glass with highly deceptive bowl (Pl.81).

Tumbler: capacity variable; a more or less cylindrical vessel on a flat base (Pl.37).
Giant Tumbler: over 10 in. in height.
Mammoth Tumbler: over 12 in. in height.

Wine: 2 oz to 3 oz.
Georgian Wine: 3 oz to 4 oz; with shortened stem; related to the rummer as the Wine is to the Goblet; only after *c.*1770 (Pl.95).

Besides the foregoing, which are purely drinking glasses, certain other types of table-glass are found.

Candlesticks and Tapersticks: in great variety.

Jelly Glasses: a parallel to the Dwarf Ale, but may have a handle or handles. Many were no doubt intended, or at least used, for drinking purposes (Pl.93).

Sweetmeat Glasses: a parallel to the Champagne (Pls 64, 83e). No sure distinction has been formulated. Broadly speaking, it is possible to drink conveniently from Champagnes, but not from Sweetmeats. The terms are used with small discrimination.
Low Sweetmeats: the same, but stem shortened (Pl.60a).

Less often collected, unless for their decorative or intrinsic usefulness, are the following:

Baskets: for dessert, e.g. fruit.

Bottles: especially wine, tea, toilet, and water bottles (carafes).
A bottle is a hollow vessel with a narrow neck and mouth; no foot or handle. Wine bottles are collected, especially when sealed.

Bowls and Basins: especially caddy, cream and milk, sugar, punch, and finger bowls.
A bowl is a vessel with concave sides with or without a foot or foot-rim.
A basin has sloping sides, the width greater than the height, with or without foot-rim. The term should be more used (Pl.39).
Standing Bowls: especially boat, harvest, and kettle-drum bowls; with foot and a pronounced stem.

Chandeliers: pendant, or for the table, walls, or mantel.

Cruets and Condiments: bottles with stoppers or caps, some with feet. Twin cruets for oil and vinegar.

Decanters, and Spirits (Bottles): for polite use at the table.

Dishes: including epergne dishes.
A dish is a shallow, concave vessel without foot or foot-rim; with or without a cover, and often with a *Stand*, which is either a tray or a solid or hollow plinth to receive the dish and give it stability.

STEM FORMATIONS
(simple)

THE KNOP PROPER

FLATTENED KNOP

ANNULAR KNOP

BALL KNOP

SWELLING KNOP

ANGULAR KNOP

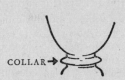

COLLAR →

BLADED KNOP

(specialized)

TRUE BALUSTER

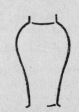

INVERTED BALUSTER

202

STEM FORMATIONS
(specialized continued)

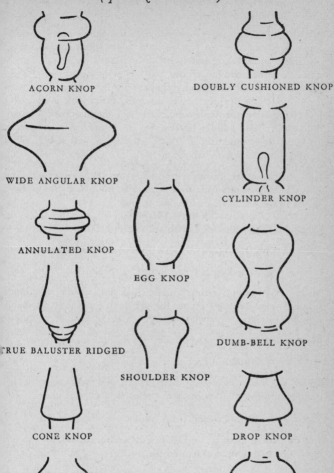

ACORN KNOP

DOUBLY CUSHIONED KNOP

WIDE ANGULAR KNOP

ANNULATED KNOP

EGG KNOP

CYLINDER KNOP

TRUE BALUSTER RIDGED

SHOULDER KNOP

DUMB-BELL KNOP

CONE KNOP

DROP KNOP

CUSHIONED KNOP

MUSHROOM KNOP

Ewers and Jugs: the former with wide, the latter with narrow mouth; with or without a foot.
A claret jug is stoppered.

Flasks: flat, oval bottles originally for travelling needs, latterly mainly decorative, or for infantile use. Gimmal flasks are of twin oil and vinegar style with short curved necks.
Saddle bottles are larger and less flat, with longer neck. Scent flasks are small and of any shape. Pilgrim bottles (Venetian) are capacious upright flasks on foot, fitted with loops for a carrying attachment; the same term is sometimes used for armpit flasks, like saddle bottles but thin and light. American flasks, for spirits, are of a high arch form, and stable; some others are of violin shape.

Jars: for preserves, honey, or ginger, and then with cover and stand. Storage jars were used for herbs, liquors, and household supplies.
A jar is a deep, wide-mouthed vessel without lip, foot, or handle. When provided with an 'ear' it becomes a piggin.

Ladles: for punch, mulled wine, or possets; both large and small.

Lamps: especially Lacemaker's lamps.

Monteiths (or Bonnet Glasses): usually small glasses with cup-topped bowls, etc., and no stem. Reputedly for salt but probably punch or cheap sweetmeat glasses (Pl.96).

Monteith Bowls: specialized punch bowls.

Patchstands: miniature *tazze.*

Phials: small bottles, usually narrow, tall, and rather unstable, for unguents and medicines from the earliest days of glass.

Plates: to be distinguished from stands; see dishes.

Pots: for tea and coffee, and then with a single handle and spout; for oil, with long spout; and for ink.

Salts: of many forms, e.g. hollow blown, trencher, and boat-shaped; with or without feet.

Salvers: i.e. trays.

Sauce Boats: of half-decker type, probably for cream or invalid use.

Stands: a circular or other plate or dish on which stands a vase or container with cover; a *tazza* on tall stem and foot to support viands on the dining table; *see also* patchstands.

Tazze: shallow saucer-shaped dishes on foot, with or without stem; or flat topped, with or without a rim.

Toddy Lifters: a decanter-bodied pipette used to transfer liquor from bowl to glass.

Toys: Implements: Apparatus: Insignia: in great variety.

Urns: which properly include comports; anciently, an oviform vase on foot, especially a pedestal or plinth, but a cinerary urn might dispense with a foot; with cover.

Vases: especially celery, flower, and ornamental vases.
A vase is a vessel, especially an ornamental one, of greater height than width, with or without a foot. Also small spherical vases for violets, primroses, etc. Often with a cover (Pl.36).

A variety of meanings has been attached to some of the foregoing terms. For instance, the *tazza* as above is often called a stand, a salver, and a waiter, so that a reader has to guess what is really meant. Other terms have come into use which appear to me redundant, even erroneous, such as 'butter cooler', 'butter boat', and 'brandy saucepan'. The lists do not include quite every article made of English glass, while some articles which might have been expected do not exist, or at least I have not seen them.

A very wide variety of terms is in use to describe stem, bowl, and foot features, and they have inevitably been inconsistently employed. The line drawings given show the main forms and shapes a collector is likely to meet with, and the captions will assist understanding of, at least, the classification which follows. Without some such guide, it would have little value.

In so far as drinking glasses and some few other types of vessel are concerned, a classification based on stem formation is wholly satisfactory until the last quarter of the eighteenth century is reached, when stem forms tend to become subsidiary to the bowl, and we find rummers, dwarf ales, jelly

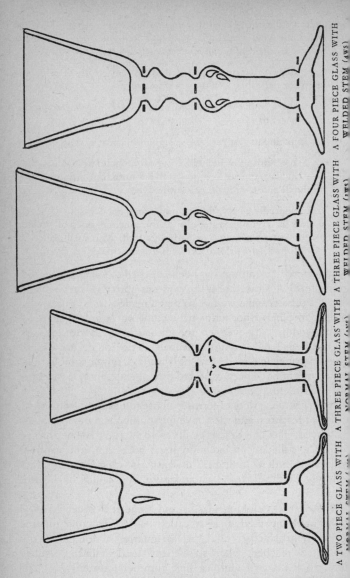

A TWO PIECE GLASS WITH NORMAL STEM (ns) A THREE PIECE GLASS WITH NORMAL STEM (ns) A THREE PIECE GLASS WITH WELDED STEM (ws) A FOUR PIECE GLASS WITH WELDED STEM (aws)

glasses, and Georgian wines and ales becoming preponderant. However, all these later types of glass have one point in common, and they can fairly and conveniently be classified under the heading of 'Other Glasses with Short or Rudimentary Stems', the word 'Other' being important because the earlier groups include varieties in which the stem is insignificant or, indeed, entirely absent.

Most glasses fall clearly within one or other of the following groups, but there are glasses intermediate between Group I and III, and others referable to either Group VI or XIII. In such cases they should be allotted to the less important category. Some arbitrary distinctions have had to be made in respect of Group III and IV, which latter is now deemed to include all glasses with multiple tears in the stem, and V, in the interests of simplicity. Practised collectors will recognize the difficulties. There are a few freak glasses which fit in nowhere, and some out-of-period glasses which are here neglected. The groupings to be recorded, then, are as under, the datings representing the effective currency of the group.

Group		
I.	BALUSTER STEMS	1685–1725
II.	MOULDED PEDESTAL STEMS	1715–1765
III.	BALUSTROID STEMS	1725–1760
IV.	LIGHT (NEWCASTLE) BALUSTERS	1735–1765
V.	COMPOSITE STEMS	1745–1775
VI.	PLAIN STRAIGHT STEMS	1740–1775
VII.	AIR TWIST STEMS	1745–1770
VIII.	HOLLOW STEMS	1750–1760
IX.	INCISED TWIST STEMS	1750–1765
X.	OPAQUE WHITE TWIST STEMS	1755–1780
XI.	MIXED AND COLOUR TWIST STEMS	1755–1775
XII.	FACETED STEMS	1760–1810
XIII.	OTHER GLASSES WITH SHORT OR RUDIMENTARY STEMS: DWARF ALES; JELLY GLASSES; RUMMERS; GEORGIAN ALES, WINES, AND DRAMS. Eighteenth to nineteenth century	

Most of these Groups can be subdivided into Sections and Subsections, according to the more precise formation of the stem, and each Section will contain a certain number of bowl and foot forms. The line drawings show and name these forms, and illustrations show the types of moulded decoration adopted by the manufacturer. The drawings showing the ways in which a glass can be built up may be found useful when considering Groups III–V.

The subdivision of the above Groups can now be dealt with. Throughout the classification it is the more familiar variations of stem, bowl, foot, and decoration to which attention is drawn, though some others of special interest are recorded.

The most useful books on English eighteenth-century glass have been mentioned. The various works by Bate, F., Buckley, Francis, Hartshorne, Honey, Powell, Thorpe, and, for Irish glass, Dudley Westropp, may all be studied with advantage.

Group I

GLASSES WITH BALUSTER STEMS
(*c*. 1685 – *c*. 1725)

If George Ravenscroft really set out to provide the people of England with sturdy glassware, he needed to have lived very little longer to see his ambitions realized. The bills of glass supplied by Apthorpe to Woburn Abbey and analysed by Mr Thorpe show how quickly the 'duble fflint' wares followed on the heels of the 'single flint' and more or less superseded them. They went on, so it seems to us now, to oust all else almost completely.

All the same, they were not the only sort made. Glasses were sold by weight, so economy would have dictated a market for light glasses if nothing else – taste or conservatism, for instance – had done so. The thinly blown glasses – I do not much like the term 'single flint' as indicative of a single gathering of metal – are scarce, though fairly well known. Parallel with these were wines and goblets of metal only slightly heavier, if at all, but with semi-hollow or completely hollow stems. The knopping on such glasses was the inverted baluster, drop knop, acorn knop, and to some extent the wide angular knop. It was impracticable to make a hollow annulated or a cushion knop, though either could have a substantial tear, while the true baluster was more often than not a solid formation. In part, the scarcity of lightly made balusters may be due to their greater vulnerability, but even so the output must have been much smaller than in the case of the balusters to which the adjective 'heavy' is often prefixed. They are better regarded as a scarce variety of their more substantial counterparts.

But it is not only a question of weight or size. I regard a baluster glass as one which had a stem wherein one knop formation markedly dominated or where the bowl had a designedly solid base. Later it will be seen that the Balustroid glasses were less heavily knopped and that, even if one knop did dominate, it

was a case of the little being greater than the less; moreover
the base of the bowl was not solid except to some extent in the
waisted bowl, and necessarily so in the trumpet.

There were transition glasses, better referred to the less im
portant category, and a few Balustroid goblets which would
have qualified for inclusion in the Balusters on every ground
except their date of manufacture. One need not be too fussy
it makes no difference to the value or interest of the glass, and
in practice there is seldom much difficulty. A few Baluster
glasses are known in soda metal (Pl.62b); apparently none in
colour.

It is not safe to date a glass on metal tint alone, but this can
be a guide. The very earliest light glasses retained something
of the soft, colourless limpidity of Ravenscroft's perfected
metal. Unfortunately, few of us have a sample at hand. Some
where around 1685 and after there was a green tint which is a
sign of early date. Before 1700, the tint had become blackish
and thus it remained until the later years of the Baluster era
when it softened in tone, to become greyish in the Balustroid
period which followed. But there will be errors in and excep
tions to any hard-and-fast rule of dating on the basis of colour
tint.

Very little engraving is found on Baluster glasses, and cer
tainly none was put on by the manufacturers for decoration
The text-books will show examples of diamond-point work
not necessarily done when the glass was new; in a commemora
tive glass that is not abnormal. Wheel-engraving is quite as
scarce as diamond-point: one would be hard put to mention
half a dozen examples off-hand. Glasses which were scratched
with a name, date, motto, or inscription are better termed
etched, not engraved. Only rarely will they have significance
as in the 'Dolly Mytton' glass (Bles, Pl.59).

There will be little or no moulding on any Baluster drink
ing glass, except that gadrooning appears on cupped wines
and goblets, as well as on tankards and punchbowls. There are
champagne/sweetmeat types with, for instance, panel mould
ing or honeycomb moulding, but they are perhaps better
referred to Group III or IV. There is moulding on some late

seventeenth-century candlesticks, gadrooning again and some ribbing. And of course there may be applied work, chain cabling or 'nipt diamond waies', on glasses that come within the Baluster period; this would especially apply to standing bowls and large tankards.

There was a larger percentage of goblets, and especially of giant goblets, in the Baluster Group than in any other. The percentage dropped as the eighteenth century grew older, until in the Facet Stem Group it became very small. Baluster ale-glasses are now extremely rare; cordials, other than the simply-knopped transition types, are scarce until the true baluster series commences when they become more frequent than is generally supposed. Gins and drams are also scarce; the squat c.f. dram is somehow rather attractive and very stable. There were no ratafia glasses.

All told the Balusters provide $5\frac{1}{2}$ per cent of our eighteenth-century glasses, i.e. of the Groups I to XII here dealt with. Group XIII includes many more nineteenth-century glasses than eighteenth-century ones; it is very numerous and of greater utility than cabinet value, and has therefore been disregarded in the computations of frequency which follow.

The Group contains twelve main stem formations, and therefore twelve Sections with varying numbers of Sub-sections.

SECTION I. *Glasses in which the Inverted Baluster is the Stem Feature (fifteen stem types)*

This covers the earliest stem formation, the Inverted Baluster, and the fifteen Subsections contain 33 per cent of the Group's glasses. This basic stem formation lasted throughout the Baluster period and considerably longer. It could be long, short, or squat, graceful or graceless, solid or with every sort of tear from a tiny bubble to an irregular cavity.

It could further be semi-hollow or truly hollow, and therefore very early in date, and there are single flint forms. It could come alone (Pl.61a) or with a basal knop, and these two Subsections are easily the commonest within the Group.

As a rule the bowl was a round funnel, deep and pointed for the earlier wines and goblets, short and wide for the dram glasses. At the beginning, too, the bowl would in wines have a solid base, even to the half-way line. Less commonly the bowl was a conical one, but this was not given the solidity of the r.f. except rather unexpectedly in a late cordial with a quite poor edition of the baluster (Pl.62e), and at least once in a companion wine. In each case the earliest foot had a narrow fold. The foot, however, looked, and was, inadequate, so the fold was soon thickened and widened; the improvement of a dome was introduced, and a 'beehive' foot was toyed with. Domed feet without a fold come late in the series, and the commonest Baluster glass is the goblet with the basal knop, round funnel bowl, and a folded foot.

SECTION 2. *Glasses in which a Wide Angular Knop is the Stem Feature (seven stem types)*

Hardly later than the inverted baluster and including 12 per cent of the Group's glasses was the attractive Wide Angular Knop which is the characteristic of this Section; it is often termed a cusped knop. It is an extremely dominant feature in its early career; on occasion it may be pleasantly elongated in a vertical direction (Pl.61b), and more rarely is a quadrilateral formation. It did, however, gradually diminish in size, but must never, for a Baluster title, be dominated by any other knopping. Glasses with this stem closely parallel those of Section 1, except that they are less frequent and provide fewer large goblets; the conical bowl is, however, relatively commoner here. As before, single flint glasses occur, and hereafter little more will be heard of these.

Of the seven Subsections that with the Wide Angular Knop at top and a Knop at base is not only the most characteristic but easily the commonest in the Section. It dates from 1690 at latest, has a conical or round funnel bowl and a folded or domed and folded foot almost exclusively. Goblets predominate. Other forms of stem are rather scarce and liable to have a smaller dominant knop.

ECTION 3. *Glasses in which a Drop Knop is the Stem Feature*
(*twelve stem types*)

Here a Drop Knop is the feature of the stem. Of the twelve
Subsections, containing 7 per cent of the Group's glasses, only
one can be regarded even as fairly frequent. That is the form
with a Drop Knop at top and a Knop at base. It comes with no
less than eight bowl forms, most frequently with the round
funnel. Again the foot is folded or domed and folded and goblets predominate. It dates from about 1700. A little later there
is a very knobbly stem for gins, wines, and goblets with Two
good Drop Knops in tandem, or one of them may approach a
true baluster. It is not common, and therefore rather a favourite with collectors, particularly as it always has a domed and
folded foot; the bowl is waisted. Other stem forms are decidedly scarce. There is a good variant of the Drop Knop in
the form of a cone, another favourite too seldom seen (Pl.
62d).

ECTION 4. *Glasses in whose Stems an Annulated Knop Appears*
(*thirteen stem types*)

This Section contains 15 per cent of the Group's glasses. The
Knop usually has three rings of approximately equal thickness;
but there may be five, seven, or even nine rings. The most frequent stem is that with the Annulated Knop at top and a Knop
at base. It can boast as many as nine bowl forms, chiefly cup,
round funnel, or a waisted type. The foot is folded or domed
and folded; also domed beneath a round funnel bowl. This
stem is fairly frequent, dating about 1710. Another form has
the Annulated Knop at the centre (Pl.62b), also with a base
Knop, and two more have an Annulated Knop over an Inverted Baluster with or without base knop. The bowl con-
tinues waisted or round funnel; the foot folded or domed and
folded. Such glasses date from 1715 and are scarce in the Baluster Group, though others of lighter character followed in some
strength and are allotted to Group III.

SECTION 5. *Glasses in which a Cushioned Knop is the Stem Featur* (*four stem types*)

Here the stem must contain a Cushioned Knop, and there ar four different types, between them accounting for but 2 pe cent of the Group's glasses. Almost always it is that with th Cushioned Knop at top and a base Knop which will be seer The bowl is a round funnel and the foot anything except plair Examples are rather early and decidedly infrequent, say from 1705.

SECTION 6. *Glasses in which a True Baluster is the Stem Featur* (*seventeen stem types*)

The stem forms of this Section, with 12 per cent of th Group's glasses, lean more towards the Balustroid glasse which follow than towards anything so far described. Ye there are a number of specimens substantial enough to ran fairly as Baluster glasses.

Throughout the Section the bowl is chiefly waisted or trumpet and the foot as in Section 5, but with a few plain fee also. The commonest stem has a Knop over a True Baluste with a Base Knop, and there may be collars beneath the bow There are stem forms with Short True Balusters in tander similar to those of the Drop Knop in Section 3. One of th rarest forms has the True Baluster only, and this is the verit able 'Kitcat' glass, with a trumpet bowl. The whole series ca be said to date from about 1715 and very rarely indeed is th baluster anything but solid.

SECTIONS 7 TO 10. *Glasses in which the Stem Feature is:*
   An Acorn Knop (*four stem types, Group frequency three per cent*)
   A Cylinder Knop (*two stem types, Group frequency two per cent*)
   An Ovoid Knop (*one stem type, Group frequency half per cent*)
   A Mushroom Knop (*one stem type, Group frequency one and a ha per cent*)

Each of these Sections has a stem with the particular specia

zed Knop noted as its feature. All are rare, and some excep-
ionally so. Section 7, with an Acorn Knop at top and Knop
.t base, usually employs a r.f. bowl and a folded foot. Speci-
nens are chiefly goblets, including hollow-stemmed and single
lint glasses; their date as a whole is 1710, and the last named
:arlier. Section 8 has a Knop and Collar over a Cylinder
Knop with either a Collar or a Knop (Pl.61c) or Twin Knops
or a small Dumb-bell at base. The bowl is a trumpet or a waisted
one; the foot chiefly domed and folded. It is rare, a collector's
oy, and it dates from about 1710. The Mushroom Knop is
nost elusive in a precise form (Pl.62a) and an Ovoid Knop
he rarest of all.

ECTION 11. *Glasses in which the Knopping is of Simple Form*
  (eight stem types)

This Section contains 10 per cent of the Group's glasses, the
nost frequently found stem type having an Angular (or Swel-
ng) Knop at centre and a Knop (or Twin Knops) at base. Its
oowl is a lipped r.f., a trumpet, or a waisted one. The foot is
nostly folded, though usually folded under a waisted bowl.
Cordials chiefly occur, most often with a Collar beneath the
oowl (Pl.61d). They are near-Balustroid glasses and are not
nfrequent; from 1715.

More like the familiar Baluster glass is a Simple stem form
vith a substantial Knop at the top. The bowl is again conical
or r.f., in that order of precedence. The foot is folded as a rule.
t is mostly dram glasses which are found, those with conical
oowls being deceptive or of true toastmaster type. Some coni-
al goblets seem to have the Knop in place of the original in-
rerted baluster; drams with a r.f. bowl look rather like cut-
lown wines, but undoubtedly many of the squat forms are in
original condition. The Subsection dates from 1700 and as a
vhole is not uncommon.

ECTION 12. *Glasses without a Stem (three types)*

This is a small Section forming but 2 per cent of the Group's
glasses, and it contains Dram glasses exclusively. The distinc-

tive form is that in which the stem and foot is replaced by a second bowl; these are the 'double-dram glasses', the bowls of different size, and sometimes different shape; the bridge between them also varies.

Another form has the stem and foot replaced by a solid cone to match the trumpet bowl above it. Specimens are rare; these come also in soda metal.

Lastly, the stem is replaced by a Heavy Knop. The bowl is conical or r.f. and the foot plain. The date of these last two Subsections may be said to be 'after 1700'. Some research and study is needed, and is also difficult, for material is scarce, before the dating is safe, and the intrusion of late or of continental specimens in the Cone-based Subsection is a possibility.

Group II

GLASSES WITH MOULDED PEDESTAL STEMS
(*c.* 1715 – *c.* 1765)

The Baluster glasses may have passed their best when George I came to his English throne, for with him came, so it is said, a glass with a stem utterly different from anything else we ever made. It was in fact a moulded pedestal, semi-hollow or with a long tear, and, strictly speaking, always inverted except occasionally in candlesticks and tapersticks. By virtue of a great variety of champagne and sweetmeat glasses, the Group contains at least 250 different glasses, but even so, it amounts to little more than 3 per cent of our eighteenth-century glasses.

The glasses form a distinctive and easily classified Group. The conventional commencing date limit of 1715 is adopted here, based on the circumstance that certain early glasses of the Group have the words *God Save King George* moulded in their four-sided pedestal stems, one word to a side. These are regarded as accession or Coronation glasses, which is the more understandable in that comparable glasses without the words have crowns or sceptres or the letters GR in the four shoulders. However, that does not prove that they were the first of the series, and there is some little evidence of earlier appearance. Plate 62f shows a smallish glass with slender, solid, four-sided stem in brown-tinted lead metal suggestive of late seventeenth-century date. Then there is Pl.62c, a magnificent giant goblet, the greenish metal and deep bowl of which both say 'early baluster', and another even larger and at least as early has been recorded.

Whatever the date, it can be assumed that the series started with the Four-sided stem. There are fifteen Sections in all: two with the Four-sided Pedestal, five with the Six-sided, seven with the Eight-sided, and one with a varying pedestal, mostly of debased form. For so small a Group this seems a formidable list, but half of them are extremely rare.

Except in the final Subsection the shoulders should be

noted. They are either rounded (sloping) or they are toppe
with bosses of pyramidal shape, here called diamonds, whic
as time went on might become quite rudimentary. The othe
point to notice, beginning with the Six-sided stems, is a for
of coil-collaring at the base of the stem; on occasion it may be
come a rounded band. Its importance lies in the fact that it
an indubitable sign of a latish date; a few early glasses have
bladed collar, but never a coil-collar. The converse is a litt
less definite, for there are late specimens referable to a New
castle house which are without the coil-collars, but not many
and such exceptions are easily recognized.

SECTIONS 1 AND 2. *Glasses with a Four-sided Pedestal Stem* (*five stem types and two stem types*)

Section 1 covers glasses with the Four-sided pedestal only (P
63b) and has a Group-frequency of nearly 6 per cent. Section
has in addition a superimposed knop and a frequency of 1
per cent. The bowl is in each case usually conical, or alte
natively a round funnel, thistle, or trumpet. The foot ap
pears always to be folded. Except for an odd goblet with th
conical bowl, only wines have been seen. A small bladed colla
at the base of the stem is possible, and it should not be con
fused with the coil-collar. The shoulders of both the Fou
sided stem types are usually rounded; in any case they ma
also carry, in the middle, small moulded crowns, diamonds, o
stars, apart from the devices already mentioned, whereas th
diamond-bosses are at the angles. It is these minor poin
which distinguish the other stem types.

SECTIONS 3 TO 7. *Glasses with a Six-sided Pedestal Stem* (*fou four, one, two, and one stem type*)

The Four-sided stems were succeeded by and probably partl
accompanied by a series of Six-sided stems, five Sections in al
The first, with 10 per cent of the Group's glasses, is the im
portant one, having the six-sided Pedestal by itself (Pl.63c
There are four Subsections, according to shoulder type an

basal collaring, but whether with rounded or diamond-topped shoulders, the uncollared stems carry the same bowls as before, with a few champagne types thrown in. A few bladed collars appear at the stem base, and stars on a very few shoulders. There is, however, a specimen or two with r.f. bowl and domed panel moulded foot, made in Newcastle, that by all ordinary experience should have the basal coil-collaring, but which do not. However, this feature only began with the Six-sided stems, and it did not develop until the Eight-sided pedestal arrived. The presence of a fair number of soda glasses with r.f. bowl, rounded shoulders, and folded foot is to be noted. A few of these have some lead in the metal, probably from the use of lead cullet, and an English origin is not impossible.

Other forms of the Six-sided pedestal have a superimposed Knop (four types of stem with a total frequency of 3 per cent), or perhaps a Teared Knop, a type of great rarity; further, there may be Two Knops superimposed (or Angular Knop and Knop) (Pl.64a), two types and a frequency of 0·6 per cent. More rarely still the Knop is Annulated, one type only with basal collaring and a frequency of 0·3 per cent. Sections 4–7 are therefore unlikely to concern anybody very much.

SECTIONS 8 TO 14. *Glasses with an Eight-sided Pedestal Stem* (*six, three, two, one, one, one, and one stem type*)

The picture changes completely when the Eight-sided stem is dealt with. The premier Section 8 has this stem all by itself (Pls 63d, 64c), with six Subsections; all told, it contains 62 per cent of the Group's glasses, but very unevenly distributed. When the pedestal is uncollared (Subsections A and C), there are twice as many drinking glasses of the early types as champagnes and sweetmeats, which are not so early. When the pedestal is collared (Pl.64b) (Subsections B and D), there are twenty champagnes and sweetmeats to every drinking glass, and these two Subsections are immensely stronger in numbers, containing 75 per cent of the Section's glasses. The other two Subsections are early, one with the Alternate Shoulders Diamond-topped and the other with them alternately Star and

Diamond-topped; there is no basal collaring and specimen
are hardly ever seen. To a large extent, therefore, this Section
includes collared champagnes and sweetmeats with a grea
variety of bowl and foot forms, and no little moulding, rib
bing, panel moulding, and honeycomb moulding. Such glasse
are unquestionably much later than the original eight-sided
pedestals, and must be given a *c.* 1750 date. Without the collar
ing, champagnes may be earlier; some, but certainly few, are o
Baluster age. Plate 62g shows a soda metal wine, named, placed
and dated; it is uncollared, as always in non-lead specimens.

Further Sections of the Eight-sided pedestal are much a
with the Six-sided, namely, a superimposed Knop (Section 9
found on a few uncollared wines and goblets (2 per cent)
one with the early lettering *God Save King Georg*; one gian
goblet and one in soda metal, and a couple of Newcastle r.f
glasses. These last are also found with coil-collaring, but no
often. There are no champagnes.

When the superimposed Knop has tears (Pl.64d) (Section
10), which now happens in 5 per cent of the Group's glasses
there is always basal collaring, and only champagnes and
sweetmeats occur. Once also the Teared Knop is beneath the
pedestal (Section 11), not above it, a fully panel moulded
champagne. Another rare form has a Knop with tears bot
above and below the pedestal (Section 12); this also is col
lared, and the one example seen had a waisted bowl and
domed and folded foot, both bowl and foot being ribbed
really as much a champagne as a goblet. There is a stem wit
an Annulated Knop over the Eight-sided pedestal (Section 13
with 1 per cent and another with a Knop, Angular Knop, an
Knop above it, rarer still (Section 14). Both these have basa
collaring and are late.

SECTION 15. *Glasses with a Pedestal of Debased Form* (*six ste*
types)

This final Section comprises 9 per cent of the Group's glasses
It divides into six Subsections. Three of these have somewha
Tapered Four-sided stems, characterized by tallish glasses wit

mall r.f. or waisted ogee bowls (Pls 65b, 20c), as well called in glasses as anything else. The latter are paralleled by similar oda glasses made and used in Normandy. Two equally rare ubsections contain champagnes with a Wrythen Pedestal, still ominally with eight sides, but the original form is lost (Pl. 5a). All these are well worth collecting if examples can be ound. A sixth Subsection has a variety of champagnes and weetmeats, but no wines or goblets, with more or less ribbed nd twisted stems, badly debased examples of the Pedestal tem, with, as is to be expected, the coil-collar (Pl.64e). They re poor stuff, the doomed remnants of a once fine array, but hey account for nearly all the 9 per cent of the Group's lasses.

t would be unfair not to mention the candlesticks and taper-ticks whereof the shaft was a moulded pedestal, usually ight-sided, but sometimes four-sided. Usually also it is nverted as in all the drinking-glasses, though one does not say o; but in the 'sticks' it is also found the right way up, with he shoulders just above the foot (Pl.65c). It is surprising that o wine tried this, bearing in mind the success of the true aluster. The shafts of the 'sticks' were embellished with nops, tears, and collars, generally speaking above and below n some symmetry. The nozzles were folded or flanged, often ibbed, and the foot a variable feature; a domed and terraced attern is attractive. Both nozzles and foot are found scalloped, hough the date of cutting may be uncertain. Of all these, per-aps the simple taperstick with a four-sided (true) pedestal is as ice as anything, devoid of the fussiness apt to overwhelm ore ambitious attempts.

Still, on the whole candlesticks and tapersticks were well esigned and well made. They are less popular now than ever hey were, and harder, far harder, to obtain. Too many have een used on the table, and too few put away in the cabinet.

Group III

GLASSES WITH BALUSTROID STEMS
(c. 1725 – c. 1760)

Of all our eighteenth-century stem types the Balustroid glasses displayed the greatest divergence in character. At first doubt fully distinguishable from the latest Balusters, they graduall deteriorated in style and somewhat in manufacture as thei market widened to include more and more people of less an less wealth. Their knopping dwindled until there might be bu a single small knop at the base of the stem; the metal worsened too, eventually acquiring a greyish, unflattering look. Ther was also quite an extensive range of poorly made but fairl well-knopped glasses in soda metal, primarily made for foreig markets; a characteristic was a high, square-domed foot. Eng lish collectors nearly always label them Dutch, for somebod in north-west Europe did make comparable glasses, but fo the most part not with exactly the same sort of knops. Ricar and de Artinano in their work *Vidrio*, of 1935, hit the nail o the head in illustrating four specimens Nos 281 and 284–6 a *Obras Inglese*, very ordinary export wares such as might hav been found in Spain; an unflattering but instructive choice.

By definition here, a Balustroid glass possesses a stem wit knopping of no particular emphasis, and a bowl base withou any particular solidity, except to some extent in the waiste bowl, and as was necessary in the trumpet. Glasses with mul tiple tears in the knopping are now excluded and placed i Group IV, the Light (Newcastle) Balusters. A certain numbe of glasses have, on paper, a claim for inclusion in more tha one Group, a claim to be resisted as far as possible on the scor of simplicity of classification, but a very few description covering Balustroid glasses will be found again in Groups and IV; the metal of these, however, and the thickness and pro portion of the stem are so different that separation is seldom a all difficult.

There are a few glasses with separately moulded bowls o

3NS form; otherwise the build-up of the Balustroids is nearly always 2NS; a very few are duplicated in every other respect by a 3WS build, a form of construction common in the Light Balusters. We may come to recognize more examples of the kind.

Moulded decoration was seldom used except on sweetmeats and champagnes, the latter not unduly scarce here. The styles noted on home market glasses and covering the whole bowl are ribbing, more or less vertical or else diagonal (wrythening) (Pl.68a), honeycomb moulding, and panel moulding. Affecting the lower part of the bowl there was plain gadrooning (Pl.68f), honeycomb moulding, and wide basal fluting. On export glasses the whole bowl might be closely wrythen or given 'beech-nut' moulding, a sort of elongated hobnail; or it might have vertical flutes rising into a honeycomb reaching to the rim.

The stems of export glasses are likely to be rib-twisted or to have a long tear, and further to be rather slender. This is probably an incomplete description of the export patterns, for lack of sufficient data, but it may be noted that the 'flutes into honeycomb' (Pl.65g) had earlier been limited to part-way moulding, with four rows of honeycombing only; this pattern was used on English air twists c. 1760 and internationally much earlier (Chapter IX). All the foregoing moulded export glasses are of 3NS build.

In addition, there was a little faint basal fluting on 2NS glasses for home use. It is a scarce decoration in the Balustroids, found only on the presumably later very simply knopped glasses. Such flutes are not too uncommon on air twist glasses, are more frequent on white twists, and still more so on plain-stemmed wines with ogee, ovoid, and r.f. bowls and on drams. One might conclude that this feature came in about 1755, rather late in the air twist series and before the white twists and smaller plain stem wines referred to were in full production, as they were in the 1760–70s.

There is small evidence of any set engraved decoration until towards the end of the series when a little 'flowered' work was put on the market. There are a few hop and barley ales in

Section 8 mentioned below (Pl.68b). But tall ale glasses are scarce in this Group, there may be one in every twenty-five specimens and few are engraved; short ales are much rarer for no apparent reason. After wines, the next commonest glass is a gin, with one example in eight, but not a fluted gin. Champagnes run parallel with the ales, with goblets twice as scarce say one in fifty glasses. It may be that some of the larger goblets find their way into the Baluster Group. Plate 69a is a case in point, where only the engraving indicates a Balustroid period glass.

Any other type of vessel is a prize, though not always a valuable one, partly because hardly anybody has real knowledge of relative scarcity. This argument applies even more strongly to coloured glasses. Green examples were made varying from a palish to a full emerald colour but not to a deep one. Some green Balustroid-like glasses are light in both tint and colour, with roemer-type bowls and high domed feet, and are presumed to have been made for the export market; they are placed in Group VIII. Others of lead metal approach or attain the full emerald tint and are true Balustroid glasses; they were knopped at top and centre, or at the centre only, and like so many green glasses, they had cup bowls. The styles are duplicated to some extent in Group IX.

The clear soda glass specimens have been mentioned. Cheaply made, they pass muster with the rest and search might produce a fair number. Apart from those obviously designed for the Continent, there were also good quality soda glasses of which Pl. 65d, e is an example. Privately etched 'A Halth to I—ms' and with a blackbird on reverse referring to the Old Claimant, it may indeed antedate the Balustroid period, and even recall the rising of 1715.

This third Group is divided here into eight Sections. A close approximation to the numerical strength of the Sections is given by the percentages. Glasses in 5, 6, and 7 do not qualify for a figure, but together total just about an odd 1 per cent. The Group includes rather over 9 per cent of our eighteenth century glasses.

SECTION 1. *Glasses in which an Inverted Baluster is the Stem Feature (twelve types of stem)*

The glasses of this Section amount to 21 per cent of the Group. Of the stem types, that with an Inverted Baluster and Base Knop is found twice as frequently as either the Baluster by itself or two formations with, respectively, a Knop, or an Angular (or Flat) Knop over the Baluster and Base Knop. All four are mainly composed of wines and gin glasses, which latter are particularly frequent with the last-named stem. The remaining stem types have different arrangements of knops and collars with the baluster and are decidedly scarce; several are extremely rare. One near-baluster stem is included here for the want of a better place. It has a strongly tapered and rather stout stem upon which there is inset a trumpet bowl with plain, folded (Pl.69c), or very occasionally a domed foot. It is a distinctive glass of good quality, some conclusively of 3NS guild.

Some of the heavier wines go back to the 1725–30 period; most are distinctly later. Stout champagnes occur, usually with collaring beneath the bowl, not a baluster feature (Pl.66a). There are a few low sweetmeats with dentated bowl-rims and and a radially grooved foot, while one extraordinary wine had a lipped ogee bowl and a domed and folded foot of three-cornered hat design. Three out of four of the feet are folded; except on champagnes, the dome or dome and fold is distinctly scarce.

Over the whole Section the waisted bowl is so firm a favourite that it outnumbers each of its nearest rivals, the r.f. and the trumpet by six to one. Its dominance would be still greater, but that a number of r.f. bowls have found their way on to the shoulder-knopped stem (Pl.66d), and also by reason of the inset trumpets already referred to. There is a mixture of champagne/sweetmeat bowls, including cup bowls, shared by some wines. Nothing else deserves mention.

A survey of the whole series suggests that the earlier glasses and the champagnes were glasses of quality, but that the remainder offered small variety of bowl or foot, and that the

waisted bowl so dominated that it must have been the glass of
the tavern and of the Age of Gin.

SECTION 2. *Glasses of the 'Kitcat' Type wherein an Inverted Baluster Usually Appears (eleven types of stem)*

These eleven Subsections comprise 10 per cent of the Group's
glasses and almost all contain an Inverted Baluster, placed at
top, centre, or bottom of the stem (Pl.66e), occasionally with
a small Basal Knop to provide variety. Rarely, the baluster becomes a ball knop, whether by accident or design it is impossible to say; such glasses are retained here as a variety, so great
is the resemblance in every other respect.

The glasses of this Section are well made of good metal and
are practically all tallish wines. The trumpet bowl predominates over the waisted by five to one, and besides these there is
only a rare ogee and a waisted r.f. which somebody will call a
thistle. The foot was as often folded as plain; the dome occurs
under a trumpet bowl once in every five glasses, and under a
waisted bowl once in two glasses. A domed and folded foot
has not been noted.

The stem may or may not have a tear, or it may be semi-
hollow. There remain a very few toasting or semi-toasting
stems. The build-up is almost always 2NS, but 3WS examples
exist. From other details it can be supposed that the series came
from a particular glasshouse, not impossibly in the north-
eastern area, and further that they were current in the late
1730s and earlier 1740s. There is hardly any engraving and
that not a set form (Pl.65h). There is no moulded decoration
at all. Glasses in soda metal have been found (Pl.65i).

SECTION 3. *Glasses in which a True Baluster is the Stem Feature (eleven types of stem)*

This is a comparatively small series of early glasses of quality
totalling but 5 per cent of the Group. They are directly related
to the true balusters of 1715; there are no degraded examples
and they include the veritable 'Kitcat' glass, a rare glass without knopping other than the baluster, and without collaring

Pl.67a). The two most familiar stem forms both have a True Baluster over a Basal Knop, one with a further Knop at top, the other without it. Another fairly frequent form has collaring beneath the bowl and directly over a Knop and the Baluster. A striking and quite scarce form has Tandem Balusters over a Basal Knop; others have a Baluster which is ridged at the base (Pl.67b) or, alternatively, set on a short Dumb-bell. These three are hard to find.

Practically all the glasses of this Section are wines; anything else but an occasional gin is exceptional. Some must be of Newcastle manufacture, and a specimen or two with an engraved rim band of the fruiting vine has been seen. No moulded decoration has been found, and no coloured or soda metal glasses. A fair amount of use was made of a neat collar or collars beneath the bowl – a happy device.

The commonest bowl is the trumpet, with the waisted form as a close runner-up; these two are used on ten out of every eleven glasses. The folded foot is nearly three times as common as the plain; the dome and the dome and fold each appear once in eight glasses. It may be noted that a quarter of the trumpet wines have a dome in the foot and one in six has the fold as well. Beneath the waisted bowl the dome seems to be absent and the dome and fold scarce. A domed and terraced foot is known and also a tripod foot beneath a tray-top tatchstand.

The build-up is 2NS in the simpler forms, otherwise 3NS, with an occasional 2WS or 4WS.

SECTION 4. *Glasses in whose Stem an Annulated Knop Appears* (*thirteen types of stem*)

Some glasses here were as early and as aristocratic as any in the preceding Section, but there was rather more deterioration in style. The thirteen stem types include 8 per cent of the Group's glasses, and most of them are scarce or rare. The usual form met with has the Annulated Knop over an Inverted Baluster with Knop at base (Pl.67c), and this stem is used on about one in every three glasses. The nearest rival has the Annulated

Knop at top and a Knop at base (Pl.67d), i.e. as the foregoin
less the Baluster. One in six glasses has this stem. One in eigl
has an Annulated Knop at top, a variable Knop at centre, an
a Knop at base. Two very rare forms have Two Annulate
Knops with or without a Basal Knop and one such specime
distinguished itself by possessing a honeycomb-moulded bow
and foot.

Two-thirds of the glasses at least are wines; champagnes fo
low in the ratio of 1 : 10. Goblets are at least twice as rare an
there is an occasional ale, gin, or *tazza*. A mead glass or lo
champagne is on record.

Very much the commonest bowl is the waisted, followed
a distance by the cup bowl and the trumpet, both 1 to 1
Further forms other than the variable champagnes are rar
One-third of the glasses have a folded foot and quite as man
have a dome and fold. Only about one in thirteen has a dom
alone. The dome and terrace may not be found, but it exists

Any sort of set engraving seems to be absent, and the litt
moulding found is almost entirely honeycombing and pan
moulding, and practically confined to champagnes and swee
meats. The rings in the knop occasionally mount to five, rarel
to seven. A tear is not much used in the stem and even so it
not conspicuous; there are some semi-hollow stems with th
cavity encroaching on the annulation, but there is reason
believe these are of seventeenth-century date and outside th
analysis. A few soda glasses have been seen with a waiste
bowl and a folded or domed and folded foot; one stem form
almost exclusively reserved for these, having a Knop an
Annulated Knop over an Inverted Baluster and base Kno
Coloured-green glasses exist.

SECTIONS 5, 6, 7. *Glasses in which a Cylinder Knop, Acorn Kno
or a Dumb-bell is the Stem Feature (two, three, and two types
stem)*

Between them, these three Sections amount to only 1 per ce
of the Group's glasses and of them that with the Acorn Kno
is the least rare; in one type the base of the bowl is protrude

nto acorn form. The Dumb-bell is included because in precise orm it is a striking formation, and even if the gaffer was think-ng of opposed balusters, the work deserves a place of its own. The Cylinder Knop (Pl.69c) seems even scarcer as a Balus-roid than as a Baluster, yet its value is considerably less, and his applies to the other two forms also. As far as it is possible o say from the very limited data available, the bowl is likely to e a waisted one and the foot folded. Wines only have been oted.

ECTION 8. *Glasses in which the Stem has Simple Knopping (thirty-three types of stem)*

On account of its numerical strength, 55 per cent of the Group, this Section is here subdivided, for ease of reference nly, according to the number of Knop formations in the tem, those with the greatest number of knops being on the vhole the earliest as well as the scarcest; in all there are four ategories.

Over the whole Section the r.f. bowl has a preponderance ver the waisted, ogee, and trumpet forms in the ratio 5 : 29 : 17 : 6, which only leaves thirteen glasses in a hundred ith any other sort of bowl, whereof the champagne types bsorb 3 per cent. But these ratios by no means hold within ne thirty-three Subsections. The feet are 75 per cent folded, 2½ per cent plain, 6 per cent domed and folded, and 5½ per ent domed, with 1 per cent for special forms. About one bowl 1 70 is of soda metal, one in 90 has faint basal flutes and the ame applies to flutes rising into a honeycomb, an export pat-ern in light lead metal. One in 150 may be wholly honeycomb noulded or deceptive. Wide basal fluting, ladder and beech-ut moulding are so rare as hardly to be assessable. A toast-aaster bowl occurs about once in every 300 glasses.

Glasses with four or more Knop Formations. Here there are six tem formations, providing 3 per cent of the Group and 5½ er cent of the Section, all having a combination of knops, nnular knops, and once a collar; one outstanding form has up to nine bobbin knops. This last includes a rare cordial with stepped bowl and domed foot; there are also patchstands and small *tazze* with as few as two bobbin knops. The only other vessel forms are wines and gins; except for a soda wine with conical bowl and the 'Blackbird' glass of Pl.65d, all have waisted one, and every one has a folded foot. They are rather an undistinguished lot for all their scarcity. The least uncommon stem has a Knop and Collar at top with Knops at centre and base. No moulding has been noted.

Glasses with three Knop Formations. In this portion of the Section examples are more frequent, with seven stem forms totalling 10 per cent of the Group and 19 per cent of the Section. Two of these are fairly common. One has a Semi-hollow stem with Knop at top, Bladed Knop at centre, and Knop at base. An r.f. ale with this stem and occasionally with hop and barley engraving is a pleasant glass (Pl.68b), as is a saucer-topped r.f. wine. Three out of four glasses with this stem have the r.f. bowl and every one has a folded foot. The waisted bowl is outnumbered by thirty to one.

The other frequent form has a solid stem with only a very occasional tear, with Knops at top, centre, and base. Here the waisted bowl outnumbers the r.f. and ogee in the proportion of 3 : 2 : 1, and nine out of ten glasses have a folded foot. A goblet with r.f. bowl and folded foot is good, as is an ogee wine with domed and folded foot. The other stem formations are very rarely seen; a good one has a Knop and Collar at top and a base Knop, a single specimen only on record with trumpet bowl and folded foot.

The proportion of the bowl forms is r.f. 48 per cent, waisted 30 per cent, ogee 15 per cent, other forms 7 per cent. About 90 per cent of the feet are folded; the remainder are equally divided into the plain and the domed and folded. Not one domed by itself has been recorded. Again there is no moulding.

Glasses with two Knop Formations. Rather more numerous, there are twelve stem forms in this category giving us 16 per cent of the Group and 27½ per cent of the Section. One is very

ommon, having a Knop or Shoulder Knop at top and a Knop
t base (Pl.66d). It comprises about half the glasses in this
ortion of the Section, and the vast majority will have either
n r.f. or a waisted bowl and folded foot; the r.f. form just out-
umbers the other by virtue of its use for export glasses. These
ave rather slender stems, often rib-twisted, and moulded
owls, all-over close wrythening, flutes rising into honeycomb
Pl.65f), and beech-nut moulding. Home glasses occasionally
ave gadrooned bowls. Only the above stem formation con-
ains any appreciable number of gin glasses; there is one for
very two wines.

The next commonest stem includes a quarter of the glasses
n this category. It has a Knop or Shoulder Knop at top and a
Knop at centre. Practically all the glasses are wines, mostly
vith the r.f. bowl, and with a folded foot. A good variety has
his bowl with strong honeycomb moulding, sometimes called
eticulation, throughout.

The only other stem form which is not quite rare has Knops
t centre and at base. Wines predominate and a cordial occurs.
'he r.f. and the waisted bowl share the honours; the folded
oot is usual, but all the usual types are found. A good glass is
cupped goblet with panel-moulded bowl and foot, and a
arity is a simple r.f. wine with wide basal flutes. There is both
bucket and a waisted bowl in soda metal. No other mould-
ng than that mentioned has been noted on this stem form.
sual forms, seldom seen, have the stem Trisected by Two
Knops or, better, by two Swelling Knops. A rarity has a
welling Knop at centre and an Angular Knop near the base.

Glasses with a single Knop Formation. This is very much the
rongest portion, which accounts for 26 per cent of the Group
nd 48 per cent of the Section. There are eight stem formations,
hereof three comprise just over four-fifths of this last cate-
ory. As many as thirteen different types of vessel are re-
orded. Of these the ratafia, cordial and semi-cordial, and
astmaster glass (Pl.68e) are extremely rare. Gins and ales
llow wines, in the proportion of 12 : 2 : 1, with champagnes
nd goblets well behind. The r.f. is perhaps the favourite bowl,

closely followed by the waisted and the ogee; the ovoid, th
pan-topped, and the trumpet each appear about once in ever
twenty glasses, the remainder being occasional only. Two ou
of every three feet are folded, and one in five is plain, one i
fifteen is domed and one in eighteen is domed and folded, an
a very few odd forms make up the balance.

Of the stem forms, that with a Knop or Angular Knop a
the centre accounts for 31 per cent of the category. Cham
pagnes are not too rare here, with one in seven. Indeed, the al
and goblet, one in fourteen and one in twenty-five respectively
can both be called scarce, and anything else is rare, no gin o
cordial of any sort being on record, though a toastmaster i
there. On this stem the ogee bowl is favourite – four times a
numerous as the waisted, ovoid, or r.f. pattern. One in ever
two feet is folded, one in every three is plain. A foot with
dome or dome and fold follows the champagne, and togethe
they appear about once in six glasses. One rarity is a dram wit
faint basal flutes and a saw-toothed firing foot; there is a ver
scarce wrythen three-piece r.f. wine (Pl.68a), and even th
champagnes – one in thirteen – are seldom moulded.

Another stem, which is nearly as frequent, has a Basal Knop
often rather a trivial one and not as Pl.68c. There are eigh
types of drinking-glass and a rare handled jelly on a tall sten
Wines are at least ten times as frequent as any other kind. Th
waisted bowl is twice as common as the r.f. and three times a
common as the trumpet type. The ogee and ovoid come nex
and anything else is quite out of the ordinary. The folded foo
is to be seen on two out of every three glasses, and the plai
foot only on one in seven. Curiously, here the domed an
folded foot is little scarcer than the plain one and twice a
common as the domed. It appears on waisted gins and sma
wines. A rarity is a domed and terraced foot on a giant gobl
with ovoid bowl, and another exceptional glass is a ta
jelly glass with a pair of 'B' handles.

The third most frequent stem here has a Knop at the top
it may be slightly shouldered, and it appears on 18 per cent c
the glasses. There are some gins which with the wines accoun
for four out of every five glasses. Ales make up most of th

balance. There are a very few low sweetmeats with radially grooved feet, and both a cordial and a toastmaster glass is on record (Pl.68e). On this stem the r.f. bowl is as easily supreme as is the ogee on the centre knopped stem and the waisted bowl on the basal-knopped stem. Otherwise only the waisted form, with one glass in four, is likely to be seen more than once in a hundred glasses. The folded foot is used on nine out of every ten glasses. Any sort of moulding is of great rarity.

Of the other stem forms, that with a Swelling Knop at centre includes about 8 per cent of the glasses here; practically all are wines, and four out of five will have ogee bowls and folded feet.

There is a definite stem form with a Knop near the base, usually carrying a waisted bowl and folded foot, and another has a Bladed Knop at the top; this will almost certainly have the r.f. bowl and folded foot. Rarest of all is a stem with a Half-Knop immediately beneath the bowl. The same form appears in air twists and in glasses with a fine incised twist, all on styles seemingly from the same glasshouse.

This concludes the survey of the Balustroid glasses. They have been given a good deal of attention and their forms statistically dealt with at some length because they have not received from collectors the consideration which is their due. They do indeed link types as far apart as the early hollow-stemmed balusters of, say, 1690, and the white twist glasses as late as 1775–80, with their small ogee bowls and 'flowered' engraving. The earlier transition Balustroids have indeed often been bought and sold as Balusters, not necessarily at undue cost, and excusably, for it is impossible to draw a secure dividing line. The glasses of Section 2 have counterparts in glasses with the composite air twist *plus* plain stems of Group v, while the more simply knopped stems can be matched in the twist glasses equally for bowl, foot, and even the decorative engraving, a considerable help when it comes to assessing dates.

Group IV

THE LIGHT (NEWCASTLE) BALUSTER GLASSES
(*c*. 1735 – *c*. 1765)

The term Light Baluster was coined to describe certain rathe
tall glasses with relatively slender stems having a series o
knops of different kinds, none of them especially dominant
Such glasses are now known to have been made on Tyneside
Very many are found with Dutch engraving, and apparentl
for that reason some authors regarded them as possibly, o
actually, continental. They are still poorly represented in th
majority of collections, but that would be inevitable in an
case, for their name is not legion.

They are distinguishable by their elegant form, carefu
manufacture, and also by their metal. This is thinner than i
Balusters and Balustroids. It is clearer, which is to say mor
free of tints, and it has brilliance without depth; once in mind
it is quite distinctive. Striations in the bowl are not consider
able. The feet have less striation than before and tend to b
flatter, usually without any fold, and are consequently liable t
be chipped. For convenience, and departing to no appreciabl
extent from the fact, all Light Balusters or Balustroids wit
multiple tears are now included in this Group.

Not all glasses referable to the Group necessarily hav
elaborate knopping. On the contrary, a certain number have
very simple stem formation and correspond exactly in descrip
tion with glasses in Groups I and III, although their aspect i
very different. Complicated knopping does not necessaril
indicate weight, though it may mean height.

The build-up varies. The simpler forms are 2NS, but her
and there a similar 3NS form appears. Of the elaratel
knopped Light Balusters, some are 2NS, and these as a whol
may be earlier in date than the rest. Most are unquestionabl
of 3WS and 4WS build, but even these are sometimes duplicate
by a 2NS form. Just how they were made probably depende
on the individual gaffer. A few glasses exist in soda metal,

ittle less well made as a rule, but a definite echo of their lead cousins.

Analysis of the more complicated stem formations does present difficulties, partly because a small knop may be imprecise, and partly because the stem can be dissected and 'read' in more than one way. Some familiarity with actual specimens, and study of the illustrations provided (Pls 69–74) will help to show how the elaborate stems have been analysed.

The dating is not satisfactorily settled. There are certainly Balusters in Newcastle style and metal, whether late or not-so-late it is difficult to say. But those were not Light Balusters and they are not included here. There is little to prove that any conventional Light Baluster was made before the 1730s, despite the existence of some quite famous specimens with signature and date. For most specimens a mid-eighteenth-century date is all that caution will permit.

The range of vessel type is much restricted. As always, wines are easily supreme; but here the larger ones merge into the goblet class to the extent that some have a deep bowl which is disproportionate in a wine, or alternatively insufficient height to make it a graceful goblet. On the other hand, some tall and a few extremely tall goblets are to be found. Otherwise there is hardly anything, even champagnes of undoubted Newcastle origin being scarce. Bowl forms are almost as unenterprising. Their incidence in the various Sections varies, but the round funnel is the most popular form; not infrequently it tends to be slightly lipped, a distinctive Newcastle touch. It outnumbers the waisted bowl by three to two or better, and the trumpet by five to one. Other forms, including such few pan types as occur and some definitely lipped round funnels, are together about as frequent as the champagnes. Hardly any bowls are of small capacity, though large ones are frequent.

As to the feet, the ratio is something like ten plain, two folded, two domed, and one domed and folded; here again the incidence varies in the different Sections. A champagne with a domed and terraced foot is known. Taking it all round, the Newcastle glasshouses were not inclined to experiment with anything but the stem; in particular, they made great use of

multiple tears in both knops and balusters, a device which
wonderfully brightened up the glass.

It seems that the bowl of the Light Baluster glass was almost
sacred to the engraver, for instances of moulding are practically confined to glasses of the pan-bowl champagne type.
Incidentally, it seems to have been a maxim throughout the
eighteenth century to avoid engraving a champagne or sweetmeat, although full liberty of moulded design was accorded.
To speak of the engraving found on wines and goblets would
be to treat of Commemorative and Social glasses once more.
Beilby used them too, indeed his best work is found thereon,
otherwise the great majority of the decorative work was
Dutch, and, one might fairly say, all the finest work.

The key to understanding of the Light Balusters is an appreciation of their extraordinary variety of stem, and also their
scarcity. It might be an over-statement to say that one
eighteenth-century drinking glass in forty is a Light Baluster,
that is roughly the list figure, but were a complete census possible, a ratio of 1 in 60 might easily be approached. As to
variety, the Sections into which the Group is divided contain
as many as 109 Subsections, that is, distinctive stem formations, and it cannot be supposed that the tally is complete. Yet
more than half of these Subsections are represented by a single
glass, and the most plentiful type, itself far in front of anything
else in the Group, has turned up about once in every 500
eighteenth-century glasses.

These Newcastle Balusters are here divided into nine Sections, which together provide less than 3 per cent of our
eighteenth-century glasses. One Section includes nearly half
the glasses of the Group, another nearly a quarter; of three
others, none exceeds 10 per cent, and the remainder have very
poor representation indeed.

SECTION 1. *Glasses in which the Knopping is Based on the Inverted Baluster (twenty-nine types of stem)*

The strength of the Section amounts to 47 per cent of the Group's glasses. It is here that the commonest stem form of the Group is found, a well-balanced graceful affair with an Angular Knop and Knop over an Inverted Baluster (with tears) and a Base Knop (Pl.71a). It would be right to say that most specimens are engraved. Here the r.f. bowl is not so far ahead of the waisted (four to three), but there is little else. There is, unusually, one domed and folded foot for every dozen plain ones, though the dome by itself is twice as scarce.

SECTION 2. *Glasses in whose Stems an Annulated Knop Appears (fourteen types of stem)*

This Section is not numerous (10 per cent) and of its fourteen Subsections the majority are rare. That most often seen has an Annulated Knop at top over an Inverted Baluster and Base Knop, and it prefers a waisted bowl and a folded foot, which is unusual (Pl.71b). Elsewhere there are a number of domed feet so that, over the whole Section, the plain foot is only just in a majority.

SECTION 3. *Glasses in which the Knopping is Based on a True Baluster (thirteen types of stem)*

Every one of the Subsections is scarce, and together they account for only 7 per cent of the Section's glasses. It may be that they came early in the series, for domed feet are as common as plain ones, and the folded as often found as the domed and folded, so plain feet are in a minority. A trumpet bowl might have been expected, but it is quite rare and even the waisted bowl is scarce. Most are round funnels, some lipped.

SECTION 4. *Glasses in whose Stems a Cushioned Knop Appears (fourteen types of stem)*

Of the fourteen Subsections only four are without multiple tears. With a 9 per cent total, specimens are just about as scarce as those in the last Section and the foot representation is repeated. Hardly a goblet is to be found, and as yet not a single champagne. The waisted bowl is here three times as numerous as the r.f. Plate 72a shows an example with a trumpet bowl.

SECTION 5. *Glasses in whose Stems a Mushroom Knop Appears* (*one type of stem*)

There is but a single representative of this Section, but rather a charming glass with a trumpet bowl (Pl.72b). It may be found once in every 4,000 of our eighteenth-century glasses.

SECTION 6. *Glasses in whose Stems a Dumb-bell is the Stem Feature* (*five types of stem*)

The Dumb-bell is not always a very pronounced feature. Its five stem types add up to but 3 per cent of the glasses of the Group, with wines and a single goblet only; the r.f. bowl, occasionally lipped, is almost universal and the same applies to the plain foot.

SECTION 7. *Glasses in which an Acorn Knop is the Stem Feature* (*three types of stem*)

This Section provides a bare 1 per cent of the Group's glasses and its distinguishing Acorn is decidedly rarer than in the Baluster Group, so specimens are hard to find, and insufficient to denote preferences as to bowl and foot.

SECTION 8. *Glasses in which the Knopping is of Simple Form* (*twenty-nine types of stem*)

The total of the twenty-nine Subsections is 23 per cent of the Group. No particular stem type stands out in point of numbers, and half of them are represented by a single specimen. The knopping varies from types with a single knop only to others with as many as six or seven formations (Pl.73d). The r.f. bowl has a long lead; domed feet are relatively frequent and the folded foot is not far behind. A fair number of soda metal glasses occur here.

SECTION 9. *Glasses in which the Stem is Replaced by Knopping
(one type of stem)*

And lastly this Section, which contains a solitary glass which
has knopping in lieu of stem, in this case a trumpet gin (Pl.
73c), a vessel form found nowhere else in the Group, and a
very happy design.

That completes the survey, leaving an impression of a
Group with a great diversity of stem formations, many of
ingenuity and beauty, and almost all of dignity. The appearance
of so much fine engraving, both wheel and diamond-point
work has perhaps tended to obscure the grace of the glasses
themselves. The same glasshouses produced equally fine specimens with the Composite, and also the various Interior Twist
Stems, readily recognizable, as is their contribution to the
Plain Stem Group. But these last, I think, gave their gaffers too
little scope, and examples are not particularly frequent.

Group V

GLASSES WITH COMPOSITE STEMS
(*c.* 1745 – *c.* 1775)

The Group is not numerous and at present can be divided
into but six Sections. Nine out of ten of the glasses belong to
one or other of the first two, combining an air twist with a
plain section of stem. The resemblance to the 'Kitcat' Balustroids will be noted. The third Section includes nearly nine-
tenths of the balance, leaving hardly more than 1 per cent for
the three remaining Sections. Indeed, within the whole Group
not more than three stem types can be called anything but
scarce, and even of the first two Sections comprising thirty-
four distinct stems, no less than twenty-six must be accounted
rare or very rare.

The general appearance of the Group, besides the preponderance of the air twist *cum* plain stem, is one of roughly
seventy wines to fourteen goblets, six ales, two champagnes,
and a single cordial. There are no other types of drinking glass
on the record. The bowl range is small, mainly waisted, trumpet, or r.f. The feet are almost always plain or domed. The
quality of the glasses is high, most bearing the unmistakable
stamp of Newcastle origin. The designs are graceful, and no
more intriguing and aristocratic Group offers itself for specialization. There are no moulded forms and relatively little engraving except of commemorative or social import. A single
specimen in soda metal has been noted.

The subdivision is as under, the whole Group providing
only 1½ per cent of our eighteenth-century glasses.

SECTION 1. *Glasses with a Plain Section of Stem over an Air Twist
Section (fifteen types of stem)*

This Section includes 24 per cent of the glasses of the Group,
and the fifteen stem types divide into three categories, a
medium or short plain section over an air-spiralled baluster or
shouldered section; a knop without or more usually with tears

over a long air twist section (Pl.75b); and a more specialized plain section (an annulated knop for instance) over a long air twist.

Rarely is the air twist other than the multiple spiral type, and only one Subsection is at all frequent. This has a Short Plain section over a Long Inverted Baluster or Shouldered section with a multiple spiral air twist (Pl.75a). By definition here, the plain section must be over half-an-inch in length to distinguish it from a normal three-piece air twist glass with a shouldered M.S.A.T. stem; that is, the neck must be long enough to be regarded as a section. Most specimens are of 3ws build; roughly half as many seem to be 2NS, including one in soda metal. But for the foregoing stem the Section would indeed be poorly represented in most collections.

The bowl is a trumpet on half the glasses and waisted on a quarter of them. The remainder are waisted buckets, r.f., or waisted r.f. Three out of four feet are plain and the rest domed. No folded or domed and folded specimen has been noted, and only wines, goblets, ales, champagnes, and cordials in the proportions 90 : 20 : 6 : 5 : 1.

SECTION 2. *Glasses with an Air Twist Section of Stem over a Plain Section (nineteen types of stem)*

This contains 66 per cent of the glasses of the Group. The expectation is roughly 75 per cent wines, 16 per cent goblets, 5 per cent ales, and the balance consists of champagnes with an odd cordial or two. The waisted, trumpet, r.f., and other bowls occur in the ratio 5 : 3 : 2 : 1. Seven feet are plain to every five domed; a folded foot appears once, on a champagne, and a dome and fold twice, in every hundred glasses. The only dome and fold recorded within the whole Group, other than on a champagne, appears here.

Half the Subsections have a long (unknopped) section of multiple air spiral stem set into a basal Knop of some sort, with or without tears and collars, or into a squat I.B. similarly. In one case the upper Long Air Twist section is Shouldered; in another it is a M.S.A.T. Dumb-bell; both are very rare. The remainder have a medium M.S.A.T. section (Pl.75) or else a short knopped or unknopped M.S.A.T. section over a balancing plain section usually composed of an Inverted Baluster with or without knop and tears. In most cases the build is 3ws. It must suffice to mention a few only.

The commonest, which includes a third of the Section's glasses, has a Long M.S.A.T. section set into a squat I.B. with tears; an ale or two and a cordial occur; the favourite bowl is a waisted one and the foot nearly as often domed as plain. A very near relation has a base knop in addition, but is much less frequent, 1 to 4; it has a trumpet bowl as often as a waisted one, and a few domed feet appear. A more attractive and slightly commoner stem than the last has the Long M.S.A.T. section let into Triple or Quadruple collars over a Basal Knop with tears (Pl.75c); 12 per cent of the glasses of the Section are like this. The bowl is more often a trumpet than a waisted one, and the foot is apparently always domed. No other stem form reaches a 10 per cent figure; ten forms score less than 1 per cent and they include some delightful specimens.

One simple glass is as rare as any, a plain-footed trumpet wine with a Short M.S.A.T. section on a Long Inverted Baluster with tears; the alternative form to that mentioned above as the commonest of the Section. One 4ws glass is not too infrequent, with a M.S.A.T. Dumb-bell on an Inverted Baluster and base Knop, both in wine and goblet size, and a fairly obvious Newcastle production.

SECTION 3. *Glasses with a Plain Section of Stem over an Opaque White Twist Section (six types of stem)*

This small Section has a 9 per cent Group frequency. Of its six Subsections, five have a knop or knops of some sort over a Long Opaque White Twist section; the sixth has a Dumb-bell in lieu of the knop. Only wines and goblets have been seen, ratio 3 : 1. The r.f. bowl and the plain foot (Pl.76c, d) outnumber the bell and the domed foot by 4 to 1. No other bowl or foot forms are on the record. Such engraving as is to be found is likely to be good Dutch work of social or commemorative import.

The least rare of the stem formations has a Knop with tears over a Long Opaque White Twist Section (Pl.76c). Both single and double series twists are available; no particular twist seems to have been chosen. As rare as any is a stem with Angular Knop and Knop set on a Shouldered section with a single spiral gauze; it is given a bell bowl and a domed foot. A second favourite has a Plain Dumb-bell over a Shouldered double series Opaque White Twist with Base Knop, bowl r.f. and foot plain. It needs careful manufacture to equal the other in attraction. All the glasses of this Section may be of Newcastle origin and they are 3, 4, or 5ws.

SECTION 4. *Glasses with an Opaque White Twist Section of Stem over a Plain Section (one type of stem)*

So far this Section can boast of a single glass only, a superb type, but once seen. It is a goblet with ovoid bowl, domed foot, and a Medium section with Multiple Opaque White Spirals set into a Medium Baluster with tears (Pl.74c).

SECTION 5. *Glasses with a Plain, an Air Twist, and an Opaque White Twist Section of Stem (one type of stem)*

Again, but one stem formation has been noted, a Knop with Multiple Air Spirals (no tears) and Plain Annulated Knop over a long double series Opaque White Twist section Knopped at top and base (long Dumb-bell), as Pl.76d, but spirals in upper Knop. With a r.f. bowl and plain foot it is a fine Newcastle goblet of 5ws build.

SECTION 6. *Glasses with a Mixed Twist and a Plain Section of Stem (one type of stem)*

The one Subsection has a stem with a Long section with Single Series Opaque White Corkscrew and a Spiral Air Gauze set into a squat Inverted Baluster, or into a base Knop. It is another goblet with waisted r.f. bowl and domed foot. Two or three specimens have been seen; build 4ws.

To sum up, there are now fully ninety varieties in this small Group, a complete series of which would be something hardly achievable. It would be difficult to point to a single ungraceful pattern, and the worst that can be said of a rewarding Group is that just occasionally one of the commoner Section 1 and 2 glasses falls short of constructional perfection. Some may comment that certain glasses in Group II, the Moulded Pedestal Stems, ought logically to be called Composite Stem glasses. That is the case, but to be logical would also raise an unnecessary inconvenience, and there is just this excuse, that the pedestal stem always forms so great a proportion of the stem that any attendant knops may be regarded as ancillary.

Group VI

GLASSES WITH PLAIN STRAIGHT STEMS
(*c.* 1740 – *c.* 1775)

Numerically this Group is among the largest. Figures on record credit it with 23 per cent of our eighteenth-century drinking glasses, and the figure does not flatter. It is an easy Group to classify, obviously in Sections according to bowl form. There are seventeen of these, the trumpet dominating with 40 per cent, the waisted, ogee, r.f., and ovoid forms absorbing another 56 per cent fairly equally, and in that order. That leaves little for the other twelve forms, of which the lipped bucket, waisted bucket, waisted ogee, and two duplex forms are indeed rarities, occurring, it seems, no more than once in every couple of thousand glasses.

Perhaps the inescapable term 'plain' is a deterrent, or the thought that as some of its glasses are abundant and therefore cheap, the Group is hardly worthy of attention. There is a fallacy there. Certainly most plain-stemmed glasses are cheap, but only a few of them are plentiful. Taking a figure of 2 per cent as a definition of 'plentiful', only ten forms would qualify; at 4 per cent only six forms. A stem tear is taken here as a factor of differentiation. Naturally there are badly made glasses, poorly proportioned, or of indifferent metal; they had to be to sell to the public for which they were intended. On the other hand, some may think that a well-designed and faultlessly made trumpet goblet is hardly surpassed in artistic value by any other glass, and a specialist could form a considerable collection without departing from this one bowl and the plain stem. Apart from this, there are enough scarce and rare varieties to keep any collector who wants them all on the *qui vive* for years and years, and good-looking glasses too.

The plain stem can vary in thickness, when it may be a toasting stem of as little as one-eighth of an inch in diameter, or up to a quarter of an inch when one may conveniently call it a semi-toasting stem. The former are rare in lead glass

(Pl.77e), and will be no earlier than 1740 in date, but are fairly plentiful in soda metal when they get given a late seventeenth-century date and a Dutch origin. Two scarce stem variations preclude any such term as 'cylindrical' in the Group title. One is something like a sausage in form, swollen in the middle and gently tapering above and below. The other is a pedestal type, thickish at the base, and it is provided with collars both at top and bottom (Pl.78f). It is an Irish pattern less often found plain than engraved, and it is a pretty glass.

Another variable factor which has no particular importance is a tear or cavity in the stem. Presuming that this started as a neat air-bead to mark the bowl base, it may be found in any symmetrical or asymmetrical shape, to the extent that for cheapness a stem might have an irregular cavity running from top to bottom. It saved weight of metal and was doubtless common and more pronounced after the Excise Act of 1745–6. But not when the stem carried certain types of bowl. There were just no rules. In glasses with a waisted bowl, the tear is practically confined to the bowl base. With the much commoner trumpet bowl, the tear or cavity is very variable and decidedly more frequent over a folded foot than a plain one. With any other bowl the tear is hardly to be found, foot-fold or no foot-fold. Try for instance to find an ogee wine with a tear, or anything but a solid stemmed r.f. wine with a folded foot. There are a very few r.f. bowl Jacobite glasses with a tear, but they have no foot-fold.

The vast majority of glasses in the Group are of two-piece make (2NS), and this includes a number with an ogee, ovoid, or round-funnel bowl, each of which may have moulded basal faint fluting. This form of decoration must be of extreme rarity on trumpet or waisted bowls and may not appear on any other than the three mentioned above. It seems never to occur in conjunction with a domed or a domed and folded foot; but on an ovoid dram with oversewn foot it is unaccountably in a very great majority and on some other drams with the stated bowls it is a modest favourite.

Other forms of moulded decoration are rather rare. They include wrythen ribbing, honeycomb moulding at base or all over (Pl.78d), and panel moulding (Pl.77c), and these patterns will be found only on 3NS glasses; the same applies to an ale with basal gadrooning (Pl.78e), mid eighteenth, not seventeenth century. There are, however, a few three-piece glasses with the faint basal fluting, an ogee form with a personality of its own as in Pl.82h. All types of vessel occur except champagnes and sweetmeats; ratafia and gin glasses are uncommon and so are large glasses with a waisted bowl. Toastmaster glasses are extremely rare.

On the other hand, and understandably on a stem type made for the people, dram glasses are rather common, and these provide some interesting foot forms, such as the flanged firing foot, found under a trumpet bowl but hardly otherwise, or with anything but a plain stem. There is the oversewn (Pl.78a) and the overstrung (Pl.60b) type of foot, the former the commoner, one in 150 glasses, the latter perhaps one in 1,000; both demand the ovoid bowl. In these, threads or strings of glass were trailed as radii from the centre of the foot over the rim to disappear beneath. There is also a substantial foot with moulded concentric rings, conveniently called a terraced foot; this again is practically confined to ogee and ovoid bowl drams.

Taken over the whole Group, the distribution of the plain, the folded, the domed, and the domed and folded foot is roughly 100 : 150 : 6 : 5, with firing feet equal to the two domed patterns added together, less than 4 per cent of the whole Group. The dome alone will be difficult to find under an ogee, and also a dome or dome and fold under an ovoid bowl. There is an occasional firing foot under a wine, and a solid conical foot which comes with a trumpet bowl, and also with a faceted stem, but it is uncommon. Deceptive bowls are widely spread but decidedly scarce.

Quite a number of the short bowl glasses, cup, ogee, ovoid, r.f. cup and saucer-topped bowls, appear in sundry shades of green metal, preferably a bright emerald, which may pale or deepen, or approach a blue. Some of these colours appear in soda metal, and the prevalence of the cup and cup-topped bowl suggests a lingering continental tradition; it seems clear that a good many of our green glasses were made for the export markets.

Soda metal glasses are also to be found, particularly with a trumpet or waisted bowl. Most are pretty crude and the origin may be uncertain, but the nearer the glasses approach a standard English form the more likely are they to have been made here. A few are to be found with an English name and date (Pl.78g), and perhaps also place; I have found such glasses in the eastern counties, and suspect they drifted south from the Newcastle–Sunderland area. Besides these, there are tall and distinctive fine-quality Newcastle glasses on a relatively slender stem (Pl.77b), mostly with trumpet bowls and some with delightful border engraving, comparable in delicacy to that found on the very best air twist glasses. They were doubtless contemporary.

Engraved decoration of set purpose is common only on wines with ogee, ovoid, or r.f. bowls, and as a rule it is rather perfunctory 'flowered' work, though somehow attractive. An interesting range of subjects is to be found, with the fruiting vine and much-discussed bird among maybe a score of motifs. The hop and barley naturally appear on tall glasses, which are accordingly called ales or short ales, and only rarely on wine-glasses, which asked for and were given the vine pattern. Waisted bowls get little decoration; it is in fact an awkward shape, lending itself ill to anything but border decoration.

Nothing could be simpler than the classification. With its 23 per cent of our eighteenth-century glasses the Group divides into seventeen Sections according to bowl form.

SECTION I. *Glasses with a Bucket Bowl*

These are not common, amounting to but 1½ per cent of the Group, but they are attractive. The bowl tends towards an ogee shape, particularly in goblets, which are relatively common. Cordials are rare, though a number exist with a heroic portrait bust of King William III, evidence of a 1750 date. Of the usual four foot forms, the dome is the rarest; specialized feet are not on record, and accordingly one finds no dram glasses.

SECTIONS 2 TO 4. *Glasses with a Modified or a Duplex Form of the Bucket Bowl*

The three bowl types on record are so rare that only consistency warrants allocation to separate Sections. The types are the Lipped Bucket, found on a plain and also on a domed and folded foot in goblet form; the Waisted Bucket, exemplified by a wine with vertical ribbing; and the Cup-topped Bucket, a single wine. Their respective frequencies vary from one in 6,000 to one in 12,000 glasses.

SECTION 5. *Glasses with a Cup Bowl*

This bowl is rather scarcer than the Bucket, with a frequency of 1 per cent of the Group, and perhaps one in every five is coloured green, usually a good emerald tint; such glasses will have a plain foot almost exclusively, while the uncoloured specimens may have any of the usual four forms, with the addition of a rare flanged firing foot applied to a dram glass.

SECTION 6. *Glasses with a Ogee Bowl*

This Section has 16 per cent of the Group's glasses, and more than two-thirds of them are the plain or 'flowered' wines with a folded foot, a favourite utility glass today for those who like to use something strong and simple and a couple of centuries old.

Analysis of many specimens records that the folded foot is four times as frequent as the plain one, yet in the case of goblets the plain foot is ten times as common as the folded. Such plain-footed goblets are about equal numerically with the plain-footed wines, but these are outnumbered ten times over by the folded-foot wines. I have no record of any dome-footed glass, and those with a dome and fold are of very great rarity.

Ales are not common, and cordials and ratafia glasses extremely rare. There are a number of solidly built ogee dram glasses to be found with a stout terraced foot. Hardly any moulded decoration exists except the faint basal fluting, and even this is uncommon except on the dram just mentioned, where it unaccountably predominates, and on folded-foot wines where its occurrence is about once in six glasses. There are some nice and quite scarce three-piece glasses like Pl.82h, and as many more in an emerald or bluish-green colour. No tear is found in any wine-glass.

SECTIONS 7 AND 8. *Glasses with a Modified Form of the Ogee Bowl*

Here there is a Lipped form and also a Waisted one, which is rarer still. A dome does occur beneath the Lipped Ogee, and the one specimen on record also possessed a tear in the stem.

SECTION 9. *Glasses with an Ovoid Bowl*

This bowl seems not to have been a popular one, and the Section contains only 11 per cent of the Group's glasses. A good many short ales occur and more goblets than one would expect; these latter always have a plain foot. In wines, plain-footed specimens are about equal in number to those with a folded foot, and basal fluting is relatively common in each case. No glass appears on record with either a domed or a domed and folded foot. To make amends, the dram glass may have a plain, folded, firing, flanged firing, terraced, oversewn (Pl.78a), or overstrung foot, the flanged and the overstrung types being decidedly the rarest. There is a good three-piece wine with wide basal fluting and a folded foot. Coloured glasses do not appear on the record.

SECTION 10. *Glasses with a Round Funnel Bowl*

This Section is only slightly more numerous than the last, with a figure of 13 per cent, yet more varieties appear than in any other section. Ales are prominent, apparently at the expense of goblets, which are few enough with a plain foot, rarely to be found with a folded one, and no more frequent with a dome or dome and fold. Short ales are fewer than in Section 8; cordials occur, but remain quite rare except with a domed foot of presumed Irish origin (Pl.77a), far more so than those with an opaque white twist stem. A ratafia may be found, the accent being on the verb. In wines the folded foot is five times as frequent as the plain foot. One with Lynn rings is known, and there are several good three-piece glasses with all-over honeycomb moulding (Pl.78d) or wrythen ribbing. Moulding over the bowl base becomes a little more frequent and diverse. A very few green glasses are known. A goblet with a 'sausage' stem is on record, in three-piece form; both a wine and a goblet may be found with a semi-hollow stem and a plain, folded, or domed foot. An ale glass with a firing foot is a curious conjunction. Dram glasses are very scarce with a firing foot and extremely rare with any specialized foot.

SECTIONS 11 TO 13. *Glasses with a Modified or Duplex Form of the Round Funnel Bowl*

As before, examples of these Sections are really rare. The forms are as follows: a Lipped Round Funnel represented by an ale glass, two goblets from Ireland and a wine, all with a plain foot; and two duplex forms, Cup-topped and Saucer-topped (Pl.78b). The first is known in green glass only, with a domed and folded foot, while the saucer-topped form, to be had on a choice of three types of foot, though probably only after long search, has been found more commonly, but possibly fortuitously, in emerald colour.

SECTION 14. *Glasses with a Trumpet Bowl*

Here we have the largest Section, with a strength of 40 per cent of the Group. Six in every ten glasses are wines; as between ales, short ales, and goblets there is not a lot to choose, but each of these is outnumbered by drams, which will usually have a firing foot or the flanged type; rather oddly, a terraced foot is a rarity. Wines and some drams come in both lead and soda metal.

Cordials remain scarce, and though ratafia glasses increase, they are just as difficult to find, and apparently always with a plain foot. Some semi-cordials turn up, where the bowl is small enough but the stem of normal thickness. The range of goblets and wines is increased by certain Newcastle examples, more slender in stem and graceful in build, not infrequently with admirable border engraving (Pl.77b).

In nearly all types of vessel tears may occur, very rarely multiple tears in small goblets, which may be presumed to be export glasses. Giant and Mammoth goblets are reasonably common, if ceremonial rather than useful.

There are toasting stems in both lead (Pl.77e) and soda metal of which some at least come from Newcastle. Toast-master glasses also occur, more like tall dram glasses than veritable wines. A few gin glasses appear here.

In this Section the tapered pedestal with its collars at top and base is first found; a scarce wine, with plain, folded, or domed and folded foot (Pl.78f). The range of goblets and of moulded decoration follows that of Section 10, but only on three-piece glasses; other than a short ale or two, no 2NS piece is on record here otherwise than plain. It should be added that many soda metal wines are to be found, not all of poor quality.

SECTIONS 15 AND 16. *Glasses with Duplex Forms of the Trumpet Bowl*

These are very rare and comprise the Cup-topped and the Saucer-topped Trumpet. The former is known in green glass and then has a domed foot; the clear glass wine has a folded foot and is rather more frequent than the Saucer-topped form, which may or may not have a fold in the foot. A goblet is known.

SECTION 17. *Glasses with a Waisted Bowl*

This is a fairly numerous Section with a frequency of 16 per cent. It is a fault that the bowl shape varies so greatly, the waist being pronounced or slight and the bowl base solid or otherwise, apart from considerable variations in its depth. Ales become rather scarce, cordials extremely rare, and rata-fias apparently non-existent. Goblets are uncommon and large ones rare; usually their foot will be a plain one. A 'sausage'-

type stem is to be found among them, very few three-piece glasses are on record, chiefly wines with panel moulded and domed or domed and folded foot which may match (Pl.77c). The collared taper stem is listed as a three-piece glass on a domed and folded foot (Pl.78f).

A single toasting stem is known and a very few soda metal wines. Dram glasses almost vanish, but a few gin glasses help to replace them.

Group VII

GLASSES WITH AIR TWIST STEMS
(c. 1745 – c. 1770)

The glasses of this Group may fairly claim a more exclusively English origin than any others. For the opaque white and coloured interior twists there were continental precedents – why did we never use a gold thread in the stem? – but it fell to us to adopt the economical use of spirals of imprisoned air as decoration. Mere tears, of course, were international, and it has been assumed that the air spiral was developed, almost accidentally, from an elongated tear. I can find no evidence to support the theory; the existence of a few imperfect twists proves nothing but the incompetence of their maker.

An exhaustive tally of the air twist glasses includes a number of knopped (Pl.82a) and unknopped two-piece specimens in soda metal. Though conventionally termed Dutch, the probability is that they were made in the north for the export market. The point cannot be laboured; as with plain-stemmed trumpet glasses, I have found them in the eastern counties and with an assuring English inscription and date. The soda metal tradition was by no means dead. It may be noted that the knopped soda glasses include formations hardly ever seen in lead metal; almost without exception the twist is the familiar 'multiple spirals'.

All classes of drinking-vessel and almost all types of bowl occur, and a careful survey of the eight Sections into which the Group now divides will show how the accent on bowl form varied as time went on. At first the trumpet or the waisted form, on two-piece glasses. Then the bell (a 3NS pattern) and the round funnel or saucer-topped r.f., with the ogee joining issue in the sixth Section, three-piece glasses with double-series twist.

There is not much specialization in foot forms, perhaps because dram glasses are relatively few. Moulded decoration is also scarce, with some very attractive exceptions, but no new devices other than a rare basal floral or vine meander and also a basal fluting which rises into a honeycomb, a pattern known on what seem to be little seventeenth-century glasses (Pl. 58a) as well as on eighteenth-century wines from Liège and France.

There is a certain amount of simple wheel-engraving, and some very fine decorative work by continental artists, but so far as the makers are concerned, I think they realized they had something new and something good, and that their lily needed no gilding. Because some of the engraved work was in fact gilded and because other decorative or inscriptional gilding is known, as well as white and shadow-white (wash-enamel) decoration, the conclusion is not affected; such work was done outside the factory by people such as Edkins or Beilby.

Some may find the types of twist of considerable interest. The multiple-spiral type was the first to appear, and it was never seriously challenged, although extremely rare in combination with any other sort of twist. The number of the spirals varies and is worth a thought; when less than five, they are much larger and a good deal nearer a corkscrew than a spiral, and because of their relatively wide cross-section and the tightness of the turns, the reflective capacity is much increased; such twists are sometimes called a 'mercury' twist, an apposite but fanciful term.

The Group contains 2NS and 3NS glasses only, and the twist must be continuous throughout the stem. Where there is a plain neck as in glasses with a shoulder-knopped stem, it is integral with the bowl and not more than – at most – half an inch in length. Glasses with a longer neck, or with a partial air twist stem, have been placed in Group v.

Here, then, is a summary of the Sections of a Group which includes about 14 per cent of all our eighteenth-century drinking glasses. The details to be given were first worked out in detail and printed in 1947. Since then a number of new stem types have been added, including some formations peculiar to soda glasses, and some additional varieties of bowl, foot, or decoration have come forward either by chance or by the kindness of collectors who have studied the list. It is rather satisfactory that the up-to-date percentages for the Sections differ very little from those ruling seven years ago.

SECTION I. *Knopped Two-piece Glasses with a Single Series Twist* (*one type of twist, eleven types of knopping*)

Partly by reason of their scarcity, for the glasses of this Section amount only to 3 per cent of the Group, it is assumed that they were the earliest air twist glasses made, though possibly contemporary with the trumpet wines of Section 2. There are some nice patterns, such as a Four-knopped stem and one with a Central Swelling Knop (Pl.79a), both duplicated in 3NS form. Much the most frequent stem is one with a Shoulder Knop or Inverted Baluster (Pl.79b), which is a lot rarer than its 3NS cousin. It comes chiefly with a waisted bowl, and the twist may continue into the bowl base, or it may be squeezed out of the neck, although reappearing above more as tears than spirals. If the weld mark cannot be seen, as sometimes happens, the glass may still be 3NS for there is a variety which has tears in the bowl base. If, however, the tears are equal in number to the spirals below it is likely to be a two-piece glass. Three stem types are peculiar to soda glasses and seven are represented by one or two examples only. Only the Multiple Spiral type of twist is employed, though the number of spirals is inconstant.

SECTION 2. *Unknopped Two-piece Glasses with a Single Series Twist* (*three types of twist*)

This is the largest Section of the Group, with a strength of 35 per cent. The Multiple Spiral Twist, is very much the commonest, and it is supplemented by a Pair of Corkscrews (Pl. 79e), and by Four of the same, both commonly called 'mercurial' twists on account of their brilliance. Their respective frequencies are 68 : 3 : 1, so that the four-corkscrew twist is decidedly scarce. There is a variety with five spirals likely to be as rare, but data are not available. For these corkscrew twists the favourite bowl is the trumpet, almost to the exclusion of all else. Beyond a few cordials with plain feet little is to be

ound but wines; the domed foot is used more frequently than
he folded.

The same bowl dominates in the multiple spiral twists; it has
the well-known waisted bowl as a competitor and about half
as frequent, and half a dozen other forms are found in ones
and twos. This trumpet bowl M.S.A.T. wine is one of our
commonest. Apart from wines there are also semi-cordials (Pl.
79d), and goblets, roughly in the proportion of 80 : 3 : 3 with
a very few short-stemmed cordials and some dram glasses.
Among the wines there are fairly frequently found nice specimens in soda metal, sometimes with as few as five or six
spirals.

Generally the foot is plain, not infrequently folded, rarely
domed, and – so it seems – never domed and folded, but that
may be my misfortune: the ratios of frequency are then
25 : 5 : 1. Some of these wines have a toasting type of stem,
permissibly thicker than is desirable in a plain stem because of
the twist, but still quite slender. Some half-hearted attempts
were made to decorate the stem with a vermiform collar half-
way up, or a double-ring collar: but it was the glasses with the
waisted bowl which shone in this way, and stem collaring to
the trumpet glasses is rare. One delightful wine, of very great
rarity, is in emerald green to which the air-twist adds a curious
attraction, a Newcastle production with good engraved
decoration.

Glasses with the waisted bowl provide no cordials or drams,
but otherwise follow the range of the trumpet variety. The
folded foot is as common numerically, and goblets relatively
as frequent, but in number deplorably few. The commonest
collaring to the stem is the vermiform collar with which two
in every seven wines are so decorated. Much rarer is the
bladed collar, and the double and the triple-ring collar
(Pl.79c), generally with a plain foot beneath. Rarest of all is a
stem with an annulated collar, and also a rounded banding
with tears; these two have only been seen over a domed
foot. Another rarity is a wine with a domed and folded foot.

SECTION 3. *Unknopped Two-piece Glasses with a Double Series Twist (five types of twist)*

Once, the assumed absence of a glass of this kind was noted with surprise, but time has made amends and enough examples have come to hand to warrant a Group-frequency of $\frac{1}{2}$ per cent. There are five types of double series twist and each has had a trumpet bowl over a plain foot; wines (Pl.82b) and cordials only.

The inner component is either a Corkscrew or a Vertical (or a slightly wavy) Column; the outer twist is more variable: Three Spiral Threads, Four Spiral Threads, Two or Four Corkscrews, and a Six-ply Spiral Band. The bowl size is usually small and the stem always stout enough, so that most of the specimens seen could almost be classed as cordials, unless a veritable cordial was at hand for comparison. Glasses of this Section are quite easy to overlook.

SECTION 4. *Knopped Three-piece Glasses with a Single Series Twist (two types of twist, twenty-seven and four types of knopping respectively)*

Here we have a Section containing 26 per cent of the glasses of the Group. There are two types of twist. The Multiple Spiral Twist has almost a monopoly; its one competitor, the Pair of Corkscrews, is known with four stem types but, as yet, with only four different glasses, including a sweetmeat with folded, prunted, and looped rim, so that examples are rarer than those of Section 3.

The general picture shows that three of the thirty-one Sub-sections together provide nearly four-fifths of the Section's glasses. First and foremost is a stem with a Knop at top (or Shouldered Knop) and a Central Knop, and here the r.f. bowl is by much the favourite (Pl.80a), outnumbering the bell by 3 to 1. Then there is a stem type with a Knop or a Shouldered Knop at the top, nearly half as frequent, but the bowl most found is the bell, in front of the r.f. by 3 to 2. Next comes a stem with Central Swelling Knop, almost as frequent as the last, and here the commonest bowl is, probably to the surprise of most collectors, the saucer-topped r.f. (Pl.80d): four of them to one of any other kind. There are two other stem types each with just under 6 per cent of the Section's glasses; the rest of the twenty-seven stem forms with the multiple spiral twist are nowhere. Of these, a Five-knopped stem is a well-recognized rarity, but there are ten others quite as rare such as the lovely acorn-knopped wine of Pl.80c and the true baluster trumpet wine of Pl.82c.

Any foot other than a plain one is scarcer than its market value would indicate. Only the shoulder-knopped stem provides any appreciable number of folded feet, which suggests that it followed or coincided with the similar form of Section 1. A firing foot is very rare, and this Section also contains the only drinking glass with a domed and folded foot of which I have a record; it belongs to a three-piece M.S.A.T. goblet with r.f. bowl. The range of vessel form is very limited. Ales are commoner than goblets, and cordials, gins, and drams very rare, as are champagnes. Some nice moulded r.f. bowls are found on the double-knopped M.S.A.T. stem referred to above; they include a somewhat indistinct vine-floral pattern, swirled basal flutes, and the commoner basal honeycomb moulding. A glass or two in emerald metal, including a fine r.f. goblet, is known.

Elsewhere, faint basal fluting rising into four rows of honeycombing is to be found. There is a fair amount of collaring beneath the bowl, a pleasant touch. There is very little moulding over the entire bowl, but ribbing and wrythening occurs. One stem type, perhaps best described as an Inverted over a True Baluster, has a central band with tears, a rare feature indeed.

The four stem types with the rare 'mercury' corkscrews are each as rare as anything else in the Section; the bowl is r.f. or saucer-topped r.f. The most spectacular is a sweetmeat glass with domed and folded foot and, once upon a time, with prunted loops rising from its folded rim. Two other types have a Ridged Knop at the base of the stem.

SECTION 5. *Unknopped Glasses with a Single Series Twist (eleven types of twist)*

This Section with 24½ per cent compares closely with the last in point of numbers. Also, there is again one twist all-dominant and two others a bad second. They are, first the Multiple Spiral Twist, with the r.f. bowl on two in every three glasses, a domed foot in every nine (Pl.81a) and a folded one in every eighteen; there is a fair range of vessel form, but anything beyond a wine, ale, or goblet is decidedly rare. A collared r.f. wine with two vermiform collars trisecting the stem (Pl.82e) is another prize.

Then comes the Spiral Gauze (Pl.81c) and the Pair of Corkscrews (Pl.81b) somewhat alike in range, though in the latter the ogee bowl is beginning to challenge the r.f. There are some good glasses with this twist, notably a diamond-moulded sweetmeat with prunted and looped rim, on a domed and folded foot, and cordials are less scarce than elsewhere in the section. The rarest twist seems to be a 2–4-ply Spiral Band. A pair of Spiral Threads and Four of the same are also quite rare, as is the Single Corkscrew (or Spiral Column).

SECTION 6. *Unknopped Three-piece Glasses with a Double Series Twist (nineteen types of twist)*

This Section contains 11 per cent of the glasses of this Group, and it is assumed to have appeared towards the end of the Air twist series. The most frequent twist is a Gauze/Pair of Spiral Threads (Pl.81d), found in one glass in four. The ogee and the r.f. bowl occur equally on nearly all the glasses, and all the feet are plain. The second favourite is a twist with a Vertical Column/Four Spiral Threads (Pl.81f) and the same two bowls in the same proportions. It is found in one glass in six and it provides a few good cordials and toastmaster glasses. Of the others, a Corkscrew/Single 6–12-ply Spiral Band is most often seen (Pl.81e), and with the widest bowl range, including a cup and a saucer-topped r.f. form. Some others are rarer, but a twist formed of a Pair of Corkscrew/Pair of 4–5-ply Spiral

Bands appears to provide five cordials or toastmaster glasses for every wine, a most exceptional state of affairs. A very occasional domed foot is to be found, and a single firing foot, but as yet not one with a fold. There is not much moulded decoration, but faint basal flutes and basal honeycombing both spread through the Section. All-over moulded ribbing appears on a quite well-known wine in green metal, rather a tall ogee glass approaching goblet size (Pl. 82d).

SECTION 7. *Knopped Three-piece Glasses with a Double Series Twist (one type of knopping, one type of twist)*

This Section is so far represented by a single specimen only, though a fine one. It is a champagne on a Shoulder-knopped stem with knop at base containing a rather malformed twist, a Pair of Spiral Threads/Pair of 5-ply Spiral Bands; the pan-topped bowl has a folded, prunted, and looped rim and is panel moulded, as is the domed and folded foot.

SECTION 8. *Unknopped Three-piece Glasses with a Triple Series Twist*

This is raised on the strength of a pair of faint fluted r.f. cordials, the twist being a Corkscrew/Corkscrew/Single 10–13-ply Spiral Band. It was quite a definite twist, and it is not necessary to infer a misplacement of the corkscrews, for no such twist as it would then be has yet come to notice. Still, one would like further examples.

Group VIII

GLASSES WITH A HOLLOW STEM
(*c.* 1750 – *c.* 1760)

This is the smallest Group, and it contains but 0·5 per cent of our eighteenth-century glasses. It divides into two Sections, for knopped and unknopped glasses respectively. Those for use at home were given a stem formed of a hollow tube, usually a cylinder, but it could be manipulated to show protuberances which for convenience may be termed knops. The hollow stem saved weight, and was a likely counter to the Excise Act of 1745–6. Yet it appears to have been unsuccessful, perhaps because of its lightness and the fragility of a plain foot, now so often notched and chipped. Yet where more pains were taken with this feature, pleasant glasses could result (Pl.83).

SECTION I. *Glasses in which the Stem is Knopped* (*three stem types*)

Examples, totalling only 15 per cent of the Group, are rare, and all those seen of the first two Subsections have been of the champagne/sweetmeat type. There may be an Angular Knop at the centre of the stem; in the one specimen on record the bowl and foot are both honeycomb moulded, and the foot is also flanged, the bowl being a waisted r.f. More frequent but still rare is a stem with Swelling Knop at centre, the ogee bowl with a dentated rim (Pl.84a) or a pan-top form over a domed and folded foot. A champagne is known with this stem, with the addition of collaring at its base. However, material is so scarce that there is no point in drawing conclusions.

A third Subsection has been raised to receive certain roemer-type wines (Pl.78c), which are presumed to be of English manufacture for export to, one would say, Holland. They are not common and the majority, perhaps, are likely to be of soda or near-soda metal; others, however, seem to fulfil all the usual tests for the presence of a substantial lead content. Parallel wines appear with an opaque white twist in the stem which is certainly glass of lead. The stem formation is not always precise, and the high domed foot significant. Despite the fact that the stem of these glasses is semi-hollow, this Group appears as suitable a place for them as any other.

SECTION 2. *Glasses in which the Stem is Unknopped (six types of bowl)*

Such as it is, the remaining 85 per cent of the strength of the Group lies here. The first Subsection has a Cup bowl with plain, domed, or domed and folded foot. The stem is not so precise a cylinder, and except for two clear metal wines with the domed and folded foot every specimen is coloured, once in blue and then with a ribbed bowl and foot, otherwise in green and anything from palish to deep emerald. As far as one can tell, the metal contained lead in each case. Specimens are not too rare, amounting to about 26 per cent of the Section. The Subsection will accommodate certain green wines with hollow stems which widen towards the base, and which possess the high domed foot. They have not been seen in lead metal, and are less certainly of English origin, but possibly deserving of provisional inclusion.

The remaining Subsections do not yet include a single coloured glass. Only odd examples have been seen with the Ogee (Pl.83a) and the Ovoid bowl, both being very rare. The Round Funnel (Pl.78g) is half as frequent as the Cup bowl, i.e. accounts for 13 per cent; all the usual four types of foot occur. Some engraving can be found here, the fruiting vine, for instance, and more unexpectedly the cut and polished circle and engraved star band to the rim. This may come on a short glass which is a close relative of glasses in Group IX, Section 2B. Lastly, the Trumpet bowl, with a strength of 52 per cent, provides an ale or two, a number of gin glasses or very small wines and as many normal wines; every foot is plain. This appears curious, after the previous diversity in this respect.

Group IX

GLASSES WITH INCISED TWIST STEMS
(*c.* 1750 – *c.* 1765)

This is another small Group, giving us just under 1 per cent of our eighteenth-century glasses. The stems have an exterior twist of closely spiralled grooving running down the stem. In the earlier and majority of specimens this grooving is fairly coarse and such glasses may be knopped (21 per cent) or un-knopped (65 per cent); the remaining 14 per cent are shorter unknopped glasses nearly always with a rather large r.f. bowl and a very fine-drawn incised twist (Pl.84e). Collectors take only a mild interest in the Knopped glasses and none at all in the very fine-drawn twists.

Somehow there seems to be little relationship between the Knopped and the Unknopped glasses. Four-fifths of the Knopped glasses are either with moulded decoration or in green metal, and three out of four of the feet are plain. A cup bowl is the commonest bowl, nearly one in every two, and always in green metal, doubtless with an export market in view, as is the case in Group VIII. The round funnel makes up most of the rest. Moulded decoration on the clear glass speci-mens includes faint flutes rising into a honeycomb, basal honeycombing, and ribbing. With all this, not much engraving is to be expected; Rose-glasses exist, however, and other Jacobite varieties, but very few 'flowered' glasses (Pl.84c).

The Unknopped glasses may be divided into those with the coarser twist, and those with the fine twist. Green glasses are much less often seen, about one in twenty being so coloured as against nearly one in two of the Knopped glasses, which themselves are less common than the straight-stemmed kinds.

SECTION I. *Glasses with Knopped Stems (six stem types)*

Not one of the Subsections but may fairly be called rare, though together they amount to 21 per cent of the glasses of the Group. The least infrequent stem type only just qualifies for inclusion, having but a small Flattened or Half-knop at the head of the stem (Pl.84c); occasionally there may be two of these half-knops. Every glass of this type except a single goblet has had moulded bowl decoration, most frequently faint basal flutes rising into a honeycomb. A second Subsection has a Central Angular Knop and, apart from a champagne and a sweetmeat with a pan-type bowl (Pl.83e), all specimens seen have had a cup bowl and have been made of emerald metal. Two ubiquitous forms have an Inverted Baluster with, or without, a basal Knop; all examples have been in green glass except for a round funnel soda metal dram moulded throughout with flutes rising into a honeycomb. Altogether it is a very mixed Section whereof a ribbed and dome-footed champagne with Central Angular Knop is the most aristocratic glass.

SECTION 2. *Glasses with an Unknopped Stem*

A. The stem with a coarse incised twist (*six bowl types*)

This is the major portion of the Section with nearly 65 per cent of the Group's glasses. The Subsection with a Round Funnel bowl is as numerous as the other five put together, and the commonest variety has honeycomb moulding at the base of the bowl. A particularly rare glass has the same bowl with deep basal flutes rising into a fruiting vine or floral meander. This form of decoration has also been seen on Air twist and Opaque White Twist glasses, but not a sharply impressed one. An odd glass or two occurs in emerald metal, the best a heavy-stemmed Cup bowl goblet on a domed foot; another with an Ogee bowl, itself unusual, had both bowl and foot ribbed. The Trumpet bowl is second favourite and here a good cordial appears. Lastly, the Waisted bowl, with very few examples in lead metal (Pl.84d), but a goodly number in soda, not too well fashioned. They probably come from the frugal North, not from a bottle-glass factory, as has been suggested. Most of these soda specimens are of 2NS form, but some are 3NS.

It is a curious thing that but for the majority of the soda

wines just referred to, not one other glass within the whole Group has, so far, been noted with a folded foot. It follows that most feet are plain; the dome is not very unusual, but the dome and fold is extremely rare. And no other Group has so large a percentage of glasses with moulded decoration.

B. The stem with a fine incised twist (*three bowl types*)

These glasses comprise only 14 per cent of the Group. As stated, they are short and nearly always with rather a large Round Funnel bowl (Pl.84e). Their aspect has a counterpart in the Air twist as well as the Hollow stem Group. But for these round funnel wines, which incline to favour moulded decoration, there is little to be found. The best glass seen long ago had a small Ogee bowl and a thin toasting stem. A semi-cordial with a Trumpet bowl has an unexpected inscription, all erased except the date, by some jealous or correcting hand, *Mifs Grace Legge Patroness 1749* (Pl.82g); the lady has not been identified, but her term of office(?) lay within the period of the loudest Jacobite clamour.

Group X

GLASSES WITH OPAQUE WHITE TWIST STEMS
(c. 1755 – c. 1780)

Having made a success of their air twist glasses, it may be
that the glassmasters sought to enhance their laurels by adding
their white and coloured enamel twist glasses. Indeed, it is
almost surprising that they did not commence with these, for
there were old Venetian and derivative precedents which must
have lain within memory, if not within actual experience;
glasses such as Pl.24b with spiral threading within its (reversed) heart and cross stem structure may well have stretched
into the sixteenth century. But by this time the objective was
sturdiness, and it may have wanted experience with the air
twist glass to teach our manufacturers that enamel twists did
not need to be fragile. Once launched, there is no doubt
that the series was an amazing success, for its relics now challenge even the ubiquitous plain-stemmed glasses in point of
number.

The dating of our Opaque White Twist glasses may represent the normal span of their popularity, even though it will be
difficult to find any specimen with any such early date as 1755;
the ordinary run of dated examples began in the earlier sixties
and persisted into the late seventies. Only a tiny percentage
was so dated or could otherwise be dated, and that holds
throughout all the Groups. It can be added that there were
good white twists made in France, as well as in England, in
the second quarter of the nineteenth century. There are also
modern specimens, legitimate editions, generally discernible
by a certain inaccuracy of the twist and sometimes by their
appearance in sets. There are specimens of the requisite age in
soda metal, and some of lead metal which can be regarded as
export glasses. An occasional phenomenon is an opalescent
stem (Pl.88a) regarded by a good many as accidental; if so it
was a rare and happy accident.

The twists were made by placing rods of opaque white (or

colour) upright in a circular mould; the clear metal was poured in and the resulting mass drawn out until of the required diameter and at the same time twisted with exact regularity. The different twists resulted from different placings of the rods, and a moment's reflection will show that every rod will remain in a constant relation with its neighbours, however much the stem is manipulated. An irregular twisting will produce tighter or wider turns of the twist, but cannot alter the relation of the various spirals. In the case of the air twist glasses, bubbles of air were used, and the regularity of those twists suggests surprising accuracy on the part of the workman or some mechanical contrivance such as a circuit of nails for placing the holes precisely.

The terminology applied to the twists has indeed been various. The illustrations provided show nearly all the varieties of twist and are named in accordance with a terminology which has now had a longish life and has met all requirements. It can be added that some twists, both single and double series, are surprisingly rare.

The twist may consist of one formation by itself or of two reciprocal spiral formations (Pl.85d); these are here termed 'single series' twists, and there are some thirty of them. More commonly, the twist is composed of two formations, the one inside the other, and these are called 'double series' twists. Rarely, there may be a 'triple series'.

By reason of the many combinations of twist, the Group contains a greater variety of glasses than any other. A schedule of the twist varieties has grown rather too long for convenience, and it may become desirable to amend it by classing as sub-varieties certain alternative formations, some rare and some imprecise. For instance, a (solid) Spiral Thread may be replaced in a goblet by a slender hollow tube, not immediately noticeable. The solid Corkscrew is an attractive and reasonable formation, but it also appears built-up of laminated plies, that is to say adjacent parallel plies which touch each other, or else in 'multi-ply' form, where the parallel plies are close to but separated from each other. For all ordinary purposes these two variations may be regarded as alternative; they are not rare, ndeed both are commoner than the solid corkscrew. Again, there is a Spiral Tape which may be an eighth of an inch or more in width; this is already regarded as an alternative to the spiral thread because it is not easy to find a dividing line. But the Spiral Tape also appears in laminated form, and not too uncommonly, and it may be better to regard it as a sub-variety; this may also be flat or concave, and again the dividing line is necessarily indefinite.

Most types of vessel occur with a white twist, as do all types of bowl, counting the bell as the three-piece equivalent of the waisted form; the round funnel and the ogee are much the most frequent, but not necessarily so in every Section. Most types of foot may be found, though variation here would be inconsiderable were it not for dram glasses and in lesser degree, champagnes and sweetmeats. Tall glasses of these last are uncommon, for the moulded pedestal stem was still ruling. Low ones are not too scarce, as they include a good many with a dentated rim (Pl.60a), a curious design which may have had a Scottish origin.

The range of moulded decoration is fairly wide, but no style other than faint basal fluting is at all common. The well-known Lynn bowl (Pls 88d 84c) nearly always has a white twist stem. Engraved decoration is not uncommon on the smaller wines, the pattern being very much like those on the concurrent plain-stem wines, but on the whole rather better executed. There is a little gilding and some enamelling which includes the pleasantries of Beilby (Pl.36) as well as his masterpieces, but which, all told, are far commoner than gilded glasses (Pl.45d).

Barring a notable trumpet wine in a private museum, every white twist glass seen of this Group has been of 3NS build. The first exception has narrow vertical *lattimo* bands rising through the stem to the rim of the bowl. A few flute (trumpet) wines appear to be 2NS, but this is because the stem and bowl are 'side-welded' together on a diagonal, not horizontally or end-welded', as is usual, consequently the twist may appear just to peter out in irregular fashion; the others are cut off horizontally as with a knife. Close inspection will usually discover the weld mark running diagonally to the axis of the stem. Except for this lack of two-piece glasses, the Group has a considerable resemblance to Group VII, as a comparison of vessel types, bowl forms, twist construction, and even extrinsic decoration will quickly demonstrate. The classification is therefore on the same lines, with five Sections comprising Knopped Glasses with a Single and with a Double series twist and Unknopped Glasses with a Single, a Double, and a Triple series twist. It must suffice if the Group, which contains 27 per cent of our eighteenth-century glasses, is dealt with rather briefly.

SECTION I. *Knopped Glasses with a Single Series Twist* (*six types of twist*)

This is a small Section, amounting to just under 5 per cent of the Group, but it includes some scarce glasses. Among the six types of twist on record, the Multiple Spiral Opaque Twist very greatly predominates, the others occurring only in twos and threes. Accordingly a wine with Four Spiral Threads is as great a rarity as a tall sweetmeat with a Lace Twist outlined, a flanged and dentated rim, and on a domed and folded foot, but its price is very unlikely to be the same.

However, the general aspect of the Section is to be seen in the M.S.O.T. Subsection, which features three favourites: centre-knopped wines with an ogee (Pl.85a) or with a round funnel bowl, and a series of rather imprecisely shoulder knopped low sweetmeats which generally have a pan type of bowl, flanged and dentated, and a foot with pressed radial grooves (Pl.60a); there may be wide basal fluting on some of these, and very occasionally indeed the pan bowl may be decorated with vertical white stripes. The grooved foot is rare under any other sort of glass, but may be found on Monteith glasses and an egg-cup. Variations occur on these low sweetmeats, such as the omission of the dentation, or a scalloped foot, or even a domed one may be provided. Either five or six grooves seem to be most used, with nine, ten, or eleven not far behind. Anything more or less appears rare. The drinking glasses mostly have a centre-knopped stem. Anything but a goblet or wine is rare; one form of the latter is seen in no other Section, a variety in which the twist rises into the solid base of a bell bowl (Pl.85b). The concourse of low sweetmeats is improved by a few centre-knopped champagnes and a sweetmeat with the rim with a circuit of loops; these have a domed and folded foot. Still more uncommon is the goblet in Pl.83b, with its single spiral gauze twist and an unusually deep bowl.

SECTION 2. *Knopped Glasses with a Double Series Twist (seventeen types of twist)*

This Section again contains nearly 5 per cent of the glasses of the Group, and it is composed almost exclusively of wines and some ales in the proportion of 9 to 1. One may fairly say they mostly came from Newcastle; the balance is made up with a few low sweetmeats as found in Section 1. Among the twists, four particular types predominate; a Gauze/Pair of Spiral Threads; a Gauze/Four 2–3-ply Spiral Bands, the favourite; a Lace Twist/Pair of Spiral Threads; and a Pair of Spiral Threads/Pair of Corkscrews. The bell bowl far surpasses all else, with the ogee, r.f., and rather unexpectedly the lipped ogee each outnumbered by four or five to one.

A grooved foot appears on the Low Sweetmeats; the rest are plain-footed, with the exception of a single bell wine which has a domed foot, one of the unspectacular but extreme rarities which go so unnoticed – if ever seen.

The Knopping is simple; either one or two knops, variously arranged, or else with three or four knops evenly spaced. It may be noted that both these latter forms are frequent in this Group, although very rare and rare respectively in the Air Twist Group. On the other hand, the air twist glasses used a number of knops, such for instance as the acorn knop, which are unknown on opaque white twist glasses.

Of late years, glasses of this Section have been becoming rather scarce, whereas formerly they seemed plentiful. Hardly any have moulding other than the low sweetmeats and few indeed are engraved. Some soda metal specimens are on the record (Pl.85c) as also in the allied Colour Twists.

SECTION 3. *Unknopped Glasses with a Single Series Twist (thirty-three types of twist)*

This Section amounts to 18 per cent of the Group, and it includes some particularly charming glasses and many rarities. More than half the recorded twists have been noted fewer than five times, and five of them are represented by single specimens. The two most numerous are the Lace Twist Outlined and the Corkscrew (laminated or multi-ply), each of which appears once in every six glasses of the Section. The range of vessel types is smaller than one might expect. Ales provide one glass in ten, goblets one in twelve, cordials one in sixty. There are still fewer champagnes and tall sweetmeats, and one may add one or two gins, drams, ratafias, low sweetmeats, and toastmaster glasses. The round funnel was the most popular bowl, with the ogee well liked; one or other occurs on two-thirds of the Section's glasses. As 95 per cent of the feet are plain there is not much scope for variation. A few glasses have folded feet, notably r.f. Lynn wines with multiple spiral twist. A dome occurs here and there on a rare cordial, and there is a cup bowl roemer type wine with a prunted knop just below the bowl, all in pale emerald except its multi-ply corkscrew stem (Pl.85f); this also has a domed foot and may fairly be regarded as an export model. Otherwise the dome and the dome and fold are reserved for champagnes and sweetmeats. Drams are equally rare with a single series twist, but may have a firing foot. Such low sweetmeats as occur have the radially grooved foot.

Rather more than their fair share of moulded decoration comes to these single series twists. Faint basal fluting is not uncommon; on the other hand, panel moulding, wide basal fluting, ribbing (Pl.88e), basal honeycombing, and gadrooning (Pl.88c) are all rare or scarce features, but they do occur on wines and goblets apart from champagnes and sweetmeats where expectation of them would be greater. A very rare device is ladder-moulding on both bowl and foot (Pl.83h).

The glasses of this Section hold a lot of attraction for their simplicity and uniform good quality, if for nothing else. They are a manageable lot with under two hundred different glasses on record. Yet it would probably take a collector's lifetime to amass as many, for at the present time no less than one hundred and thirty have been seen but once.

SECTION 4. *Unknopped Glasses with a Double Series Twist (ninety-three types of twist)*

If a complete collection of Section 3 glasses is so formidable a task, what then of the possibilities of securing all the twists in this one? The Section accounts for 72 per cent of the glasses of the Group, and it contains over six hundred and fifty different glasses. The picture is very much as in Section 3, with certain twists very much more popular than all the rest. Here there are four favourites: a Pair of Spiral Threads/Single 10-20-ply Spiral Band (13 per cent), a Gauze/Pair of Spiral Threads (12½ per cent), a Gauze/Four Spiral Threads (9 per cent), and a Lace Twist/Pair of Spiral Threads (8 per cent). They make a total of 42½ per cent, though a certain number of soda metal glasses are included in the third mentioned. At the other end of the scale there are twenty-eight definite twists seen but once only, and not for lack of search.

Somewhere or other in the Section there is pretty well every type of vessel and bowl, and almost every type of foot and moulding; the foot ribbing on Pl.88e is extremely rare. Nothing is to be deduced from a scrutiny of the very small Subsections except that that particular type of twist is rare; but there are enough in the larger ones to give a fairly good idea of the manufacturer's predilections. Some preferred one kind of bowl and some another, and it is the same with their choice of vessel. A ratafia (Pl.88f) will occur just a little more frequently than once in every hundred glasses of the Group, yet in one smallish Subsection it comes once in every twelve glasses. Many similar examples could be cited, and though they would not be impressive on paper, together they do much to suggest that various houses had their pet twists. Witness for instance the (Newcastle) Lace Twist Outlined of Section 3, used so much by Beilby, and the Pair of Spiral Gauzes found on Privateer glasses of Bristol origin.

The incidence of bowl, foot, and vessel varies with the twists, but, over the whole Section, wines, ales, and goblets occur in the ratio roughly of 16 : 2 : 1, with a dram glass just unplaced. Low sweetmeats, fairly frequent earlier in the Group, now appear once in a thousand glasses. The ogee bowl is a little commoner than the round funnel, one or other occurring on two out of every three glasses. Next come the trumpet and the ovoid, each once in every ten glasses. The foot range is fairly wide, thanks to the drams, but twenty-one in every twenty-two glasses are plain-footed. A folded foot was once thought a rarity, but now attracts too little attention. Here it occurs about twelve times in a thousand glasses and most often on a Lynn wine. The firing and the terraced foot are somewhat more frequent, but only on dram glasses. A rarity is the over-strung foot (Pl.60b), and a really heavy foot too, only on a dram. The dome occurs on cordials, but the dome and fold only on sweetmeats and champagnes, themselves very scarce in this Section.

A few striking varieties come to mind, a 'half' Lynn and engraved wine (Pl.83c); a round funnel wine with a basal meander of vine or floral moulding; a hexagonal r.f. and an octagonal ogee bowl (Pl.83a); and a wine of roemer type with prunted knop beneath a cup bowl, all in pale emerald, as Pl.83f. Somewhat of a curiosity are a wine and a goblet with a hollow stem, the wall of which contains a white twist, but there an almost inexhaustible subject must be left.

Engraving of a general character is confined to the 'flower-ed' work, whereof a considerable number of motifs are to be found; they tend to be treated like the twists, a single and a double series according to whether the reverse of the glass is engraved, the subject coming alone or in differing pairs. The subjects for wine include chiefly and naturally the fruiting vine; a bird in flight often occupies the reverse. The work is no more than pleasant, yet it retains its appeal. The hop-and-barley design is found on ale glasses, in surprising variation whereof collectors are taking increasing notice. Two versions, one grave, one gay, of the miniature-like portrait on Pl.83d have been seen, conjecturally representing Mrs Siddons.

Gilding is to be found, and again the fruiting vine and the hop and barley designs are more effective than the isolated posies and insects put on, so it may be, by the Michael Edkins enterprise. Much more frequent is enamelling in white or in colours, notably by the Beilby outfit. Here again there are arresting designs of which something has already been said in Chapter VIII.

SECTION 5. *Unknopped Glasses with a Triple Series Twist (four types of twist)*

This final Section is tiny indeed but intriguing, for it contains glasses which seem to have gone entirely unrecorded, if not unnoticed, in the past. An example has occurred about once in every three hundred white twist glasses, a considerable improvement on the position as stated in the first edition of this book, but, by a fortuitous circumstance, now too flattering a calculation. Three of these twists are based on the Vertical Column and have a 15-ply Spiral Band as the outer component, the intermediate one being respectively Four Spiral Threads, Four Corkscrews, or Eight Corkscrews, the last formation occurring nowhere else. In the last instance, a model of fine placing, some ales have been found. The fourth twist has a Pair of Spiral Threads/Four Spiral Tapes/Single 16-ply Spiral Band, found on a round funnel wine only whereof an engraved example is known. Clearly enough from the components of the twist, the whole series emanated from a single glasshouse, probably from a single chair.

That completes an all-too-short survey of our Opaque White Twist Glasses, but enough has been said to dispel the idea that one White Twist is as good as another. It is really not enough, even as a mere sample of the Group type, to have single specimen of the commonest wine, and may be too much to have a specimen of the finest white twist champagne. Neither a bestarred general nor a private of the Line can be regarded as representative of so multitudinous an army, with a variety of uniforms and facings.

Group XI

GLASSES WITH MIXED AND COLOUR TWIST STEMS

(*c*. 1755 – *c*. 1775)

In collector's parlance a Mixed Twist is one partly of air and partly of opaque white spirals, or columns, and a Colour Twist is one which contains a coloured component. But since a Colour Twist is usually found with opaque white, sometimes with air, and every now and then with both, there seem no grounds for giving them any separate grouping. The Group comprises but 2½ per cent of our eighteenth-century glasses.

Within the whole Group there is only one glass which is even fairly common. Most varieties are rare, and a surprising number have been recorded in the lists once only. As a whole, there is little to choose in rarity between the conventional Mixed Twist and a Coloured Twist; the detailed records show that there are roughly forty Mixed Twists to every fifty Colour Twists, and two varieties to every five, so there is clearly a smaller choice if the search is for a Mixed Twist, though at present a less expensive one. A single rare type has a composite stem incorporating a Mixed Twist, and this has been placed in Group v.

The twist colours most desired by collectors are canary, emerald green, and purple, but all intense colours are welcomed. Some greens, blues, and ruby tints are translucent and may be ill-defined, as a result of the use of coloured glass rods instead of enamel, that is to say opaque rods. Newcastle used them with effect in its knopped glasses with a double-series twist. There is a rubber-red colour, quite extensively used; a good pink is found, and there is also a paler pink which is now included in the list, but it is often regarded as an accident, even though it may appear in conjunction with the usual dense opaque white. There are a few special spirals, such as an opaque white tube banded with a blue spiral; a laminated corkscrew with alternate blue and white plies, and another with a symmetrical arrangement of plies in three colours interspaced by white. These are extensions of the common practice of edging a white corkscrew with a coloured ply, or giving it penultimate plies in colour. Another trick was to back a coloured ply with opaque white. As will be seen, the number of twists with a colour component is impressive, in view of the modest strength of the Group; nevertheless, the possible and even likely number of combinations of colour and style of twist might be far greater, and the tally here does in fact increase with more regularity than anywhere else.

Goblets and cordials occur, but not often; ales are still less frequently found and apparently never with Mixed Twists; the same applies to candlesticks. Bowl forms are rather more restricted, but otherwise much as for the other three-piece interior twists; the bell, however, is relatively rather more frequent, and it has been looked upon with some disfavour by collectors, partly because it is not infrequently ill-proportioned and partly because of a misty legend that Colour Twists with this bowl might be Netherlandish in origin. There is nothing to show that Colour Twists are any earlier, or any later, than the others. There are insufficient data to justify precise dating within the Group, dated or datable specimens being very infrequently found. Those vaguely in mind were of the early seventies, but many must be earlier than that. Conventionally, they have been regarded as a later development in the twist series. No doubt the white twists followed the air twists, which is not to say that all white twists are later than air twists. On the contrary, they must have reigned jointly for at least fifteen years, and it may be that both mixed and colour twists were made as soon as the white twist arrived.

Some of the soda metal specimens are quite good, and as with the knopped soda Air Twists, which tried to be exclusive, there is a twist seemingly reserved for unknopped soda glasses with a double series colour twist. It is quite a simple one, an o.w. Gauze/four Spirals, two ruby, two white, and of the six bowl *cum* stem varieties which had this, not one of some thirty casually found specimens is glass of lead, although the forms can be matched several times over in lead metal but only with a different twist.

The Group divides into five Sections, some being sub-divided for convenience.

SECTION I. *Glasses with a Combined Air and Opaque White Twist*

A. With unknopped stem and a single series twist (*four types of twist*)

B. With unknopped stem and a double series twist (*eleven types of twist*)

This Section comprises the conventional Mixed Twists with air and opaque white components only within the stems, and in total it numbers 45 per cent of the Group, the ratio of Sub-sections A and B being rather less than 1 to 3. As all glasses in the other four Sections have a colour component it follows that Mixed Twists are scarcer than Colour Twists, and the number of their different twists is far smaller.

In Subsection A about every other twist found has a Spiral Air Gauze and a Single Opaque White Spiral Thread, and the bowl is usually a bell, less often a waisted bucket, with three other forms. A distinct variety has the same Spiral Air Gauze with a heavy O.W. Spiral (Pl.89a) and this also favours the bell bowl. The waisted bucket appears in three of the four twists, and a saucer-topped bucket twice, giving a delightful cordial always with a domed foot.

Subsection B is divided into two parts, according to whether the inner component of the twist is an air twist or an opaque white twist. In the first category there are seven twists with roughly another quarter of the Group's glasses, generally an Air Gauze with either Two (Pl.89b) or Four O.W. Spiral Threads around it; in the first case the round funnel is preferred; in the second it is a bell. No foot other than a plain one has been noted here. In the second category there are only four twists, but it still provides half the glasses of the Section. This is because of the relative frequency of a particular twist and a particular glass, namely an O.W. Gauze/Pair of Air Spirals, given to a tall flute glass with trumpet bowl (Pl.90c), a wine, not an ale glass, and this is the only frequent glass of the whole Group. It has two scarce variants, appearing with triple or quadruple collars at the base of the bowl or more rarely with a semi-toasting stem. Two of the other twists are a development of the first twist of Subsection A, an O.W. Vertical Thread being inserted as an inner component: in these, only the ogee and round funnel bowl have been noted. The fourth twist deserves mention as it provides the only case of the Multiple Spiral Air Twist being used in conjunction with any other twist; it is placed outside an Opaque White Corkscrew on saucer-topped r.f. wines, and makes a very desirable glass (Pl.90e).

SECTION 3. *Glasses with a Combined Air and a Colour Twist* (*three types of twist*)

The omission of Section 2 is intentional, it is being reserved for twists in colour only, known to exist if only in a somewhat attenuated form whereof no record has been retained. It could also accommodate glasses with a single-series twist in pale pink.

Section 3 contains less than $2\frac{1}{2}$ per cent of the Group's glasses, and so far all have had a single Series Twist and an Unknopped Stem. Such examples as come into view will almost certainly have a Spiral Air Gauze and a Single Spiral, either blue or green, and they will be wines with a bell bowl.

SECTION 4. *Glasses with a Combined White and a Colour Twist*

A. With a knopped stem and a single series twist (2 *per cent, two twists*)

B. With a knopped stem and a double series twist (11 *per cent, five twists*)

C. With unknopped stem and a single series twist (19 *per cent, seventeen twists*)

D. With unknopped stem and a double series twist (60 *per cent [a] sixteen plus [b] twenty-four plus [c] nine twists*)

E. With unknopped stem and a triple series twist (2 *per cent, two twists*)

Section 4 contains just over 50 per cent of the Group's glasses, but very unevenly distributed among its five Subsections: their percentage of strength is noted above.

Subsection A contains few glasses indeed, but they are most attractive. A Shoulder-knopped stem carries a bell bowl and has a twist formed of an O.W. Corkscrew edged in Purple. The other glass worth mention had a double-knopped stem (at Top and Centre) and a twist of Six Spirals, in Blue, Mauve, White, and Yellow. Anything qualifying for inclusion here will be a prize.

Subsection B derives such strength as it has from certain double-knopped bell bowl wines of indubitable Newcastle origin; their twists being based on the O.W. Gauze with either three or four spirals outside in varying combinations of blue, green, red, rubber-red, and white. Two soda metal wines are included. Outside the foregoing, a notable Shoulder-knopped glass possessed a translucent Green Column/Pair of Laminated O.W. Corkscrews with edges in carmine.

Subsection C provides a variety of neat glasses. The twists have O.W. Spiral Gauzes with similar Corkscrews edged in colour; Three or Four Spiral Threads in O.W. and colour; Laminated O.W. Corkscrews with vari-coloured edges, sapphire, green, blue, grey-blue, or ruby. Further O.W. multiply Corkscrews incorporate some plies in colours such as canary, carmine or ruby, blue, grey-blue, a rubber-red, and one with a few further elaborations it is unnecessary to describe. The bowl in this Subsection seems usually to be an ogee or r.f., though some of the solo Corkscrews have the bell. Not enough examples of any particular twist are on record to warrant any more definite statement.

It is in Subsection D that the bulk of our colour twists are found, and for convenience of classification, they are subdivided into three portions according to the nature of the inner component.

(*a*) The Inner Twist component in Opaque White (38 per cent).

Eights twists are based on the O.W. Gauze, vertical or spiral, single or pair; outside it, there will be found Two or Four spirals, both or two of which will be in colour. A trumpet dram glass with firing foot has the O.W. Gauze/Two O.W. and Two Green Spirals. The commonest twist in the whole Section appears here, the O.W. Gauze/Two O.W. and Two Ruby Spirals already mentioned as being used only for glasses in soda metal, and it would surely be strange if the commonest colour twist we know was anything but English. Three twists are based on an O.W. Lace Twist with white and/or coloured Spirals outside; in these no bell bowl has been noted. Four further twists are based on a Multi-ply or Laminated O.W. Corkscrew with pairs of coloured spirals outside. No bowl preference can be given, but a waisted bucket appears and a good ale with r.f. bowl.

(*b*) The Inner Twist Component in Opaque White and Colour (51 per cent).

The twists can only partially be mentioned. Two, Three, or Four Spiral Threads, in colour or backed with colour, have O.W. Spiral Threads or an O.W. Spiral Band or Bands outside. O.W. Corkscrews edged in colours are partnered with Pairs of Spiral Threads, usually both O.W. (Pl.89c), but sometimes one is in colour. There are sixteen variations of this last formation. The bowl is a bell, ogee, ovoid, r.f., or occasionally a trumpet, which has been seen over a semi-toasting stem. The dram in Pl.90d has a green-edged Corkscrew within a special type of O.W. Spiral Band.

(*c*) The Inner Twist component in Colour only (11 per cent)

This subdivision includes some of our most popular colour twists. The outer formation is to all intents and purposes always in white, and the inner coloured component can be striking. We have, for instance, a Blue Gauze within a Pair of O.W. Spirals, fairly frequently seen; a Rubber-red Corkscrew/Pair of O.W. Spiral Cables, a very fine design; and a Dark Green Column inside a Pair of O.W. Corkscrews whereof the outer edges are in blue. The bell bowl tends to disappear, leaving the field largely to the round funnel.

Subsection E to complete Section 4 provides two types of twist only, the best glass being a cordial with faint fluted round funnel bowl, possessed of a twist formed of an O.W. Gauze/Pair of Blue Spiral Tapes/Pair of O.W. Spiral Gauzes. The stem seemed a little overburdened, but it was a brilliant glass.

SECTION 5. *Glasses with a Combined Air, Opaque White, and a Colour Twist*

A. With unknopped stem and single series twist (*one type of twist*)

B. With unknopped stem and a double series twist (*one type of twist*)

In this last Section there are fewer glasses than in any other, and together they will barely amount to 1 per cent of the Group.

Subsection A is known by a single ogee wine, and the twist was a Spiral Air Gauze and a Single Opaque White Spiral partnered by an Orange Spiral.

Subsection B is more likely to be seen, though still extremely rare. The bowl is a faint fluted ogee and the twist an O.W. Vertical Thread/Spiral Air Gauze and a Single Blue Spiral (Pl.89d). The basis of both these will be found in Section 1.

Group XII

GLASSES WITH FACETED STEMS
(c. 1760 – c. 1810)

The date of our first Faceted Stem glasses has been given with authority as certainly 'pre-Excise', that is to say before 1745–6 and indeed materially earlier. That there were faceted German glasses even before the 1730s is beyond dispute; that there were English ones is more a question of faith than of evidence. Hartshorne figures what must surely be a Lauenstein glass engraved with a crowned monogram allocated to Frederick Lewis Prince of Wales, 1729–51, and father of George III, of the nearby House of Hanover, and there is a faceted Newcastle wine engraved *Prosperity to Houghton* and *1735*, the year in which the house was rebuilt. The tribute may not have coincided with the rebuilding. In any case, we are concerned rather with the glassmaker's production than the special job of an outside hand or shop. An example of what could happen is provided by a goblet (Pl.90b) which is an English baluster type with a plain foot made no later than 1740. The cutting is exceptional and must be attributed to a German, whether working in England or elsewhere it is difficult to say; the engraving and inscription is Dutch and somewhere in the 1750s, featuring a brewery at Amsterdam, the 'Haystack', and its potential profits.

One would be hard put to it to find any cut drinking glass much earlier than the faceted Britannia goblets and wines (Pl. 91f) issued to commemorate the Peace of Paris of 1763 which concluded the Seven Years War in, to Britain, such an embarrassingly satisfactory manner that we made all decent haste to rid ourselves, not for the first time, of as many of our cumbersome acquisitions as we could. If then we attribute the earliest facet-stem glasses to the 1760 prelude, and the body of them to the 1780 invasion of Ireland by English glassmasters, we ought not to be far wrong. Their style persisted into the nineteenth century, but they are not particularly frequent and fine specimens are scarce.

This particular classification excludes after-cut glasses and also cut sweetmeat glasses and champagnes, partly because of the difficulty of deciding when they were cut, and partly because the intricacy of shape and cutting makes a written description very difficult of understanding, but this does not mean that the excluded glasses are not desirable; on the contrary, they comprise some of the best glass English glass-masters ever made or English glass-cutters decorated. All elaborately cut rims should be examined for signs of re-cutting or re-touching; as a rule the wheel will have left variable 'flats' on the cross-sections of the glass, and often light chamfers along the edges. It is not to be expected that many such rims on either bowl or foot can have survived unscathed.

The range of drinking glasses is uninteresting. In the Group as a whole, and more or less so in the Sections, the ratio of wines to goblets is 10 to 1. Yet by reason of a superiority in Section 2, ales are rather commoner than goblets. Some glasses with very small bowls qualify as cordials even though the stem is less thick than in the interior twist glasses. There are odd drams, short ales, and one glass in a hundred may be a ratafia.

Bowl forms vary within the Sections, but in general the ovoid and round funnel greatly predominate. Because of the cutting, it is often a moot point whether the bowl is an ogee, ovoid, or r.f. Doubtful specimens have been taken as ovoid to the possible enhancement of its position. There are lipped ogee and lipped r.f. forms, some trumpets, not always beyond suspicion of after-cutting, but little else indeed.

As to the foot, one in thirty-five may have a firing type, but this mostly means a solid plain foot, rather flat beneath, a variation occasionally found on a plain-stemmed glass. A fold occurs once in a hundred glasses, and some of these may be old plain-stemmed stock cut to a later taste. A dome-footed r.f. bowl, rather wide in the mouth, is a collector's favourite.

Knopping of the stem is curiously limited to almost the fewest possible forms, a centre-knopped stem being the usual thing. And since two-thirds of the glasses come from four

particular Subsections, it may be fairly inferred that other
stem-cuttings are scarce; some elaborate devices have been employed. One stem feature has had no notice I am aware of. In
the faceting there is nearly always a circuit of six facets, and it
is the same with the vertical flutes. But occasionally there is a
seven-facet circuit, which may have been an easier problem by
eye than by mathematics. Cutting of the foot includes scalloping the rim, i.e. petal cutting; and an arch and point rim
sometimes termed rose-cutting, an attractive style sadly vulnerable and now seldom found in good condition. The surface of the foot may occasionally be 'bridge-fluted', i.e. given
short wide vertical flutes to link stem and foot; the junction of
stem and bowl is nearly always so treated. Or the foot surface
may be flat-cut in broad radial zones, or with a clover lea
(sprig) pattern at the rim: these surface cuttings may be horizontally sliced.

Moulded decoration is very scarce and strongly suggests an
after-cut glass, for the Group consists almost entirely of 2N
glasses. Wheel-engraving on the bowl is rather extensive; very
common is a border of stars and polished circles (or ovals).
The circles may be linked by festoons. 'Formal tulips', looking rather like a row of reversed exclamation marks, are found
on glasses late in the series, especially smallish trumpet Georgian wines, though much commoner on rummers yet to come
(Pl.95g). The bowl base more often than not has decorative
cutting above the bridge-fluting: a row of circles, ovals, or a
row of sprigs, or arches, for instance, but most frequently one
or more rows of scale-cutting. The more rows there are the
later the glass, I suggest, and the less frequently found. One
very unusual glass had the whole bowl cut with a series of
scales separated by short grooves, with a resultant aspect of
large-celled honeycomb moulding. Rarely, the whole bowl is
diamond-faceted, a solid affair (Pl.91a). Gilded glasses are to
be found, but not too many good ones, and of course, there is
the stippled work which is dealt with elsewhere. Large glasses
with really elaborate cutting are extremely scarce; work of that
sort postulated a substantial glass and most examples of the
Group are quite small.

The Group divides quite comfortably into four Sections and all told comprises only 6 per cent of our eighteenth-century glasses.

SECTION 1. *Glasses with Knopped Stems* (*two types of knopping*)

   A. The stems with knop at top or shoulder knop (*seven types of cutting*)

   B. The stems with knop at centre (*thirteen types of cutting*)

As a whole the Section includes nearly 19 per cent of the glasses of the Group and also the finest of them. There is only one glass in Subsection A for every five in B, and the most frequent cutting to its Shoulder-knopped stem is Diamond Faceting with the Knop cut Vertical Flutes. Nothing other than a wine is likely to be seen. Four of the styles of cutting are extremely rare. In so far as the bowl is concerned, the round funnel is practically universal and every glass seen has had a bridge-fluted bowl, that is, the upper facets of the stem are extended over the bowl base, as is the usual but not invariable practice throughout the Group. Bridge-fluting of the foot is very much the exception, but as often seen here as elsewhere. Above the bridge-fluting of the bowl every glass in Subsection A has scale cutting or another device; the foot may further be given wide radial flutes.

Subsection B is notable in that it includes wines, cordials, goblets, and ales in the proportion of 30 : 4 : 3 : 2, the cordials being distinguishable from wines only by reason of their small bowls, for their stems are not especially stout or of greater length. The most frequent Subsection is that with Diamond Facets, taking the Knop in their stride, so to speak (Pl.91b). Six out of ten glasses will have this cutting, with the ogee bowl on two-thirds of them, and the ovoid making a first and unimpressive appearance; most glasses have scale cutting. Of the other Subsections, one with the stem cut Vertical Flutes and the Knop with something like a Relief Diamond on each face (Pl. 90a) is represented chiefly by cordials with lipped r.f. bowl and rose-cut foot rim; arches over circles decorate the bowl and the foot receives a sprig circuit or scale cutting. Another similar form of cutting, but with the alternate angles of the fluting given grooves is represented only by waisted ogee bowls, not otherwise seen in the Group, and nearly all the feet are bridge-fluted with a flat sprig circuit and rim treatment. The other forms of cutting include four further types of vertical fluting with the angles or alternate angles grooved or notched; they are quite scarce.

SECTION 2. *Glasses with Unknopped Stems and Diamond Faceting*

These glasses may be regarded as numerous enough, with 41 per cent of the Group, to be given a Section to themselves. They are simple glasses, and three out of four are wines, the balance being mainly ales and goblets in the proportion of 2 : 1 with oddments of gin glasses, drams, short ales, and a very few cordials and ratafias. The commonest bowl is the ovoid, with the r.f. not far behind; together they include 85 per cent of the Section, the goblets favouring the ovoid type and the ales naturally having the round funnel (Pl.91d). The ogee can provide a figure of 11 per cent, which leaves very little indeed for the cup, saucer-topped r.f., and the trumpet. Rarely, a domed foot may appear under an r.f. bowl, and both the popular bowls receive an occasional firing foot of the type seen on plain-stemmed trumpets, namely a solid conical foot. In this particular Section the folded foot is the rarest feature. It is possible that a certain number of after-cut glasses may be included in the lists.

SECTION 3. *Glasses with Unknopped Stems and Hexagon Faceting*

These glasses also are given a Section to themselves. They are little less numerous than those just described and account for 38 per cent of the Group. While there are many very simple and inexpensive wines, the Section can boast some first-class specimens such as Pl. 91e, f. The proportion of wines is 80 per cent with goblets just over and ales just under 7 per cent. The bowl range is considerably extended with as many as nine forms, with the r.f. in first place and the ovoid not far behind, between them appearing on four out of every five glasses. Of the others, the ogee has fallen away; an octagonal bowl has been seen in tall wine or ale form; and a very definite waisted bowl, which may be after-cut. Bowl decoration is much as in Section 2, though perhaps rather simpler. Many glasses have the engraved star and polished circle band just below the rim, as in Pl.91b, but this is regarded as engraving, not cutting: it was a good and attractive device. Except that bridge-fluted feet are almost unknown here, such foot forms as occur are very much as in Section 2; the folded foot is now less rare than the domed, and it remains to find a domed and folded foot anywhere in the Group, and that would probably hold good for sweetmeats.

SECTION 4. *Glasses with Unknopped Stems and Vertical Flute Cutting (five types of stem cutting)*

This final Section is only able to provide 1½ per cent of the Group's glasses for all that it can boast is five kinds of stem cutting. The most usual form is simple Vertical Fluting; wines, drams, ales, and short ales are on record, and the ovoid, round funnel, and trumpet bowl. The other Subsections have the vertical flutes horizontally sliced, or the angles or alternate angles notched or grooved. They may perhaps be late in the series of Facet Stem glasses, but they are still good glasses, hard to come by and undoubtedly hardly ever represented in a collector's cabinet. They seem more in accord with Section 1 than either of the other two; material, however, is too scarce to permit of any deduction.

Group XIII

OTHER GLASSES WITH SHORT OR RUDIMENTARY STEMS
(eighteenth – nineteenth century)

Hitherto the Groups have contained glasses of the same character, whereas this present Group not only covers a longer period than any other, not less than a hundred years in some cases, but it has been allowed to include glasses of different kinds. It is indeed five Groups in one. In their presumed order of seniority we have Jelly glasses; Monteiths; Dwarf Ales; Georgian Ales, Wines, and Drams; and Rummers, though there is little difference in age and style between the last two groups, and many rummers are no more than Georgian goblets. To the foregoing must be added a number of scattered Dram glasses which may fairly be termed Tavern Drams, unaccompanied by similar wines or ales.

Hitherto also, the system of classifying by stem formation has been quite satisfactory, even though here and there regard has been necessary for glasses with a bowl or with a knop or knops in lieu of the stem. Now, however, there is a very large Group of non-stemmed or short-stemmed glasses, mainly the product of the later eighteenth and the earlier nineteenth century.

By far the greater number of specimens now to be dealt with were made after 1780, and some, more or less correct for style but as late as 1840 or even 1850, have been admitted to the list. They are therefore not included in any calculation which affects our eighteenth-century glasses.

Jelly glasses have been given a very early date, no doubt with some justice; Pl.96c is suggestive, in hard medium lead metal, with a folded pedestal foot (a very close reproduction of Morin-Jean's form 102 of third to fourth-century date); so too is Pl.96a with its pair of handles coinciding with those of the posset pots of Pl.54b, but I do not know that they are definitive. Any made before 1740 must by the nature of things be scarce, and to this period belong plain glasses with double

290

'B' type handles (Pl.93f), no doubt closely followed by diamond-moulded examples (Pl.96b) and others, including one with a single 'B' handle. This is unique in my experience and it may precede both the double and the single swan-neck types (Pl.93), some of which probably stretch into the nineteenth century. The attractive diamond-moulded patterns of around the middle of the century were followed or accompanied by panel-moulded, ribbed, and wide-fluted types. There were plain specimens as well, but how to distinguish them from the greater majority seemingly of the last quarter of the century, and around 1800, is another matter. It is quite difficult to give assured datings to all the rudimentary stemmed glasses in this Group, largely because there is so little stem to act as a signpost, and hardly any dated specimens (outside Rummers) or specimens datable by engraving exist, while their general insignificance has deterred serious investigation. So far as Jelly glasses are concerned I would suggest that the third quarter of the eighteenth century is quite early enough for the great majority, and that the simpler plain ones continue into the Victorian period.

Not many posset glasses (Pl.96g) will be seen, perhaps because of an inherent vulnerability, but they are obviously linked with the jelly glasses, and may be dated accordingly.

To a large extent the same 1750–75 commencement holds for the little Monteiths, often called 'bonnet glasses' and sometimes punch glasses, and used for, should one say, salt, confectionery, olives, almonds, or vaguely as convenient adjuncts for a well-provided table. I do not know why they are called Monteiths unless it be that their frequently scalloped (petal-rimmed) foot recalls the famous hem of M. Monteith's early eighteenth-century gown; there were, in fact, glass Monteith bowls (Pl.51c) of the 1760–70 period, though I have never succeeded in hanging any glass by its foot to the castelated rim of the bowl or understood why anyone should try to do so. One may then date the earliest Monteiths to about 1760 and agree that they were made continuously until 1820, particularly in Ireland, and that elaborately cut forms with square feet were still just current in early Victorian times. But the

cup-topped moulded patterns (Pl.96d), and the plain Irish-made
glasses of similar shape (Pl.96e), are regarded as belonging to
the eighteenth century, and are both attractive and useful. I
may be observed that while diamond-moulding is common
and often rises from short basal flutes, as in certain Balustroid
wines, definite honeycomb moulding is scarce. Really rare
varieties exist both as to bowl decoration and foot form (Pl.
96f). There are blue-rimmed specimens and a few wholly in
blue metal; a deep amethyst example is known. It seems that
the type was made in America in a greater range of colour.

Dwarf Ales are assumed to follow, and here again contro-
versy could arise as to dates of origin. Those with a fairly
short stem at the top of which is a propeller-like formation
with four or five pinched wings are conventionally regarded
as of late seventeenth-century date. So, too, are some without
the wings. They have folded feet and forms of gadrooning
plain, sunken, and flammiform, and bear some resemblance to
certain glasses with spiked gadrooning rare and much more
safely regarded as of that early period. But there are gadrooned
plain-stemmed ales (Pl.78d) of no earlier a date than 1750 at
best, and there are flammiform and otherwise gadrooned
Dwarf Ales with plain feet which are a hallmark of c. 1800. Pl.
94d with its winged stem, bowl decoration, and presumptive
1790–1820 date is either an extraordinary anachronism or a
documentary specimen. For very often Dwarf Ales will be
wrythen or given what can be called ribbing swirled rather
sharply on approaching the rim; there is little real difference
except in aspect, and there are plenty of intermediate forms.
Other decorative devices are wide basal flutes, and swirled
basal flutes, which bear much the same relation to one another
as do the two foregoing styles. The faint basal fluting so common on 1760–70 wines is rarely seen. Lastly, there are Dwarf
Ales set on the same domed square feet as are Rummers,
though far less commonly; just a very few have a six-sided
pedestal, on a hexagonal foot. One of the latter had a six-
rayed star impressed beneath with twelve scallops on the
under-edge of the foot rim. An octagonal foot is also to be
found, under a dome (Pl.96i).

The other styles of glass included in this Group are Georgian Ales, Drams and Wines, and Rummers, which are closely allied, often built on such similar lines that they might be called Georgian Goblets. They can be divided into two classes, those having stems without, and those having stems with a merese or reinforcement at the top; this is usually a sharp collar except under rounded bowls when it is virtually a thin pad at their base. The former are the earlier, scarcer, and pleasanter, and one might not be too far out in calling the non-reinforced glasses pre-1800 and the reinforced ones post-1800, though naturally there will be errant specimens. Lastly, the Tavern Drams already referred to must be placed here, rather a heterogeneous lot, none really numerous, and they run into Victorian times.

Dating once more presents its difficulties, but a first date of 1770 for the earliest of the three Georgian types (Pl.94g), as well as of the Rummers (Pl.95c), is good enough; they continue until 1830, and then the former began to lean towards an elongated style which one calls 'flute wines' but which could be used for cordials, waters, or for ale, though rarely committed to such a plebeian drink by engraving. The shorter glasses with bucket forms of bowl (Pl.94h) were outmoded after 1820 by heavier glasses made for cutting. The Rummers were so useful and popular that they went on after 1830 with little change of style except that they became heavier and more clumsy in design, some with unattractive U-shaped bowls all too often of soda metal, and I am not referring to modern tavern glasses. Plain ones are found with etching dated as late as the 1850s. The more polite rummers were cut, often elaborately, and are much sought after now for table use. Of necessity, they also had to be more heavily fashioned.

As to decorative moulding, wide basal fluting is the only serious attempt. Throughout there is a fair range of soda metal specimens while colour occurs in a very limited degree. Among the various small glasses of tavern quality one finds a substantial semi-deceptive dram with a corrugated bowl (Pl.95d), something like wrythening, but much coarser and normally ceasing just below the rim of the bowl.

Something must be said as to the special forms of foot which are practically confined to Rummers, Monteiths, and to the Dwarf Ales already dealt with. After the normal circular foot, the commonest style is a domed square foot, mostly cut round the four edges, but much nicer when left alone. A special form of the square foot has a row of narrow pressed indentations all round, giving it the appearance of a corrugated step. The dome may be solid or it may be hollow and impressed beneath with what is called a mushroom pattern, in reality the counterpart of the common radially ribbed mushroom stopper; other impressions may be found such as a star pattern. The dome is usually plain, the upper part with a more or less distinct ridging (Pl.95f), actually a reinforcement, but on occasion the dome can be terraced (Pl.95g), and good examples are desirable. I call this 'terrace-domed' to distinguish it from 'domed and terraced', where the dome is plain and the remainder of the foot terraced. An approach to this occurs in cases where the square foot is stepped, but there is some doubt whether the few specimens in mind are true rummers or rummer-shaped comports which have lost their cover. There are rummers and also possible comports (Pl.95i) on a four-sided spreading pedestal and square foot, no dome then being possible; the pedestal is mushroom-moulded or concave beneath, or just solid.

The classification is simple enough, with five Sections, which will be found to feature one or two of the five classes of vessel just described. The Tavern Drams may crop up anywhere. Specimens are not regarded as belonging to the eighteenth century because fully half could never have done so; hence the exclusion when calculating the percentage of our eighteenth-century glasses in the twelve earlier Groups.

SECTION I. *Glasses without Stem and Foot*

A. The stem and foot replaced by a bowl
B. The stem and foot replaced by a solid cone or trumpet

All told, this Section contains too few glasses to be safely given a percentage. Subsection A contains only dram glasses with a pair of opposed bowls, a resurrection of the double drams of the Baluster Group.

Subsection B is no more frequent, and so far each of the few specimens handled has been of soda metal, and, as in Subsection A, no thing of beauty. Whether foreign – for there are such foreign glasses – or otherwise it is hard to say, but there is no reason why the type should not have been made in England.

SECTION 2. *Glasses in which the Bowl is Set Directly on the Foot (nine types of bowl)*

This Section contains a relatively small number of glasses, the bowl being set directly on one or another form of foot. They are attractive stable glasses, not particularly common, and all told amounting to between 5 and 6 per cent of this very large Group. Three out of four are Jelly glasses, with eight different bowl forms of which the commonest is a conical/trumpet form, seldom with any moulded decoration. The rim will nearly always be flanged (Pl.93c) and often also folded either upwards or downwards. Some are set into a milled thistle foot and will have a folded rim. A waisted bowl is also quite frequent, with some moulded decoration and more than the usual number of domed feet. The dome and fold is scarce in this Section. Of other bowl forms, only the lipped r.f. is other than very scarce.

Parallel with these Jellies, as far as the conical/trumpet bowl is concerned, is a series of Dwarf Ales, not large, but including gadrooned examples, mainly of the flammiform type (Pl.94b) and mostly with plain feet. Wrythening in whole or in part occurs (Pl.94d).

The remainder of the Section is formed of odd specimens

and types, many quite scarce. Good gadrooning over a domed or a domed and folded foot is rare, and so is a Jelly with a hexagonal bowl on a domed foot, although in the next Section it will not be scarce. Rare, too, is a Jelly with waisted bowl on a very solid overstrung firing foot (as Pl.60b), but in soda metal. A good and early Jelly glass with a pair of 'B' handles and a domed and terraced foot (Pl.93f) may go back to the early eighteenth century; indeed, it is reasonable to regard handles of this type on plain specimens as indicative of an early date. Incidentally, handles are practically confined to Jelly glasses, though very occasionally seen in pairs on a rummer, a small loving-cup, perhaps. A few posset glasses of the first half of the eighteenth century come into this Section, with a lipped r.f. bowl.

SECTION 3. *Glasses with Knopping in Lieu of a Stem (sixteen types of knopping)*

Glasses of this Section are not uncommon, amounting to about 21 per cent of the Group. Let it first be said that the Section contains to all intents and purposes Jelly glasses and Monteiths only, in the proportion of 3 to 1. Of the sixteen different knoppings or Subsections, one particular type is found on four out of every five glasses, namely Subsection A with a Half-knop, Flattened Knop, or Rudimentary Knop. It may be noted that when a bowl is mould-blown, the Knop is nearly always moulded also, though there are exceptions; when the glass is plain, the Knop is never moulded. There are nine possible bowl forms; a lipped r.f./waisted form and a more definitely waisted bowl are equally plentiful; one or other of these is used for three glasses out of four. An interesting form is the hexagonal bowl, usually on a domed foot (Pl. 93d); a saucer-topped r.f. bowl is commoner (Pl.93e) and only just prefers a plain foot to anything else. Here and nowhere else do the Monteiths congregate (Pl. 96d, e, f), and they are much more numerous than Jelly glasses with the same bowl.

It will hardly be necessary to refer to Monteiths again, so let it be recorded that but one in ten is quite plain, diamond moulding very common, and ribbing and wide fluting also found. A great rarity is a specimen with ribbing vertically and the whole bowl overlaid with fine horizontal threading. There is little variation in bowl form, cut examples being disregarded, but the feet have considerable interest. One is known with the pressed radial grooving common on Low Sweetmeats. Scalloping or petal-moulding is frequent, the number of petals varying from five to eleven. A rarity is an octagonal foot pinched at each angle, and so is a star pattern foot mentioned in Section 5. The domed square foot occurs, so far as I know, only in cut examples which would be contemporary with the similarly-footed rummers, but it lasted longer.

The remaining fifteen Subsections are rare save for two which contain Jelly glasses only. First, the same Flattened or Half-knop as before, but with Multiple Tears (Pl.93h). Here the waisted bowl is easily dominant among half a dozen forms; panel moulding is added to the repertoire, single and double swan-neck handles occur, and double 'B' handles. More unexpectedly still, I have no record of any glass in this Subsection, whatever the bowl, with a folded foot, and hardly any with either a plain foot or a domed and folded one; practically all have the simple dome. The other Subsection of some frequency has a very Rudimentary plain Stem with a sharp Collar beneath the bowl. It may be regarded as a reinforcement. Beyond a couple of waisted bowls only saucer-topped trumpets occur, and here the domed and folded foot is four times as common as the domed, with no other variation.

One of the prizes, if you like Jelly glasses, is a specimen with a multiple spiral air twist in the Knop or Half-knop. This is quite distinct from the Teared Knop already mentioned. There are Jellies with an Opaque White Twist in the Half-knop, rare enough. Another, with a Teared Knop, has a stepped r.f. bowl which is ribbed, and so is the foot. One with a waisted bowl and single reeded swan-neck handle was ribbed and then given fine horizontal threading throughout. One cannot describe all the rarities, so suffice it to say that there is ample material in this Section, both among the Monteiths and the Jelly glasses, to provide an intriguing collection of fine quality.

SECTION 4. *Glasses with Short Knopped Stems (nineteen types of knopping)*

Here are included all such glasses as have Short Knopped stems, and it is a very numerous Section, comprising 36 per cent of the Group. Eleven of its nineteen Subsections are insignificant. As a whole, the Section is composed thus: Dwarf Ales 36 per cent; Georgian Ales, Wines, and Drams 44 per cent; Rummers 19 per cent; and oddments 1 per cent, that is to say practically all drinking glasses.

Two particular Subsections, equal in numbers, contain two-thirds of the glasses. One, a stem with Knop at top and Knop (or cyst) at base is primarily concerned with Dwarf Ales whose features have already been given, though a single specimen with faint basal fluting may be mentioned. The other has an Angular or Bladed Knop at centre with a base Knop and the stem is 'reinforced', that is to say, there is a merese beneath the bowl and attached thereto where possible (Pl.94h), or else a sharply bladed collar or disc when the bowl is pointed (Pls 94d, 95g), as in the ovoid/ogee form. It is, to my mind, a second and stronger edition of the same stem without the merese, but a less elegant edition, and the distinction applies to half a dozen of the stem forms. The particular reinforced form now in question may very occasionally have as an alternative to the Bladed Knop an Annular Knop, a relic of the similar non-reinforced stem. This Knopping is not used for Dwarf Ales, only for Georgian Ales (rather plentifully), Wines and Drams, and for Rummers. Comment is hardly needed as to bowl forms, the Dwarf Ales using mainly a conical/r.f. or a conical/trumpet form, the other glasses preferring chiefly bucket varieties and some conical/trumpets. Earlier enterprise in respect of the foot had completely died out. Folded feet are frequently seen otherwise than on Rummers and on quite late glasses, but a dome or dome and fold is of extreme rarity, strangely so after the profusion of such forms in Section 3. Moreover, firing feet do not occur in either of these popular Subsections; a thick tavern type is frequent.

Two other stem types merit a word or two; the non-reinforced stem with Knop at centre and Knop or cyst at base contains 12½ per cent of the Section's glasses which here are practically all Georgian Wines and Drams. In this case no Ales or Rummers occur worthy of mention. The other worthwhile stem is the prototype of the reinforced stem with a central Bladed Knop already described as so plentiful. It has, of course, no reinforcement, and the central Knop is practically always annular; it carries some well-proportioned bucket, incurved bucket (Pl.94g), and cup-topped bucket bowls, and the vessels are as in the reinforced edition, but less numerous. But they are as early as any of the Georgian series. Strangely and extremely rare is a comparable form, both reinforced and otherwise, with an Annulated Knop at the centre (Pl.95a), and two intriguing types, earlier and barely warranting the description of 'Georgian', are represented by a few Drams with either an Inverted Baluster and a Base Knop, or a True Baluster over a base Knop (Pl.95b). The latter can have a reinforcement and the bowl tends to be a lipped round funnel, but specimens are too scarce to justify any more definite statement.

SECTION 5. *Glasses with Short Plain Stems* (*four types of stem*)

This final Section is very numerous (37½ per cent) but with four Subsections only. There is the Short Plain Stem without (Pl.95c) and with the upper reinforcement (Pl.95f), in the proportion of 5 to 8. The earlier form contains Georgian Wines and Drams with half a dozen bowl forms of which the conical/trumpet is the commonest, plentiful with a folded foot, and also an equal number of Rummers, all (except a single much-prized specimen) with a plain foot. The Georgian Ale has almost disappeared, a few firing feet have crept in and so have a few glasses in various shades of green and in blue. Some non-reinforced glasses have longer stems than usual, and for this reason, and also their scarcity, may be earlier than is supposed, of the 1770s perhaps.

The second Subsection with reinforced stem is more numerous still. Less than 10 per cent are Dwarf Ales with plain conical bowl and the merese; about a third of them have a square foot, while the remainder of the glasses are to all intents and purposes Rummers with twelve different kinds of bowl and six varieties of domed square foot. Among the few Dwarf Ales and Jelly glasses is a handful of specimens with a hollow-domed octagonal foot (Pl.96i). Monteiths appear again, not commonly, with a ribbed r.f. bowl, the rim and ribs notch-cut (Pl.96f), a factory process; the foot is hollow-domed and square.

The series ends with two very small Subsections. The one has a Four-sided Pedestal on a square foot (Pl.95i), numbering some Rummers with ovoid or ovoid/ogee bowl within its ranks; were cut forms included the number would increase. A very few Monteiths can be added, the ribbed r.f. bowl notch-cut as to ribs and rim as before. The other has a six-sided pedestal (Pl.96h), is scarcer, and includes Dwarf Ales and Monteiths only. They are attractive glasses and bring the thought that more could have been done with feet of this order. Something, indeed, was done, for there is a Monteith with a moulded foot described as a large four-pointed star, the 'points' sufficiently large and rounded to permit of delicate scalloping (Pl.96f). Other patterns may well exist.

POSTSCRIPT

Check Lists of nearly all the Groups are already in print and may be had from Messrs Arthur Churchill Ltd. They include every variety known at the time of compilation and provide an approximate valuation of each item. Similar Check Lists of the remaining Groups are in preparation to complete the series.

INDEX

Absolon, 115, 128
Adams, L., 120
Aldrevani beaker, 51, 56
Ales, bowl forms of, 249–53
 cutting, 285, 287–9
 dwarf, 205, 207, 290, 292
 engraved, 223–4, 248, 275
 fluted, 289
 foot forms of, 250, 252, 259,
  285, 289, 292, 296, 298–300
 Georgian, 197, 293, 298
 short, 196
 stem forms of, 211, 227–8, 231–
  5, 260–1, 263, 271, 274, 278,
  282, 288–9
Aleppo, 56–8, 111
Alexandria, 25–6, 33, 59
Altarists, 48, 52, 63–5, 74–9, 150
America, 77–8, 81, 88, 119, 123,
 130–2, 140, 151, 204, 292
Amsterdam, 70, 77, 86, 89
Antwerp, 70, 77, 86–7, 148
Apthorpe, 209
Artas, 28

Baccarat, glasshouse, 81, 101,
 133–4, 136–7
Bakhmeteff, 100
Banding, 69, 113, 258, 260, 263,
 269
Baskets, 25, 88, 201
Bate rummer, 186
Beads, 18–19, 22, 25–6, 72, 151
Beakers, ancient, 25–6, 29–30, 39,
 43–4, 55–6
 Bohemian, 128, 133
 bun-foot, 96–7, 113, 121
 cameo, 135
 early blown, 84, 86, 89
 German, 104–6, 113, 116
 Islamic, 53

Beakers, *latticinio*, 89, 103
 modern, 70
 Roman, 140
 waisted, 97
Becker, 94
Begram, 30, 44, 111
Beilby, William and Mary, 114–15,
 127, 151, 236, 255, 269, 274,
 275
Belgium, 86, 130
Bellingham, John, 156
Berovieri, 66, 179
Bigaglia, Pierre, 137
Bishopp, Hawly, 160–2
Bohemian glass, ancient, 31, 103
 carving of, 124
 cristallo of, 88
 cutting of, 131, 133
 enamelling of, 104–5, 114
 engraving of, 91–2, 121
 gilding of, 128
 goblets of, 105–6
 nineteenth-century, 121, 140
 painting of, 107–8, 114, 116
Bonhommes, 88
Bonnet glasses, 204, 291
Bott, J. T., 116
Bottles, 135–6, 162, 201, 204
 Bohemian, 107, 114
 cameo, 135–6
 canister, 107, 114
 double-walled, 138
 early, 17, 19–21, 25, 29, 33, 44,
  49, 53, 68, 139
 English, 146–7, 151, 162, 204
 Irish, 130, 133
 Russian green, 100
 Spanish, 84
 sprinkler, 53–4, 57
 Venetian, 65
Bowes, Sir Jerome, 146, 148
Bowls, 197, 200, 205

Bowls, base, 133, 210, 212, 246, 251, 293, 295
bell, 242, 254, 258, 269, 271, 278, 279–83
bridge-fluted, 287
conical, 212, 215, 218, 295, 298
corrugated, 293
cutting, 52, 135, 285
cylindrical, 135, 154
deceptive, 230
deep goblet, 217, 235, 271
double-blown, 152
duplex, 245, 249, 251
early, 26, 39, 57, 67–9, 179
engraved, 133, 179, 236, 248, 285
gadrooned, 231, 295
German, 104
hexagonal, 296
Irish finger, 130–1
lattimo, 269
mould-blown, 129, 296
moulding, 90, 230–1, 236, 259, 262, 265, 296
Netherlands, 89–90
notch cut, 300
octagonal, 289
opposed pair, 295
press-moulded, 129
roemer-type, 224
Scandinavian, 97
short, 247
thistle, 218, 226
toastmaster, 229, 260
U-shaped, 293
Venetian, 117, 130
windowed, 109
wrythening, 223, 231
Bowls, bucket, 88, 231, 248, 293, 298
cup-topped, 249
lipped, 245, 249
waisted, 241, 245, 249, 279, 282
Bowls, cup-topped, 90, 292
baluster stem, 213
balustroid stem, 225, 228, 231–2
faceted stem, 288

Bowls, cup-topped, hollow stem, 263
plain stems, 247, 249, 291
twist stems, 264, 265–6, 274, 281–2
Bowl, ogee, 94
balustroid stem, 223, 226, 230–3
faceted stem, 285, 287–9
hollow stem, 262–3
lipped, 225, 250, 271, 285
moulded pedestal stem, 221
plain stem, 298, 299
saucer-topped, 254
short stem, 298, 299
twist stem, 254, 260–1, 262–3, 266, 269–72, 280, 282–3
waisted, 245, 250, 288
Bowl, ovoid, balustroid stem, 223, 231–2
composite stem, 243–4
faceted stem, 285, 287–9
plain stem, 245, 249–50, 250–1
short stem, 298, 299
twist stem, 274, 282–3
Bowl, round-funnel, 106
baluster stem, 212–15
balustroid stem, 223, 225–6, 229–33
composite stems, 240–3
cup-topped, 251, 260
faceted stem, 285, 288
light Newcastle, 235, 237–8
lipped, 215, 237, 251, 285, 288, 295, 299
moulded pedestal stem, 221–2
plain stem, 245–6, 247–8, 250–1
saucer-topped, 251, 254, 260–1, 288, 296
twist stem, 254, 259–61, 266–9, 270–2, 274, 275–6, 280, 282–3
waisted, 265
Bowles and Lillington, 162
Briati, 72
Bristol, 88, 107, 115, 127, 196, 274
Britannic glasses, 284
Brunoro, 151

Buckingham, Duke of, 155–6
Byzantium, 32, 40, 42, 52, 92

Calsedonio, 66
Cameo, 26–7, 125, 135–6
Candlesticks, 80, 201, 221, 278
Carafes, 30, 95, 97, 99
Carré, 143, 145, 148
Carving, 27, 52, 54, 117, 123–5
Catalonia, 38, 51, 82–3
Champagnes, 197, 217, 219–20, 223–5, 240–1, 247, 259, 261, 262, 274, 285
Collars, 87, 96–7, 215, 218–21, 225–6, 229, 251–2
  blade, 218, 294
  candlestick, 221
  coil, 219–20
  vermiform, 97, 139, 257, 260
Colour in composite twists, 254, 263, 277, 280, 282–3
  metal as date guide, 210
Comports, 205, 294
Constantinople, 33–4, 40, 43, 51–2, 61, 102
Cordials, 197, 200, 231
  baluster stem, 215, 229, 233,
  bowl, 252, 287–8, 293
  foot forms, 251–2, 257
  plain stem, 248, 249–50
  twist stem, 256–7, 260, 272, 274, 278–9
Cordons, 71, 139, 154, 157
Crackle-glass, 66
Cristallo, 67–8, 70, 88, 105, 113, 143, 145
Crizzling, 80–1, 105, 124, 159, 160–1
Crusades, 50, 55–6, 60–1, 75
Crystal glass, 68, 88, 93–4, 99, 135, 148, 158–9
Crystallo-ceramie, 136
Cups, covered, 88
  early, 21, 26, 43, 49, 52, 66
Cups, English, 197, 247

Cups, German, 107–8
  Gothic standing, 63
  marriage, 66, 179
  modern coloured, 70
  Roman, 25, 27, 29, 178
Cutting, after, 285–6, 288–9
  Bohemian, 108, 133
  calligraphic, 117–18
  cameo, 125
  early, 26, 45, 52, 54
  flat, 117, 286
  flute, 289
  German, 106, 108, 284
  Irish, 133
  Islamic, 131
  lustre, 193
  notch, 307
  patterns, 286, 287–8
  relief, 52, 54
  spiral, 139
  Victorian, 291
Czechoslovakia, 102, 140

Da Costa, 151
Damascus, 41, 45, 55–8, 63, 111
decanters, 130–1, 135, 173, 201
decay, carved glass, 124, 127
de la Cour, John, 156
de Lysle, Anthony, 118, 146, 148
Denmark, 92–3
de Puymarin, Marcassus, 134
Desprez, 135–6
dishes, 29, 67, 117, 149, 201
drams, bowl forms, 249–50, 265, 293
  decoration, 115, 285, 289
  double, 216
  foot form, 216, 249–50, 272, 282
  Georgian, 200
  stem forms, 211, 258–9, 274, 282, 288, 290, 298–9

Edkins, Richard, 115, 255, 275
Egermann, Friedrich, 108

Egypt, 18–21, 24–7, 32–3, 41–2, 52, 59, 63, 117, 126
Elmzel, William, 99
Elstermann, Kristoffer, 96
Enamelling, Bohemian, 104–5, 107
  early, 27, 55–6, 67, 79, 111
  English, 114–16, 180
  German, 67–8, 105, 111–13, 116
  Russian, 100
  Spanish, 82, 84, 114
  Venetian, 65, 70
England, air twist glasses of, 88–9
  glassmakers in, 132, 142–4, 284
  Italian style in, 67, 73, 118
  lead glass in, 120, 122, 176, 193
  wines, oil gilding of, 127
Engraving, 117 ff., 139
  acid, 134–5
  Bohemian, 105
  commemorative, 175, 180, 240
  diamond-point, 91, 114, 117–19, 148, 170, 180, 210
  English, 115, 123, 167, 175, 223–4, 264
  German, 96–7, 107, 109
  hand-tool, 117
  Russian, 92, 122
  Scandinavian, 93, 94–6
  Scottish, 130
  Spanish, 83–4
  wheel, 91, 117, 120–4, 180
Ennion, 28
Erard, 116
Etching, 31, 71, 128, 210, 300
Ewers, 31, 53, 80, 86, 130, 204
Excise Act, 131–2, 140, 246, 262, 284
Exeter flute, 156

Faceting, early, 26, 30–1
  stem, 133, 169, 207, 211, 285–9
Festooning, 69, 115, 139, 286
Flashing, 21, 31, 54, 75, 79, 86, 100, 114, 204
Flasks, 80, 86, 109, 124, 130, 139

Flutes, 90, 156, 200, 279, 293
Fluting, 69, 130, 286–8, 292
  basal, 130, 223, 229, 246–7, 249–50, 255, 259, 261, 269–70, 272, 292–3, 298
  vertical, 223, 287–8, 289
  wide, 291, 292
Foot, beehive, 212
  bun, 96–7, 113, 121
  conical, 288
  decoration of, 225, 254–5, 257–8, 265–6, 270–1, 272–3, 286–8, 297–8, 300
  firing of, 247, 249–52, 272, 274, 285, 288, 299
  hexagonal, 292
  hollow block, 147
  octagonal, 292, 297, 300
  oversewn, 246–7, 250
  overstrung, 247, 250, 274, 296
  pedestal, 97, 113, 290
  square, 97, 222, 291, 294, 299–300
Foot, domed
  baluster stem, 212–14, 235, 237–38
  composite stem, 240–2, 243
  faceted stem, 288
  moulded pedestal stem, 218–19
  plain stem, 247, 250–1, 252
  short, 295–6, 299
  square, 222, 292, 294, 297, 299–300
  terraced, 227, 235, 296
  twist stem, 257, 260, 263, 265, 270–2, 274, 279
Foot, domed and folded
  baluster stem, 213–14, 235, 237
  balustroid stem, 224–5, 226–7, 230–1
  composite stem, 241–2
  faceted stem, 285
  hollow stem, 261–3
  moulded pedestal stem, 221
  plain stem, 246–7, 249
  short stem, 294–5, 296–7, 298–9

Foot, domed and folded, twist stems, 49–53, 258–60, 266, 270–2, 274

Foot, folded
  baluster stem, 212–15, 235, 237–39
  balustroid stem, 226–32
  composite stem, 241–2
  faceted stem, 285, 288–9
  hollow stem, 262
  moulded-pedestal stem, 218–19
  plain stem, 246–7, 249–53
  Scandinavian, 96–7
  short stem, 292, 298–300
  twist stems, 257, 262, 274

Foot, plain
  baluster stem, 216, 235, 237–8
  balustroid stem, 231
  composite stem, 240–3
  hollow stem, 262–3
  plain stem, 246–7, 249, 250–3
  short stem, 295–6, 299–300
  twist stems, 257–9, 260–1

Forest glass, 66–7, 104, 111

France, 78–82
  cameo cutting, 125
  dip moulding, 130
  early glass, 47, 111
  fluted wines, 255
  lead glass, 157
  modern glass, 140
  paperweights, 137–8
  press moulding, 131
  social glasses, 179
  twist glass, 267

Fransysk, Kristoffer, 96, 188

Gadrooning, 71, 88, 95, 97, 139, 157, 210–11, 231, 247, 272, 292, 296

Gallé, 27, 82, 125

Germany, 102 ff.
  carving of, 125
  commemorative glass of, 178–80
  cutting of, 133–4, 284

Germany, enamelling of, 27, 67, 111–12
  engraving of, 117–18, 120
  glass paste of, 135
  goblets of, 134
  Italian style glass of, 103

Gilding, Bohemian, 115
  Bristol, 115, 127
  commemorative, 180
  early, 38, 55–6, 67, 179
  firing, 125–6
  German, 108, 115, 122
  oil, 96, 126
  protection of, 126, 128
  Russian, 101
  twist glasses, 255, 269, 275
  Venetian, 65–6, 69

Gins, 200, 211, 221, 224–5, 230, 232, 239, 249, 252, 259, 263, 272

Glass, disease, 105–6, 161
  early, 17–18, 24–6, 30–3, 45, 51, 54, 58, 76, 139
  metal, 68, 80, 121, 161, 193, 209, 248, 262
  prepared mould, 180
  trade routes of, 103

Glasshouse sites, England, 142–4, 147

Glassmakers, emigration of, 32, 61–3, 132
  guild of, 51, 62
  licensing of, 86–7
  travelling of, 28, 48

Glass Sellers' Co., 154 ff., 161

Glazewyth, 144

Goblets, 200, 232, 290, 299
  baluster stem, 211, 213, 215, 224, 234–5, 238
  Bohemian, 105, 133
  bowl form, 227–8, 231, 232, 250–2
  composite stem, 240–1, 242–3
  covered, 93
  decoration of, 109, 210, 231–2, 272–3
  faceted stem, 284, 287–9

Goblets, German, 104–5, 124, 134
  Gothic, 63, 65–6
  Jacobite, 186
  latticinio, 90
Goblets, lead metal, 157, 160, 193
  light, 209, 234–5, 238, 240–1
  moulded pedestal stem, 217–18, 220
  Netherlands, 88–9
  plain stem, 248, 249–50, 252–3, 257
  short stem, 290
  twist stem, 257, 259, 260, 274, 278
  zwischengoldgläser, 104
Gold-inserts, 31, 68, 128–9
Gondelach, Franz, 124–5
Gottlob, Samuel, 116
Grave-glass, 29, 30, 38–9, 47–8, 50
Greene, 66, 72, 73, 97, 157, 158, 161
Greenwood, Frans, 119
Grooving, 26, 264, 271–2, 288, 297

Hall, 103–4, 118, 148
Hennezel, 143
Hope glass, 56, 67–8
Humpen, 104, 112–13
Hyalith glass, 108
Hydrofluoric acid, 117, 125, 134–5

Ireland, 130–4, 246, 251, 284, 291
Islamic glass, 46–7, 51, 53, 131, 148, 179
Italy, 33, 37, 38, 41, 51
  glass exports of, 92, 118, 154
  paperweights of, 137

Jacobite glasses, 123, 127, 164 ff., 176, 186, 250
Jäger, Heinrich, 124

Jelly glasses, 201, 205, 232, 297
  stem forms of, 207, 290, 297, 298, 300
John le Alemayne, 76, 143
Jugs, 26, 49, 100, 135, 159, 162, 204
Jung, Melchior, 95

Keith, James, 93
Killinger, 121
Kilner, J., 138
Kitcat glasses, 215, 226–7, 240
Knop, acorn, 209, 228–9, 238, 259
  angular, 209, 212–13, 215, 219
  annulated, 209, 213–14, 219, 220, 227–8, 229–30, 237, 241, 243, 298
  bladed, 230, 233, 298
  collar and, 229–30
  cushion, 209, 214, 237–8
  cylinder, 228–9
  cyst, 298
  drop, 209, 213
  dumb-bell, 228–9
  flat, 296
  German wines of, 134
  half, 233, 265, 296
  hollow, 96
  multiple, 87, 90, 212–13, 229–30, 258–61, 269–71
  mushroom, 238
  pear-shaped, 90
  pillar and, 70, 87, 90
  shoulder, 231, 232, 255, 256, 258, 261, 281
  simple, 215–16, 229, 232, 234, 238, 271
  stem form, 209–10, 214, 222, 229, 243, 254, 264, 270–1, 280, 285–7, 296–7
  swelling, 215–16, 231, 233, 256, 258, 262
  teared, 219, 220, 240–3, 298
Kohler, W. A., 94
Kothgasser, 104, 108, 116, 127

Kreybich, George, 92
Kunckel, 105, 107, 196

Lalique, 82
Lamps, 26, 29, 43, 52, 57, 63, 76
Latticinio, 83, 87, 89–90, 103
Lattimo, 66, 69, 269
Lauenstein, 107, 122, 161, 284
Laurence Vitrearius, 49, 50, 75, 142
Lead metal, 68, 80, 93, 122–3, 160,
    193, 196, 217
    cullet, 39, 218–19
    Newcastle, 91, 120, 263, 267
Lehmann, Caspar, 120
Liège, 70, 74, 80, 86–8, 157, 255
Lithyalin, 108
Locke, J., 116
Lomonosoff, Prof., 99
London, 77, 92, 132–3, 143–5, 196
Lotharingians, 74–8, 84–6, 88, 113,
    135, 143, 145
Luteri, Ogniabene, 143
Lynn glasses, 251, 269, 272, 274

Maltzoff, Thomas, 99–100
Mansell, Sir Robert, 70, 150 ff.
Mazzola, 150
Merovingians, 39
Mildner, Joseph, 115, 129
Millefiori, 26, 66, 137
Mirrors, 72, 79, 151, 156
Mohn, Samuel, 116
Mongarda, 87
Monteiths, 204, 290, 291, 294,
    296–7, 300
Montferrat, 48, 51
Morelli, 72–3, 158
Mosaics, 22, 26, 32, 42
Mould-blowing, 33, 43, 53, 154
    modern, 129–30, 296
Moulding, 81, 130, 254–5, 296
    beechnut, 88, 223
    diamond, 291–2
    dip, 130

Moulding, honeycomb, 88, 220,
    223, 228, 231, 246, 251, 259,
    262, 264–5, 286, 292
    ladder, 273
    mushroom, 294
    panel, 219–20, 228, 231, 247,
    261, 272, 291, 297
    petal, 291, 297
    ribbed, 261
Murano, 51, 70, 72–3, 77–8, 87,
    150, 158

Nailsea flasks, 69
Neck, 204, 241, 255, 291
Netherlands, 76, 86–91, 111, 144–5
    commemorative glass of, 179–80
    cutting of, 133
    engraving of, 91, 118–19, 120,
    122–3, 234, 284
    painting of, 113–14
Newcastle glass, 91, 120, 144, 151,
    196
    decorated, 127, 133, 284
    stem forms of, 219–20, 234–9,
    240, 252, 271, 277
Normandy, 42, 48–9, 75–6, 79–80,
    142
Nuremberg, glass
    decoration of, 91, 113, 120–1, 135
    goblets of, 87, 104–5, 121

Oppenheim, Mayer, 196

Painting, 27, 110 ff.
    Bohemian, 107–8, 114
    Bristol, 115
    cold, 110, 180
    cristallo glass, 113
    early, 30–1, 55, 66, 111
    German, 104, 107, 115
    Netherlands, 114
    protection of, 128
    transparency of, 127

Palm cups, 39, 49, 53, 104, 139
Paper-weights, 135–8
Paris, 30, 48, 79, 140
Pellat, Apsley, 135–6
Persia, 41–2, 44–5, 52–5
Peter the Great, 98–9
Peytowes, 143
Pfohl, Karl, 124
Picardy, 28, 48
Polishing, 117, 120–1, 125, 176–7
Portrait glass, 115–16, 135–6, 167, 172
Posset pots, 157, 162, 200, 284
Potsdam, 97, 103, 105, 108, 122, 124
Prague, 103, 120
Preissler, 113
Press-moulding, 24, 129–31, 180
Privateer glasses, 123, 274
Prunts, 44, 49–50, 83–5, 95, 139, 272, 274
Punchbowls, 210, 291

Ratafias, 200, 231, 247, 249–53, 273, 285, 288
Ravenscroft, George, 21–2, 107, 157–62, 179–80, 193, 209–10
Reticulation, 231
Rhineland, 32–3, 39, 49–50, 74, 84, 102, 118, 139
Ribbing, 220, 272, 291
    bowl, 297
    early, 69, 70
    latticinio, 90
    radial, 129
    spiral, 88, 130
    stem, 223, 259, 263–4, 265
    vertical, 249, 297
    wrythen, 246, 251
Ricart, 84
Rim decoration, 127, 140, 261, 271, 285, 287, 294–5
Roemers, 50, 85, 90, 97, 102
Rome, 22, 25, 28–9, 69
    clear glass of, 68, 139

Rome, glass decoration of, 117, 131, 139, 178
    western empire of, 32, 35–6, 38, 42
Rose glasses, 176–7, 186
Rummers, 97, 119, 123, 130, 135, 286, 290–1, 293–4, 296, 298–9
Russia, 91–2, 98, 100–1, 122, 136, 188

Sang, Jacob, 122
Saracenic glass, 46–7, 57, 63, 92, 111
Saucers, 70, 108, 197
Savoy glass-house, 159–61
Scalloping, 140, 221, 286, 291, 297, 300
Scandinavia, 39, 92–8, 122, 188
Schaper, Johann, 113
Schmelzglas, 66–7
Schmidt, H. W., 121
Schurterres, 30, 143–4
Schwanhardts, 120–1, 134
Schwinger, 121
Scotland, 130, 138, 150, 157, 172–4
Scudamore flute, 156
Seals, 159–60, 162
Sidon, 28, 55, 60
Silesia, 103, 106, 121, 124, 126
Silver, 116, 128, 138–9, 152
Simm, Anton, 121–2
Soda lime glass, 68, 106, 121
Soda metal glass, 107, 133, 137, 161
    Newcastle, 196, 234–5, 238, 240
    stem forms of, 210, 219–20, 222, 226, 229, 245–8, 254–7, 265–7, 272–3
    wines of, 252–3, 262
Spain, 40, 51, 82–4, 87, 111, 114
Spiller, Gottfried, 124–5
Sprinklers, 53–4, 56–7, 83
Staining, 55, 110
Stem, air twist, 28–9, 69, 89, 94, 175, 207, 223, 233, 254–61, 265

Stem, baluster, 106, 207, 209–15, 226–7, 259
  balustroid, 207–10, 222–33
  bridge-fluted, 286
Stem, classified, 196, 205–8
  collared, 218
  composite, 207, 233, 239–44, 279
  convoluted, 71
  cylinder, 263
  drop knop, 213
  faceted, 133, 169, 207, 211, 234–9
  filigree, 132
  German, 89, 96, 105
  hollow, 154, 207, 209, 211, 233, 262–3
  incised twist, 207, 233, 264–6
  inverted baluster, 211–12, 225–6, 240, 242–3, 256
  light Newcastle baluster, 93, 207, 222, 234–9
  mixed colour twist, 207, 277–83
  moulded, 260
  moulded pedestal, 68, 97, 207, 217, 246, 269, 294
  octagonal, 220
  opaque white, 89, 207, 223, 233, 249, 265, 267–76
  plain, 207, 223, 245–53, 292, 297, 299–300
  prunted, 85, 97
  reinforced, 293
  rib-twisted, 89, 223, 231
  Roman, 29
  rudimentary, 207, 290–300
  sausage, 246, 251, 252
  semi-hollow, 207, 209, 211, 217, 226, 227–30, 251, 263
  semi-toasting, 280, 282
  serpent, 154
  short, 290, 300
  shoulder knopped, 225, 232, 241, 255–6, 259, 261
  tapered, 211, 251–2
  teared, 211, 217, 223, 226, 242, 245–6, 250
  toasting, 226, 252, 257, 266

Stem, toastmaster, 231–2
  Venetian, 68, 70, 154
Stippling, 117, 119–20, 186, 286
Stourbridge, 116, 140–1, 144, 196
Stringing, 69, 71, 83, 139
Sulphides, 81, 136
Sweatmeats, 131, 201, 210, 217, 221, 222, 225, 259, 262, 265, 269–72, 274, 285
Syria, 20, 24–5, 27, 29, 33, 40, 42–3, 51, 53, 57, 61, 63
  glass decoration of, 27, 56, 126

Tableware, 90, 107–8
Tankards, 97, 114, 200, 210–11
Tapersticks, 201, 220–1
Tassie, James, 135
Tavern glasses, 290, 293–4, 298
Tazze, 104, 127, 148, 157, 162, 228, 230
tears, 219–20, 234, 236, 237, 245
Threading, 53, 69–70, 297
Tilson, Thomas, 156
Tyneside, 114, 130, 150–1, 176
Trailing, 20, 43–4, 54, 88, 95, 113, 139
  patterns of, 71, 83, 139, 154, 247
Tumblers, 81, 84, 97, 121, 158, 200

Unguentaria, 21, 25, 43, 44
Urns, 29, 154, 205

Van Heemskerk, 118
Varnishing, 110
Vases, 19, 27, 29, 43, 54, 57, 81–3, 117, 130, 136, 138–9, 205
Venice, Syrian glassmakers, 55, 61–2
Venetian glass, 55, 60, 63–7, 71–3, 78, 82, 87–8, 98–9, 117–18, 120, 126, 131, 145, 148–9
Verre de fougère, 48–9, 76, 78–9, 147

Verzelini, 118, 143, 145–6, 148–9, 154, 179
Vignettes, 109, 114
Vinter, Villas, 94
Visscher, Anna Roemers, 118

Waldglas, 49, 76, 85
Weald glasshouses, 144, 147–8
Welding, 269–70
William le Verrier, 142–3
Window-glass, 32, 42, 48, 50, 76, 79, 142–3, 147
Wines, baluster stem, 212, 223–5, 226–7, 232
  Bohemian, 106
  bowl forms of, 250–3, 286, 293
  classification of, 197, 200, 205
  composite stem of, 241–2
  decoration of, 71, 127, 210, 231, 288–9
  engraved, 123, 248, 274, 275
  faceted stem, 284, 286, 288–9

Wines, French, 80
Wines, Georgian, 127, 205, 286, 293, 299
  green metal, 261, 263
  hollow stem, 263
  Jacobite, 170, 173
  Kitcat, 227
  latticinio, 103
  Mansell, 151
  metal weight, 209
  moulded-pedestal stem, 218
  Netherlands, 87, 89, 113
  Newcastle, 94, 235, 257–8
  roemer-type, 262
  Russian, 99
  short stem, 290, 299
  soda metal, 157
  twist stem, 94, 257, 260, 270–1, 272–3, 282
Winging, 87–8, 90, 139, 154
Winter, Martin, 124
Wolff, David, 119
Wrythening, 221, 223, 231, 246, 251, 259, 292, 293, 295

*A variety of Pelican books
which may interest the reader
is described on the
remaining pages*

Wines and Spirits

L. W. MARRISON

A383

The world produces over four thousand millions of gallons of wine each year, equivalent to nearly two gallons for each human being. Although it is all made in much the same way as was the wine that Noah and the Pharaohs drank, a great many refinements of the old methods have been introduced during the last century or two. Much also has been discovered in the last few decades of how the fermentation process is carried on by the wine-yeasts. The process of making spirits was discovered, perhaps by the Arabs, some twelve centuries ago, possibly in an effort to temper the rigours of the Dark Ages.

Wines and Spirits attempts to give a factual account (with thirty-two plates and eighteen maps) of the making of these alcoholic drinks, and when the author deviates from purely factual description it is only in order to offer some guidance on the selection of good wines.

European Painting and Sculpture

ERIC NEWTON

A 82

The object of this book is to provide a short account of the development of the fine arts, and in particular of painting, in Europe from the earliest times to the present day. The author's aims have been three – brevity, continuity, and a sense of proportion. He has kept as close to the limits of justifiable compression as possible. Each artist or group of artists is treated not as an isolated phenomenon but as a link in the growing chain of tradition. The emphasis is rather on the evolution of the chain than on the individual link.

The opening chapters contain a brief exposition of the author's attitude to works of art in general and an explanation of the characteristics of European art as a whole. The book has been recently revised and contains thirty-two pages of plates.

Landscape Into Art

SIR KENNETH CLARK

A 369

Sir Kenneth Clark has shown the belief that art is part of our general consciousness and gives a special value to all our experiences. In this book, which is based on his first course of lectures as Slade Professor at Oxford, he is concerned with man's relation to nature as reflected in the history of landscape painting. In the first part he considers the acceptance of descriptive symbols, the curiosity about facts, the creation of fantasy to relieve his fears, and a belief in a Golden Age of order. The great landscape painters of the nineteenth century, Constable and Corot, Turner and Van Gogh, Cézanne and Seurat, are treated in detail. Finally he considers the future of landscape painting at a time when the more vital artists have turned away from nature.

'The importance of this book to art criticism and to the history of art can scarcely be exaggerated. Ruskin and others have written notable pages on the art of landscape painting, but no such complete work on it as a separate branch of art has appeared in English.' – *Cambridge Review*.

The Age of Elegance

ARTHUR BRYANT

A411

In *The Age of Elegance* Sir Arthur Bryant brings to a climax the saga of the Napoleonic Wars. It opens in 1812 with Napoleon marching into Russia and Wellington's men knocking open the door into Spain behind him. It describes first the brilliant campaigns which brought the dictator to his knees and then the splendid and opulent island capital and the rich countryside from which for a generation resistance to Revolutionary France had stemmed. Thence the scene shifts to the peace-makers at Vienna and the field of Waterloo, of which the author draws a battle-piece of unforgettable clarity.

In the second and longer part of the book Arthur Bryant surveys the England that had emerged after so many years of struggle and development. It was an England rich, powerful, and victorious, overflowing with energy and self-confidence. He describes how the revolution which the English had mastered in battle nearly overwhelmed them in peace, and closes with a glimpse of the spirit which was able to mitigate the social wrongs and move on to the making of the future.

The Aesthetic Adventure

WILLIAM GAUNT

A386

The Aesthetic Adventure is an account of the aesthetic movement in Victorian England and the part played in it by Rossetti, Ruskin, Swinburne, Pater, Whistler, Wilde, and many others. The personalities of the artists and writers are depicted with such reality that we almost feel ourselves taking part in their quarrels and lawsuits and being involved for or against 'art for arts sake', especially as their cutting witty words are often quoted. The social climate in which they lived is brought to life so well that we come to feel at home in it.

'Of all that has been written about the nineties no book has set forth that distinctive period in art so comprehensively and so wittily as *The Aesthetic Adventure*.

'All the familiar names from Baudelaire to Sickert come under review – with the amusing things they said and the extraordinary things they did – in a book which is eminently sane and entertaining.' – *Daily Telegraph*

NOT FOR SALE IN THE U.S.A.

Porcelain Through the Ages

GEORGE SAVAGE

A 298

This is the first study of the art and history of porcelain to be published in an inexpensive edition. The art of pottery is older than history, but 'porcelain' is a comparatively recent development. In this volume George Savage traces it from its beginnings in China more than twelve hundred years ago, through its European apotheosis in the eighteenth century, to its emergence as a factory-made product in the nineteenth and twentieth centuries. He discusses a number of aspects which are related to the subject, such as the numerous existing forgeries and reproductions of valuable porcelain, and the better-known methods of identifying the factory origin and the artist responsible. A list of the more common marks is appended as an aid to identification, and there is a comprehensive bibliography of the European literature on the subject. The book is illustrated with sixty-four plates of important specimens.